Big Data and Artificial Intelligence for Healthcare Applications

T0332607

Edited by
Ankur Saxena, Nicolas Brault, and Shazia Rashid

CRC Press
Taylor & Francis Group
Boca Raton London New York

CRC Press is an imprint of the
Taylor & Francis Group, an **informa** business

First edition published 2021
by CRC Press
6000 Broken Sound Parkway NW, Suite 300, Boca Raton, FL 33487-2742

and by CRC Press
2 Park Square, Milton Park, Abingdon, Oxon, OX14 4RN

Library of Congress Cataloging-in-Publication Data

Names: Saxena, Ankur, editor. | Brault, Nicolas, editor. | Rashid, Shazia, editor.
Title: Big data and artificial intelligence for healthcare applications / edited by Ankur Saxena, Nicolas Brault, and Shazia Rashid.
Description: First edition. | Boca Raton : CRC Press, 2021. | Includes bibliographical references and index.
Identifiers: LCCN 2020056220 (print) | LCCN 2020056221 (ebook) | ISBN 9780367554958 (hardback) | ISBN 9781003093770 (ebook)
Subjects: LCSH: Medical informatics--Technological innovations. | Medical telematics--Technological innovations. | Big data. | Data mining. | Artificial intelligence--Medical applications.
Classification: LCC R858.A3 B54 2021 (print) | LCC R858.A3 (ebook) | DDC 610.285--dc23
LC record available at https://lccn.loc.gov/2020056220
LC ebook record available at https://lccn.loc.gov/2020056221

ISBN: 978-0-367-55495-8 (hbk)
ISBN: 978-0-367-55497-2 (pbk)
ISBN: 978-1-003-09377-0 (ebk)

Typeset in Times
by Deanta Global Publishing Services, Chennai, India

Big Data and Artificial Intelligence for Healthcare Applications

Big Data for Industry 4.0: Challenges and Applications

Series Editors

Sandhya Makkar, K. Martin Sagayam, and Rohail Hassan

Industry 4.0 or fourth industrial revolution refers to interconnectivity, automation and real time data exchange between machines and processes. There is a tremendous growth in big data from internet of things (IoT) and information services which drives the industry to develop new models and distributed tools to handle big data. Cutting-edge digital technologies are being harnessed to optimize and automate production including upstream supply-chain processes, warehouse management systems, automated guided vehicles, drones etc. The ultimate goal of industry 4.0 is to drive manufacturing or services in a progressive way to be faster, effective and efficient that can only be achieved by embedding modern day technology in machines, components, and parts that will transmit real-time data to networked IT systems. These, in turn, apply advanced soft computing paradigms such as machine learning algorithms to run the process automatically without any manual operations.

The new book series will provide readers with an overview of the state-of-the-art in the field of Industry 4.0 and related research advancements. The respective books will identify and discuss new dimensions of both risk factors and success factors, along with performance metrics that can be employed in future research work. The series will also discuss a number of real-time issues, problems and applications with corresponding solutions and suggestions. Sharing new theoretical findings, tools and techniques for Industry 4.0, and covering both theoretical and application-oriented approaches. The book series will offer a valuable asset for newcomers to the field and practicing professionals alike. The focus is to collate the recent advances in the field, so that undergraduate and postgraduate students, researchers, academicians, and Industry people can easily understand the implications and applications of the field.

Industry 4.0 Interoperability, Analytics, Security, and Case Studies
Edited by G. Rajesh, X. Mercilin Raajini, and Hien Dang

Big Data and Artificial Intelligence for Healthcare Applications
Edited by Ankur Saxena, Nicolas Brault, and Shazia Rashid

For more information on this series, please visit: https://www.routledge.com/Big-Data-for-Industry-4.0-Challenges-and-Applications/book-series/CRCBDICA

Contents

PART I   Conceptual

PART II   Application

PART III   Ethics

Preface

The word Artificial Intelligence (AI) was coined by John McCarthy in 1956. However, the possibility of machines being able to mimic human actions and think was posed earlier by Alan Turing who created the Turing test to distinguish humans from machines. Since then the power of computation has evolved to the point of instant calculations and the ability to analyze new data, in real-time. Over the years AI has grown to be overused and misused to include all kinds of computerized automated systems, including logical programming, probability algorithms and remote-controlled surgical robotics. Machine Learning (ML) is a branch of AI, where the system is trained by introducing data to its learning algorithms, from which it uncovers patterns, builds models, and makes predictions based on the best fit model. Big data is another branch of AI involved in managing extremely large data sets that are too big and complex to be dealt by traditional data-processing application software and maybe analyzed effectively using computational tools to reveal patterns, trends, and associations, especially relating to human behavior and interactions.

Health care is a dynamic research field that is continually confronted by issues with the acquisition, distribution, and utilization of a vast volume of information. These struggles partially emerged as a consequence of the incorporation and use of methods which create big data. Furthermore, there are persistent demands, such as improving access to medical care, reducing operational costs and improving outcomes of treatment. Instead of concentrating on patient safety, the stress of adjusting the workflow to ever-evolving requirements and protocols raises the dissatisfaction of healthcare professionals and causes professionally qualified experts to waste more and more hours on paperwork. The extreme shortage of healthcare practitioners is also attributed to the tremendous growth in indicated medical treatments and exams. With such burden on healthcare systems, AI, ML, and Big Data have been incorporated into healthcare services to improve patient care by speeding up procedures and ensuring greater accuracy, paving the door to provide improved overall healthcare. ML is evaluating radiological images, pathology slides, and patients' electronic medical records (EMR), assisting in the process of diagnosis and treatment of patients and increasing the skills of physicians. ML and AI have varied applications and healthcare has come up as a major area that has benefited from these advanced tools and techniques. Some of the areas where AI is predicted to have a major influence are in the prediction of population health outcomes for formulating smart personalized health plans, Clinical decision support (CDS) which will provide a framework for precision medicine, medical imagining, and diagnostics, drug discovery and digital patient engagement platforms to promote preventive care practices for chronic disease management. AI has the potential to ease the human resources crisis in healthcare by facilitating diagnostics, decision-making, big data analytics, and administration, among others. Big data analysis in medicine and healthcare includes the integration and analysis of large volumes of complex heterogeneous data, such as omics data (genomics, epigenomics, transcriptomics, proteomics, metabolomics, pharmacogenomics, interactomics, diseasomics), biomedical data, and data from electronic health records. Coupled with related technologies, the use of mobile health devices (mobile health/mHealth) promises to transform global health delivery by creating new delivery models that can be integrated with existing health services. These delivery models could facilitate the delivery of health care to rural areas where access to high-quality care is limited.

Despite the great potential of AI and ML research and development in the field of healthcare, new governance requirements have been raised by the ethical challenges induced by its applications. The establishment of an ethical global governance structure and functionality, as well as special guidelines for AI applications in health care, is needed to ensure "trustworthy" AI systems. The roles of governments in ethical auditing and the roles of participants in the framework of ethical governance are the most significant elements.

With a multi-disciplinary approach, this book focuses on the principles and applications of AI, ML, and Big Data in different areas of health care and highlights the current research in these areas. This book also covers the associated ethical issues and concerns in using these technologies in healthcare. This book will be useful for programmers, clinicians, healthcare professionals, policymakers, scientists, young researchers, and students and can provide information to each stakeholder in their areas to develop, implement, and regulate these modern revolutionary technologies.

Editors

Ankur Saxena is currently working as Assistant Professor in Amity University Uttar Pradesh (AUUP), Noida. He has 14 years of wide teaching experience at graduation and post-graduation levels and 3 years of industrial experience in the field of Software Development. He has published 10 books with international reputed publication. He has published 40 research papers in reputed national and international journals. He is Editorial Board Member and Reviewer for a number of journals. His research interests are Cloud Computing, Big Data, Artificial Intelligence, Machine Learning evolutionary algorithms, software framework, design and analysis of algorithms, and Biometric identification.

Nicolas Brault is Associate Professor in History and Philosophy of Science, Institute Polytechnique UniLaSalle, France. He is Research Associate at SPHERE Research Unit, and Part-time lecturer for Data science and Biotechnology in Society at various Schools in Paris Metropolitan. He obtained his PhD in Epistemology from SPHERE Research Unit, University Paris.

Shazia Rashid is working as Assistant Professor in Amity Institute of Biotechnology (AIB) and Adjunct faculty at Amity Institute of Molecular Medicine and Stem Cells (AIMMSCR), Amity University Uttar Pradesh, Noida, India. Dr. Rashid has 10 years of teaching and research experience in the area of Cancer biology and Drug Discovery. She received her PhD in Biomedical Sciences from University of Ulster, United Kingdom, after which she worked as a post-doctoral fellow at University of Ulster and later at University of Oxford, United Kingdom. She later joined Amity University Uttar Pradesh, Noida, India, and has since been involved in teaching undergraduate, postgraduate, and PhD students and carrying out research in the areas of women-associated cancers, specifically HPV infection and cervical cancer. She has published a number of research papers and book chapters in reputed international and national journals. She is a strong advocate of women's health and is involved in various outreach activities such as spreading awareness about HPV infection in women.

Contributors

Isha Agarwal
Bioinformatics
Amity University
Noida, India

Vandana Bhatia
Department of Computer Science
    and Engineering
Amity University
Noida, India

Nicolas Brault
Interact Research Unit
UniLaSalle Polytechnic Institute
Beauvais, France

Anveshita Deo
University of Glasgow
Glasgow, United Kingdom

Benoit Duchemann
Sphere Research Unit
University of Paris
Paris, France

Rajiv Janardhanan
Amity Institute of Public Health (AIPH)
Amity University
Noida, India

Rajesh Jangade
Amity University
Noida, India

Neha Kathuria
Amity Institute of Biotechnology
Amity University
Noida, India

Alejandra Rodríguez Llerena
Institut Supérieur Des Biotechnologies
    De Paris
Paris, France

Jai Prakash Mehta
SEQOME Limited
Ireland

Nita Parekh
IIIT
Hyderabad, India

Urvija Rani
Netaji Subhas University of Technology
New Delhi, India

Priya Ranjan
Department of Electronics and
    Communication Engineering
SRM University
Guntur, India

Shazia Rashid
Amity Institute of Biotechnology
    (AIB) and Adjunct faculty at Amity
    Institute of Molecular Medicine and
    Stem Cells (AIMMSCR)
Amity University
Noida, India

Bhawna Rathi
Amity University
Noida, India

Suba Suseela
International Institute of Information
    Technology
Hyderabad, India

Aditya Narayan Sarangi
Computational Genomics Lab
CSIR-Indian Institute of Chemical
    Biology
Kolkata, India

Ankur Saxena
Amity Institute of Biotechnology
Amity University
Noida, India

Mohit Saxena
Institut Pasteur
Paris, France

Harpreet Singh
Indian Council of Medical
    Research (ICMR)
New Delhi, India

Smitha Mony Sreedharan
Amity Institute of Microbial
    Technology
Amity University
Noida, India

Arti Taneja
Amity Institute of Information
    Technology
Amity University
Noida, India

Neha Taneja
Amity Institute of Public Health (AIPH)
Amity University
Noida, India

Amit Ujlayan
Gautam Buddha University
Noida, India

Part I

Conceptual

1 Introduction to Big Data

Ankur Saxena, Urvija Rani,
Isha Agarwal, and Rajesh Jangade

CONTENTS

1.1 BIG DATA: INTRODUCTION

The current scenario in the world tells us the importance of data that is collected in our daily lives in various forms. The data is collected in unimaginable size every minute of the day. When one half of the earth sleeps, the other half starts their morning with web surfing. So, one can say that data never sleeps. A 2018 article from Forbes tells us that 2.5 quintillion bytes of data are created each day, and the number is increasing with every year ahead. All this data is being collected from Netflix, Amazon, Google, office meetings and messages and emails, hospital records or health records, financial firms, the entertainment world, government sector, social networking sites, shopping sites, etc. The amount of data helps in making personalized experiences for humans, and all this is because of big data [1, 26].

"Big data" is a term that covers large and complex datasets that cannot be processed using traditional methods of data management. All this vast data can be stored, processed, and analyzed computationally to get useful results. There is no exact range of which data can be considered as big data, but the more data one has, the more meaningful and resourceful it is. But according to a few, any data that cannot be treated with traditional management models can be treated as big data. This big data concept gathered momentum in the early 2000s. Big data has brought major changes in the information management industry. So, one needs to know how to make this data informative and knowledgeable [2, 27].

Big data undergoes various stages, the last one of which is the analysis of the data, which gives all the information that one can extract from that dataset. Traditional data analysis methods included exploratory paths that consider the past and the current form of data, but big data analysis is a predictive analysis that tends to focus on the current phase and future outcome of the data; earlier, analytics was a model-driven process, but now it is a data-driven process [3, 28]. Another difference between traditional and new management methods is that nowadays data analysts tend to use structured and clean data for building a model, but they want to try that model on unstructured data, which is not possible using traditional data management methods. Models are built using statistical and probabilistic methods while analyzing big data, which help effectively in making real-time predictions and detecting anomalies that were not possible before. Real-time data found around us in our day-to-day lives can be in any form such as finance or government records, research or biological data, and many more. All this data is useless unless it is filtered and a conclusion is made out of it. I have dealt with healthcare data to understand how big data can be used to gain knowledge and derive conclusions [4, 29].

1.2 BIG DATA: 5 VS

Big data was first defined using 3 Vs, but with the expansion of the term, it is now defined with 5 Vs. These Vs are Volume, Velocity, Variety, Veracity, and Value. These are all the characteristics of big data, or we can say that these are the parameters that are used to define whether data is big data or not [5, 30].

1.2.1 VOLUME

As the name suggests, big data comprises large chunks of data, which ultimately defines the word "volume." These large chunks of data can be of any volume. It plays an important role in interpreting the worthiness of data, which means to consider a chunk of data as big data volume plays a very important role. In the case of the healthcare sector, a huge amount of data concerning an individual is generated on a daily basis. This huge amount of data is needed to be handled properly. So, here big data comes into use.

1.2.2 VELOCITY

Since the amount of data is very large, it is necessary that the rate of collection of data should also increase. That's why the term "velocity" is introduced in the context of big data. Velocity in big data is very important because there is continuous circulation as well as building up of data, so it is necessary to process and analyze these data at the same rate so that we can gain valuable information from these chunks of data.

Suppose a survey is being held to know the actual cause of malnutrition among children below the age of 5. This data is collected as well as interpreted simultaneously to know about each and every reason which is responsible for causing malnutrition.

1.2.3 VARIETY

It defines the diverseness of the huge amount of data that is being collected. In the context of big data, "variety" tells us about characteristics of data, that is whether the data is sorted, which means data of the same category are in the same group, or unsorted, which means data are not arranged at all—there is no relationship that can be established between them.

1.2.4 VERACITY

It is related to the affirmation of data. It tells us about the reliability of the chunk of data, which means whether the collected data can be useful for the establishment of any useful relation or not and whether any useful interpretation can be made or not. Veracity is very helpful in checking the credibility of data as well as in ensuring that the interpreted information does not have any error. In the case of healthcare, multiple examinations are done on an individual so that the diagnosis of a disease has no room for error and treatment can be provided accordingly.

1.2.5 VALUE

It is the most important among the five Vs. This is so because the other four Vs are dependent on it. Without value, there is no interpretation, no analysis of data, and no affirmation of data. There would be no use of volume also because volume shows how huge a chunk of data is and if this chunk of data can't be processed further, then there is no use in collecting it either (Figure 1.1).

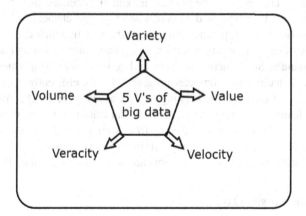

FIGURE 1.1   Five V's of Big Data.

1.3   BIG DATA: TYPES OF DATA

Variety, which is one of the Vs, is the cause of the emergence of the different types of big data, as variety itself defines the diverseness of the huge amount of collected data in the context of big data. There are three different types of big data: structured data, semi structured data, and unstructured data. These three types of big data are defined below.

1.3.1   STRUCTURED DATA

Structured data is one of the types of data that comes under the "variety" category of big data. As the name suggests, it comprises a group of data that are assembled in such a way that they belong to some criteria and show some meaningful relationship among them. These types of data show a particular pattern among themselves. They are easy to be retrieved and analyzed by any individual or any type of computer program. The structured data is arranged in a tabular manner, i.e. in rows and columns, to define the characteristic feature of the dataset. In big data, structure query language, i.e. SQL, plays a crucial role in the arrangement of the structured data. This tabular arrangement of data leads to the generation of a database. This type of data is very helpful in affirming the security of the data. It also helps in modifying the data easily if it is required. In the case of the healthcare sector, structured data is very valuable in maintaining the clinical records of an individual for the treatment of disease [7, 31].

1.3.2   SEMI STRUCTURED DATA

Semi structured data is the second type of data that comes under the "variety" category of big data. As the name suggests, it comprises a particular group of data which shows a particular arrangement but fails to define a relationship between them. This type of data does not show the arrangement of data in a tabular manner, which helps in defining the attributes. The relation type of database can be generated from the given semi structured datasets. This type of data comprises tags and elements which are being used to gather data of one type and also explain the way in which data is being kept. The same type of data belongs to a certain group that is assembled and arranged in a hierarchical manner. Since there is no sure and certain relationship among the datasets, it causes difficulty for a computer program to work efficiently. Due to the semi structured nature of the data, the keeping of data has become tough. The size of the characteristic features may be varied in a particular criterion. It can be understood in situations such as when a person suffering from stomach pain is prescribed to do a blood test and X-ray of bone. The results from these two tests are well structured in their criteria, but the relation between them cannot be established at all [8, 32].

1.3.3   UNSTRUCTURED DATA

Unstructured data is the third and last type of data that comes under the "variety" category of big data. As the name suggests, it comprises a group of data which cannot be arranged, nor can any type of relationship be established between them. Unlike structured data, the dataset belonging to this type cannot be arranged in a tabular manner. So, there is no generation of a database. Due to the lack of a well-defined structure of data, a computer program is restricted to access it. This type of data lacks a particular type of pattern in its datasets. Since there is no well-established relationship, the processing and analysis of this type of data is very difficult. It is a very time-consuming process if we want to infer any kind of information from it. This type of data is very helpful in handling the diverseness of data present in a group of datasets. But this type of data does not guarantee the security of data. The process of modification of the dataset is also restricted due to its nature. Generally, this type of data can be handled with the help of extensible markup language, i.e. XML [6].

1.4 BIG DATA ANALYSIS: TOOLS AND THEIR INSTALLATIONS

The processing and analysis of big data can be done with the help of tools such as Apache Hadoop, Hive, and HBase.

I. **Hadoop** is an open-source platform provided by Apache. It provides a platform on which a huge chunk of data can be processed and interpreted. It is written in Java and the processing and analysis of data are done in offline mode. Hadoop has its architecture based on the data being processed and analyzed, which is composed of Hadoop Distributed File System, i.e., HDFS and MapReduce. Hadoop mainly focuses its work on nodes that consist of one master node and several slave nodes. HDFS mainly focuses on the master-slave framework. It has a name node, which acts as a master node that plays a role in controlling each step of the task processing, and a data node, which acts as a slave node that follows the commands given by the name node [9].

MapReduce is also a part of the Hadoop architecture that has a role in making a large amount of data concise to get valuable information as there may be many redundancies in the datasets. Thus, MapReduce takes the input, maps the input, reduces the mapped input, and finally gives the accurate and concise output [10].

Hadoop Installation

Hadoop generally supports Linux/Unix environment, but it can also work on Windows using Cygwin. The following are the steps for Hadoop installation [11]:

Step 1: Check whether Java is installed or not using "java-version." If not, then it can be downloaded from www.oracle.com. A tar file is downloaded.
Step 2: Extract the tar file using the following command:

```
#tar zxf jdk-7u71-linux x64.tar.gz
```

Step 3: Make Java available to all users using the following command:

```
# mv jdk1.7.0_71 /usr/lib/
```

Step 4: In ~/.bashrc use the following command for setting up the path:

```
# export JAVA_HOME=/usr/lib/jdk1.7.0_71
# export PATH=PATH:$JAVA_HOME/bin
```

For confirming the installation, use the "java-version" command.

Step 5: Create Hadoop user for the further purpose of SSH installation using the following command:

```
# useradd hadoop
# passwd Hadoop
```

Step 6: Map nodes by putting the IP address and their names (Master-Slave architecture of Hadoop) with the help of the following commands:

```
# vi /etc/hosts
```

After executing the above command, enter the following lines:

```
190.12.1.114 hadoop-master
190.12.1.121 hadoop-salve-one
190.12.1.143 hadoop-slave-two
```

Step 7: Set up an SSH key in master and slave nodes so that they can interact smoothly with the help of the following commands:

```
# su hadoop
$ ssh-keygen -t rsa
$ ssh-copy-id -i ~/.ssh/id_rsa.pub tutorialspoint@
hadoop-master
$ ssh-copy-id -i ~/.ssh/id_rsa.pub hadoop_tp1@
hadoop-slave-1
$ ssh-copy-id -i ~/.ssh/id_rsa.pub hadoop_tp2@
hadoop-slave-2
$ chmod 0600 ~/.ssh/authorized_keys
$ exit
```

Now, our main focus is to install Hadoop.

Step 8: Download the latest version of Hadoop from "hadoop.apache.org". A tar file will be downloaded. Now, extract this tar file to a particular location with the help of the following command:

```
$ mkdir /usr/hadoop
$ sudo tar vxzf hadoop-2.2.0.tar.gz ?c /usr/hadoop
```

Step 9: Edit the ownership of Hadoop with the help of the following command:

```
$sudo chown -R hadoop usr/hadoop
```

Step 10: Make changes to the configuration file of Hadoop in the following way:

Files required for the configuration are available in the path "/usr/local/ Hadoop/etc/Hadoop".
In hadoop-env.sh file, execute the following command:

```
export JAVA_HOME=/usr/lib/jvm/jdk/jdk1.7.0_71
```

At core-site.xml, execute the following commands:

```
<configuration>
<property>
<name>fs.default.name</name>
<value>hdfs://hadoop-master:9000</value>
</property>
<property>
<name>dfs.permissions</name>
<value>false</value>
</property>
</configuration>
```

In hdfs-site.xml, execute the following command:

```
<configuration>
<property>
<name>dfs.data.dir</name>
<value>usr/hadoop/dfs/name/data</value>
<final>true</final>
</property>
<property>
<name>dfs.name.dir</name>
<value>usr/hadoop/dfs/name</value>
<final>true</final>
```

```
</property>
<property>
<name>dfs.replication</name>
<value>1</value>
</property>
</configuration>
```

Make changes to Mapred-site.xml in the following way:

```
<configuration>
<property>
<name>mapred.job.tracker</name>
<value>hadoop-master:9001</value>
</property>
</configuration>
```

Finally, update $HOME/.bahsrc with the help of the following commands:

```
cd $HOME
vi .bashrc
Append following lines in the end and save and exit
#Hadoop variables
export JAVA_HOME=/usr/lib/jvm/jdk/jdk1.7.0_71
export HADOOP_INSTALL=/usr/hadoop
export PATH=$PATH:$HADOOP_INSTALL/bin
export PATH=$PATH:$HADOOP_INSTALL/sbin
export HADOOP_MAPRED_HOME=$HADOOP_INSTALL
export HADOOP_COMMON_HOME=$HADOOP_INSTALL
export HADOOP_HDFS_HOME=$HADOOP_INSTALL
export YARN_HOME=$HADOOP_INSTALL
```

Step 11: Now install Hadoop on the machine that will act as a slave with the help of the following commands:

```
# su hadoop
$ cd /opt/hadoop
$ scp -r hadoop hadoop-slave-one:/usr/hadoop
$ scp -r hadoop hadoop-slave-two:/usr/Hadoop
```

Step 12: Configure the master node and slave nodes with the help of the following commands:

```
$ vi etc/hadoop/masters
hadoop-master

$ vi etc/hadoop/slaves
hadoop-slave-one
hadoop-slave-two
```

Step 13: Finally, format the data nodes and initialize the daemons in the following way:

```
# su hadoop
$ cd /usr/hadoop
$ bin/hadoop namenode -format

$ cd $HADOOP_HOME/sbin
$ start-all.sh
```

II. **Hive** is one of the tools that come under the Hadoop environment. It acts as a data repository for the structured type of datasets. As structured data support structure query language (SQL), in which data can be stored in a tabular form, in which there is room for retrieval, addition, and removal of data to establish valuable relationships among data, these features are also available in Hive. The analyzing process is very fast. It can also function in a compressed file that is present in the Apache Hadoop environment. But it is not suitable for performing the analysis of real-time data [12].

Hive Installation

The following are the steps of installation of Hive [13]:

Step 1: Before proceeding with the installation of Hive, install Java and Hadoop beforehand. To check whether they are already installed or not, we can execute "java-version" and "Hadoop version." If they are not installed, we can follow the steps that have been mentioned previously.

Step 2: Download the latest version of Hive from "hive.apache.org".

Step 3: Extract the files using the following command:

```
tar -xvf apache-hive-2.3.7-bin.tar.gz
```

Step 4: Now, open the bashrc file using the following command:

```
$ sudo nano ~/.bashrc
```

Step 5: Provide the path to Hive using the following command:

```
export HIVE_HOME=/home/codegyani/apache-hive-2.3.7-bin
export PATH=$PATH:/home/codegyani/apache-hive-2.3.7-bin/bin
```

Step 6: Update an environment variable:

```
$ source ~/.bashrc
```

Step 7: To work with Hive, just type "hive" in the command line.

```
$ hive
```

III. **HBase** is also a very useful tool that comes under the Hadoop environment. It is mainly a column-based type of database. It also has a feature of adding any number of columns to it at any span of time while processing. It is more suitable for scattered types of datasets, which means it is very useful in datasets that have multiple null values to an attribute. It provides a very good platform for saving and providing data without any restriction to its access. It only allows read and write operations on datasets, with the option of updating or modifying it. It has an important characteristic of automatic failover in which whenever the system faces any problem while performing the task, it puts the computation on hold [14].

HBase Installation

The following are the steps of HBase installation [1515]:

Step 1: Before proceeding with the installation of HBase, install Java and Hadoop beforehand. To check whether they are already installed or not, we can execute "java-version" and "Hadoop version." If they are not installed, we can follow the steps that have been mentioned previously.

Step 2: Download the latest version of HBase from "hbase.apache.org". A tar file will be downloaded.

Step 3: Extract the files using the following command:

```
$tar -zxvf hbase-2.3.1-hadoop2-bin.tar.gz
```

Step 4: Now, login as a super user:

```
$su
$password: enter your password here
```

```
mv hbase-2.3.1/* Hbase/
```

Step 5: Configure HBase in stand-alone mode with the help of the following commands:

```
cd /usr/local/Hbase/conf
gedit hbase-env.sh
```

Substitute the already present JAVA_HOME value with the latest one.

```
export JAVA_HOME=/usr/lib/jvm/java-1.7.0
```

Within /usr/local/Hbase, get hbase-site.xml. For this we need to add the following code in between configuration.

```
<configuration>
//Here you have to set the path where you want HBase
to store its files.
<property>
<name>hbase.rootdir</name>
<value>file:/home/hadoop/HBase/HFiles</value>
</property>

//Here you have to set the path where you want HBase
to store its built in zookeeper files.
<property>
<name>hbase.zookeeper.property.dataDir</name>
<value>/home/hadoop/zookeeper</value>
</property>
</configuration>
```

Step 6: Initialize HBase using the following command:

```
$cd /usr/local/HBase/bin
$./start-hbase.sh
```

IV. **Apache Pig** is also a component of the Hadoop environment. It acts as a possible alternative to the MapReduce tool in case of highly complex structured data. It has the advantage of handling all three types of big data: structured, semi structured, and unstructured. It also provides an option of built-in operators such as sort, filter, and joins. It allows access for creating a user-defined function in which the user is free to use his logic to solve the problem. It also provides nested data types, i.e., tuple, bag, and map [16].

Pig Installation

The following are the steps of Pig installation [17]:

Step 1: Before proceeding with the installation of Pig, install Java and Hadoop beforehand. To check whether they are already installed or not, we can execute "java-version" and "Hadoop version." If they are not installed, we can follow the steps that have been mentioned previously.

Step 2: Download the latest version of Pig from "pig.apache.org". A tar file will be downloaded.

Step 3: Extract the files using the following command:

```
$ tar -xvf pig-0.17.0.tar.gz
```

Step 4: Open the bashrc file using the following command:

```
$ sudo nano ~/.bashrc
```

Step 5: Give the path to PIG_HOME in the following way:

```
export PIG_HOME=/home/hduser/pig-0.16.0
export PATH=$PATH:$PIG_HOME/bin
```

Step 6: Use the following command for updating the variable of environment:

```
$ source ~/.bashrc
```

Step 7: Finally, check whether the Pig has been successfully installed or not using the following command:

```
$ pig -h
```

1.5 BIG DATA: COMMANDS

There are several commands that are frequently being used in big data. Some of these commands are as follows:

HDFS Commands

- **ls:** This command is used to show all the files present in the folder or all the folders present in the directory.

  Syntax:

  ```
  bin/hdfs dfs -ls <path>
  ```

- **mkdir:** This command is used to make a new directory.

  Syntax:

  ```
  bin/hdfs dfs -mkdir <folder name>

  creating home directory:

  hdfs/bin -mkdir /user
  hdfs/bin -mkdir /user/username -> write the username of your computer
  ```

- **touchz:** It is used to make an empty file.

  Syntax:

  ```
  bin/hdfs dfs -touchz <file_path>
  ```

- **cat:** This command is used to show what is written in the file.

  Syntax:

  ```
  bin/hdfs dfs -cat <path>
  ```

- **mv:** This command is used to shift the files in between HDFS.

  Syntax:

  ```
  bin/hdfs dfs -mv <src(on hdfs)> <src(on hdfs)>
  ```

- **cp:** This command is used for copying the content of file in between HDFS.

  Syntax:

  ```
  bin/hdfs dfs -cp <src(on hdfs)> <dest(on hdfs)>
  ```

- **du:** This command helps in giving the size of a particular directory that is mentioned.

  Syntax:

  ```
  bin/hdfs dfs -du <dirName>
  ```

- **stat:** This command is used to provide us the time at which the changes can be made in a file or a directory.

  Syntax:

  ```
  bin/hdfs dfs -stat <hdfs file>
  ```

Hive Commands

- For generating a database:

  ```
  hive>create the database emp
  >WITH DBPROPERTIES ('name' = 'XYZ', 'id' = '101');
  ```

- For checking if there is any new database:

  ```
  hive> show databases;
  ```

- For getting required information from database:

  ```
  hive> describe database extended emp;
  ```

- For deleting database:

  ```
  hive> drop database emp;
  ```

- For making an internal table:

  ```
  hive> create table emp (Id int, Name string, Salary float)
  row format delimited
  fields terminated by ',';
  ```

- For making an external table:

```
hdfs dfs -mkdir /HiveDirectory
hdfs dfs -put hive/emp_details /HiveDirectory

hive> create external table emplist (Id int, Name string, Salary float)
row format delimited
fields terminated by ','
location '/HiveDirectory';
```

- USE statement in Hive: The USE statement in Hive is used to select the specific database:

  Hive >USE Employee;

- DROP DATABASE in Hive:

  Hive> DROP Employee;

- ALTER DATABASE in Hive: This is used to change the metadata associated with the database in Hive:

  Hive> alter database Employee set OWNER ROLE admin;

  - ALTER TABLE in Hive:

  hive> ALTER TABLE college. Student RENAME TO college.college_students;

  hive> ALTER TABLE collge. college_students SET TBLPROPERTIES ('creator'='Emp');

  hive> ALTER TABLE college.college_students SET TBLPROPERTIES ('comment'='this table is created by Student');

HBase Commands

- **Create:** This command is used to generate a new table.

  hbase(main):002:0> create 'emp', 'personal data', 'professional data'

- **Put:** This command is used for inputting the data.

  hbase(main):002:0> put '<table name>' ,'row1', '<colfamily:colname>', ' <value>'

  hbase(main):005:0> put 'emp','1','personal data:name','Nitin'

  hbase(main):006:0> put 'emp','1','personal data:city','Delhi'

  hbase(main):007:0> put 'emp','1','professional data: designation','manager'

  hbase(main):007:0> put 'emp','1','professional data:salary','70000'

- **Scan:** This command is used to show the data that are already present in the table.

  hbase(main):003:0> scan 'emp'

- **Get:** This command is used to show the data that is asked in the query.

  hbase(main):012:0>Get '<table name>' ,'row1'

  hbase(main):012:0> get 'emp', '1'

1.6 BIG DATA: APPLICATIONS

In our daily life, zillions of data are being generated constantly. Every minute there is a constant need to handle these data carefully for further processing. These data can be generated in any sector of our daily life such as marketing, healthcare, research, banking, and many more. Therefore, big data has a very responsible job for performing the task of handling, processing, and analyzing the data that are constantly being produced over a period of time very precisely. Let's focus on the healthcare sector to know what are the tasks which are needed to be taken care of with the help of big data, which ultimately shows the divergence of application of big data in the case of healthcare management:

- An enormous number of images are being generated every second in the healthcare sector, whether they are in the form of CT scan, MRI, X-ray, ultrasound, and many more. These images are constantly being stored and updated for a particular individual who is being diagnosed with some disease in a database of healthcare centers. The storage of this kind of data is very helpful in keeping the records of a patient so that the history of his disease can be understood carefully and also ease the way of his/her treatment [18].
- Apart from the continuous generation of various healthcare images, there is a constant generation of vital signals of a patient too. These vital signals comprise heart rate, pulse rate, level of oxygen in the blood, and many more. These data are very crucial in constantly monitoring the seriousness of a patient. Since at a time in a hospital many patients are there, so here the task of big data is to not only collect the information regarding these vital signals but also assign them to the correct patient record [19].
- There is a lot of research work happening around the world. These research works generate a large amount of desirable or undesirable outcomes. These outcomes are generally stored in a repository called the database. Thus, big data performs the task of regularly maintaining and storing these data so that if some other person wants to refer to a particular work that has already been performed, then he can have easy access to it [20].
- Another role of big data can be seen during the clinical trial. A clinical trial is a process where a drug is tested on an individual to know about its efficacy and efficiency. There is a lot of documentation work done during

a clinical trial as a record of each and every step of it must be recorded for analyzing the drug. Therefore, big data has a very important role in handling these records [21].

- Another big data application that helps in managing the big data and giving useful outputs is Cloudera. It provides a flexible, scalable, and integrated platform to store and get a reasonable output for a variety of big data. Cloudera products and solutions enable us to deploy and manage Apache Hadoop and related projects, manipulate and analyze data, and keep the data secure [24]. Cloudera provides a number of tools form, a few of which are listed below [25]:

  1. *CDH:* Cloudera Distribution Hadoop is an Apache Hadoop Distribution. It also includes Cloudera Impala and Cloudera Search with many other related projects. Cloudera Impala is a parallel processing SQL engine, while Cloudera search provides real-time text exploration, indexing, and other search operations.
  2. *Cloudera Manager:* While CDH is busy with deployments, Cloudera manager keeps a check on all the deployments performed by CDH. It manages, deploys, monitors, and diagnoses various issues encountered in CDH deployment.
  3. *Cloudera Navigator:* It works from end to end to manage and secure CDH platform. This tool helps in robust auditing, data management, lineage management, life cycle management, and encryption key management in Cloudera Navigator.

All this helps in big data analytic, the most modern tool used for big data analytic is Cloudera's Enterprise data hub.

Not only the healthcare sector has a requirement of big data but other sectors are also in need of it. For example, in the banking sector, big data is being used to track the record of the account of a customer; in companies, big data is being used to track the record of the employees, projects as well as profit and loss; in the stock market, big data has a role in tracking the price of stocks that are available in the market and whether there is an increment in price or not, and many more.

1.7 BIG DATA: CHALLENGES

Even though big data many uses and advantages, there are still some problems related to it which are needed to be solved carefully. Some of the challenges of big data are as follows [22, 23]:

- One of the most basic problems related to big data is continuously growing up in its volume. A very large amount of data are regularly being generated. So, there is a constant question of which tool is the best one to handle this.
- Even after so much development in the field of big data, there is a constant question being raised related to handling real-time data. As mentioned earlier, the data is increasing every second in multiple folds, so the tool

includes the features of velocity and veracity because not only the rate of collection of data but also the type of data that is collected is important.

- Data security is one of the most important challenges related to big data. Not only data handling and processing but also its security is important. If the tool used for big data does not focus on the security aspect, then the user's information is sacrificed and some unauthorized users can take advantage of it.

- Since this field of big data is still in progress, there is a scarcity of skilled individuals who know how to use tools for big data handling.

REFERENCES

1. Fernández-Manzano, Eva-Patricia, Neira, Elena & Gavilán, Judith (2016). Data management in audiovisual business: Netflix as a case study. *El Profesional de la Información* 25: 568. 10.3145/epi.2016.jul.06.
2. Mehta, Tripti, Mangla, Neha & Guragon, Gitm (2016). *A Survey Paper on Big Data Analytics using Map-Reduce and Hive on Hadoop Framework.*
3. Oguntimilehin, Abiodun & Ademola, Ojo (2014). A review of big data management, benefits and challenges. *Journal of Emerging Trends in Computing and Information Sciences* 5: 433–438.
4. Adam, Khalid, Adam, Mohammed, Fakharaldien, Ibrahim, Mohamad Zain, Jasni, & Majid, Mazlina. (2014). Big Data Management and Analysis. In International Conference on Computer Engineering & Mathematical Sciences (ICCEMS 2014).
5. Ishwarappa, Anuradha J. (2015). A brief introduction on big data 5Vs characteristics and Hadoop technology. *Procedia Computer Science* 48: 319–324.
6. Eberendu, Adanma (2016). Unstructured data: An overview of the data of Big Data. *International Journal of Computer Trends and Technology* 38: 46–50. doi: 10.14445/22312803/IJCTT-V38P109.
7. Acharjya, D. P. and Ahmed, P. Kauser (2016). A survey on big data analytics: Challenges, open research issues and tools. *International Journal of Advanced Computer Science and Applications(IJACSA)* 7 (2): 511–518.
8. Adnan, K. and Akbar, R. (2019). An analytical study of information extraction from unstructured and multidimensional big data. *Journal of Big Data* 6: 91.
9. Beakta, Rahul. (2015). Big data and hadoop: A review paper. *International Journal of Computer Science & Information Technology* (2) e-ISSN: 1694–2329 | p-ISSN: 1694–2345.
10. Buono, D., Danelutto, M., and Lametti, S. (2012). Map, reduce and MapReduce, the skeleton way. In *Proceedings of International Conference on Computational Science, ICCS 2010, Procedia Computer Science* 1: 2095–2103.
11. Shah, Ankit & Dr. Padole, Mamta (2019). Apache Hadoop: A guide for cluster configuration & testing. *International Journal of Computer Sciences and Engineering* 7: 792–796. doi: 10.26438/ijcse/v7i4.792796.
12. Chandra, Shireesha, Varde, Aparna & Wang, Jiayin. (2019). A Hive and SQL Case Study in Cloud Data Analytics. doi: 10.1109/UEMCON47517.2019.8992925.
13. Available at: https://www.javatpoint.com/hive-installation.
14. Patel, Hiren (2017). HBase: A NoSQL Database. doi: 10.13140/RG.2.2.22974.28480.
15. Available at: https://www.javatpoint.com/hive-installation.
16. Swa, Cdsa & Ansari, Zahid. (2017). Apache Pig–A data flow framework based on Hadoop Map reduce. *International Journal of Engineering Trends and Technology* 50: 271–275. doi: 10.14445/22315381/IJETT-V50P244.

17. Available at: https://www.javatpoint.com/pig-installation.
18. Dash, S., Shakyawar, S. K., Sharma, M. et al. (2019). Big data in healthcare: Management, analysis and future prospects. *Journal of Big Data* 6: 54.
19. Belle, A., Thiagarajan, R., Soroushmehr, S.M., Navidi, F., Beard, D.A., & Najarian, K. (2015). Big data analytics in healthcare. *BioMed Research International* 2015: 370194. doi: 10.1155/2015/370194. Epub 2015 Jul 2. PMID: 26229957; PMCID: PMC4503556.
20. Belle, Ashwin, Thiagarajan, Raghuram, Soroushmehr, S.M. Reza, Navidi, Fatemeh, Beard, Daniel, & Najarian, Kayvan. (2015). Review article big data analytics in healthcare. *Biomed Res Int.* 370194. doi: 10.1155/2015/370194.
21. Ristevski, B. & Chen M. (2018). Big data analytics in medicine and healthcare. *Journal of Integrative Bioinformatics* 15 (3): 20170030. doi: 10.1515/jib-2017-0030.
22. Patgiri, Ripon. (2018). Issues and challenges in big data: A survey. 10.1007/978-3-319-72344-0_25.
23. Hariri, R. H., Fredericks, E. M. & Bowers, K. M. (2019). Uncertainty in big data analytics: survey, opportunities, and challenges. *Journal of Big Data* 6: 44.
24. Pol, Urmila. (2014). Big data and Hadoop technology solutions with Cloudera Manager. *International Journal of Advanced Research in Computer Science and Software Engineering* 4: 1028–1034.
25. Available at: https://docs.cloudera.com/documentation/enterprise/5-10-x/PDF/cloudera-introduction.pdf.
26. Jain, S. & Saxena A. (2016). Analysis of Hadoop and MapReduce tectonics through Hive Big Data. *International Journal of Control Theory and Applications* 9 (14): 3811–3911.
27. Saxena, A., Kaushik, N., Kaushik, N. & Dwivedi, A. (2016). Implementation of cloud computing and big data with Java based web application. *2016* 3rd International Conference on Computing for Sustainable Global Development (INDIACom), New Delhi, 1289–1293.
28. Saxena, A., Kaushik, N. & Kaushik, N. (2016). Implementing and analyzing big data techniques with spring framework in Java & J2EE. Second International Conference on Information and Communication Technology for Competitive Strategies (ICTCS) ACM Digital Library.
29. Saxena, A., Chaurasia, A., Kaushik, N., Dwivedi, A. & Kaushik, N. (2018). Handling big data using Map-Reduce over hybrid cloud. International Conference on Innovative Computing and Communications Springer, 135–144.
30. Nagpal, D., Sood, S., Mohagaonkar, S., Sharma, H. & Saxena, A. (2019). Analyzing Viral Genomic Data Using Hadoop Framework in Big Data. *2019* 6th International Conference on Computing for Sustainable Global Development (INDIACom), New Delhi, India, 680–685.
31. Saluja, M. K., Agarwal, I., Rani, U. & Saxena, A. (2020). Analysis of diabetes and heart disease in big data using MapReduce framework. In D. Gupta, A. Khanna, S. Bhattacharyya, A. E. Hassanien, S. Anand, & A. Jaiswal (eds.), International Conference on Innovative Computing and Communications. *Advances in Intelligent Systems and Computing*, vol. 1165 (Springer: Singapore). doi: 10.1007/978-981-15-5113-0_3.
32. Saxena, Ankur, Chand, Monika, Shakya, Chetna, Singh Gagandeep Singh Saggu, Gagandeep, Saha, Deepesh, & Shreshtha, Inish Krishna. (2020). Analysis of big data using Apache Spark (April 4, 2020). Available at SSRN: https://ssrn.com/abstract=3568360.

2 Introduction to Machine Learning

Ankur Saxena, Urvija Rani, Isha Agarwal,
and Smitha Mony Sreedharan

CONTENTS

2.1 INTRODUCTION TO MACHINE LEARNING

In today's world, everyone wants quick and effective solutions to every problem in every field. All that humans want is computers that work like the human brain. The desired accuracy and speed intended for all human activities is achieved with the help of machine learning (ML).

The term Machine Learning was coined in 1959 by Arthur Samuel, an American pioneer in the fields of computer gaming and Artificial Intelligence (AI). He said, "It gives computers the ability to learn without being explicitly programmed." In 1997, Tom Mitchell gave a "well-posed" definition that "A computer program is said to learn from experience E concerning some task T and some performance measure P, if its performance on T, as measured by P, improves with experience E" [1].

Machine Learning (ML) is nothing but a set of methods that contain models that work and learn like the human brain. It is a branch of Artificial Intelligence that requires minimal human interventions to give predictions of complex datasets [2]. Earlier, Machine Learning made use of pattern matching, but with advancements in computer functions and configurations, this technique has found applications in various fields. The input data can be of any type, for example, biological data involving gene sequences, or measurements of various attributes of a disease, or information on how different chemical reactions occur. The data can also be of various origins, such as financial or banking service sectors, retail market, government data, transportation, and entertainment. In all these fields, one can find a trend of a particular thing and such a trend can help in further research, provide ways to save expenditure, assist government in making improvements in providing public services and amending in rules and regulations(e.g., Traffic rules), or show personalized suggestions or recommendations based on previous data (e.g., Netflix or Amazon). These data are nowadays collected using different sensors put everywhere in the form of fitness bands and cameras or tracking devices or different applications that humans use in their day-to-day life.

All these data collected are in large quantities and cannot be handled using the basic programming language. And this enormous amount of data is called big data. Machine learning assists in deriving meaning out of big data [3].

2.2　ARTIFICIAL INTELLIGENCE

Artificial Intelligence is a science of how computers mimic the human brain, while deep learning, Machine Learning, and natural language processing are the methods of how to implement this science [6]. Artificial Intelligence, which was introduced in the 1950s, works on large datasets and has been the world's most popular branch of computer science for many years. There are a lot of examples of AI present in our daily life like navigations, robotics, automatic cars, and Siri on iPhone. Artificial Intelligence is a science that implements and can be understood using topics like Machine Learning, deep learning, and neural networks. The term Artificial Intelligence implies that it is the intelligence exhibited by a machine artificially. This science deals with building machines that can simulate the human brain; also, this term can be given to any machine that functions like the human brain in solving problems and making tasks easier. With AI, a machine first learns and reasons the topic and then it helps in problem-solving, giving a new perception to the topic [4].

There are two ways by which Artificial Intelligence works: the symbolic/ top-down approach and the connectionist/bottom-up approach. In the top-down approach, symbols are given to a machine and then data is given to the machine to predict the output; but in the bottom-up approach, the reverse is done; that is, the machine is fed with each attribute first, and it learns automatically, and then the test is performed to predict the output [5].

AI is of three types:

a. *Strong AI:* It is used to build a machine that can think for itself[8].
b. *Cognitive AI:* It is for information processing. It aims to build smart systems and applications [7].

c. *Applied AI:* This is applied on computers to test theories defined by humans and also which are based on the human brain [9].

All these theories are applied in various fields of medical science, banking and finance, gaming, cars, mobiles and systems, and government surveillance, and also on advancing technologies to ease human efforts.

Machine Learning models are made using Python language. They can also be built using SAS which is Statistical Analysis Software. Python language is used because it facilitates easy importing of libraries and various datasets using Jupyter Notebook. Python language also provides easy and comprehensive programming. Python is a general-purpose interpreted, interactive, object-oriented, and high-level programming language created by Guido van Rossum during 1985–1990 [10]. Like Perl, Python's source code is also available under the GNU General Public License (GPL). Python is a scripting language, that can be easily read because it uses frequent English conversions and has less punctuation and syntactical constructions than other languages.

2.3   PYTHON LIBRARIES USED IN MACHINE LEARNING

Python has made it easy to perform complex programming in Machine Learning with a vast collection of libraries that the program code uses to manage the dataset. Various libraries and uses are described below [11]:

i. *NumPy*

NumPy is a very popular library in Python. It is used for large multidimensional matrices and arrays because it contains high-level mathematical functions. It is imported when scientific calculations are performed in arrays or matrices in Machine Learning. It makes calculations faster and efficient. NumPy assists in sorting, selecting, random selection, manipulation, data cleaning, and many other functions. It works on the Object-oriented Programming Concept and can integrate many other languages like C and C++.

ii. *TensorFlow*

It is widely used in many fields as it is an open-source library developed by Google. It defines and performs computations on tensors as the name suggests. It is the best library in Python to make models in Machine Learning as TensorFlow makes model building easier and faster. TensorFlow helps in natural language processing, deep neural network building, image search, speech and text recognition, etc.

iii. *Pandas*

It is also one of the most used libraries in Python, but it is not directly related to building Machine Learning algorithms however, it helps in tasks related to data preprocessing like data extraction, manipulation, and processing, which can include handling missing data, encoding data, merging and joining data, data alignment, and a few others.

iv. *Scikit-Learn*

It is also a widely used library because it has algorithms related to classification, regression, model selection, and clustering, and these algorithms help to build models using different methods. It is simple to use because it can be integrated with NumPy and Pandas very easily.

v. ***Theano***

This library is used to optimize and define mathematical expressions, which is done by optimizing the usage of GPU instead of CPU. It is a robust library in Python and is very powerful to perform mathematical functions related to a multidimensional array. It helps in the rapid and efficient development of several algorithms due to its strong incorporation of NumPy, as well as many other libraries like Keras and Blocks.

vi. ***Matplotlib***

This library, as the name suggests, is used for plotting graphs and output visualizations. Like Pandas, this library is also not directly related to Machine Learning but helps to visualize different patterns in the form of plots and graphs in Machine Learning. A library named Pyplot is among the most used under Matplotlib.

vii. ***Keras***

It is used in neural network programming and works on top of Theano and TensorFlow. It is a popular open-source library that provides open-source prototyping. Keras was also developed by Google.

viii. ***PyTorch***

It was developed by Facebook, and is in close competition with TensorFlow as it is also used to compute tensors but with GPU, which makes it more enhanced in speed and accuracy. PyTorch is an open-source library that also helps to build graphs and is based on Torch, which works on C and C++ interfaces.

Apart from these, many libraries come in handy while building Machine Learning models.

2.4 CLASSIFICATION OF MACHINE LEARNING BASED ON SIGNALS AND FEEDBACK

Machine Learning works on the system of signals and feedback.Signals are are sent to a machine which happens after machine haslearned the statistics from a set of data, and feedback is the response which machine gives to the signalprovided. Based on signals and feedback, Machine Learning implementations can be classified as follows [1].

2.4.1 SUPERVISED LEARNING

In supervised learning, the algorithm learns from the data provided and the responses are given to it in the form of labels or tags or values to predict the correct response when new data is provided, i.e., provide all the necessary patterns to the machine that needs to be matched instead of it determining. The approach is similar to how the human brain processes new information received from a teacher or an expert and applies that knowledge to a related field. This is also referred to as providing trained datasets to the machine. The method finds various applications such as detecting fraudulent transactions. [12].

2.4.2 UNSUPERVISED LEARNING

In this algorithm, the machine is provided with datasets but not the labels that define the pattern to be matched; i.e., they are provided with untrained datasets. This type of learning helps humans to get a new perspective on the datasets, which may not be possible through a visual search alone. The datasets used in this do not have any historical background and so no tags are known. The human brain learns to identify different objects by detecting their various features. This feature can be applied to machine learning, which can find different patterns in a dataset; for example in biological data, it can help categorize genes sharing similar structures under one class. [13].

2.4.3 REINFORCEMENT LEARNING

In this type, the algorithm is provided with unlabeled datasets as in unsupervised learning, but certain outcomes are provided ranked. This way the algorithm has no or little room for errors and provides maximum output. This method learns by trial and error. Reinforcement Learning has three components—agent, environment, and actions—where the agent is the learner who learns and makes the decision, the environment is the component with which the agent interacts to give accurate predictions, and actions are the different paths that the agent takes to get the maximum score. This type of learning is used in robotics, gaming, and navigation, where each path to a single destination is first analyzed and then the best one is selected [14].

2.4.4 SEMISUPERVISED LEARNING

In this type, some part of the data is labeled while the rest of the data is unlabeled. This method is transduction where the whole learning is done first, but few of the unique cases are missing from labeled data set. The simplest example of this is of labeled and unlabeled files in a folder, where prediction is made using only the labeled files in a step-by-step manner; i.e., first the unlabeled data is labeled and then the algorithm is applied to other files [15].

2.5 DATA PREPROCESSING USING PYTHON IN MACHINE LEARNING

Data preprocessing is the first step in building a good Machine Learning model. The data imported is first refined, because the raw data collected is a bit messed up and can't be directly fed to the algorithm in further processes. This process is performed to achieve better results in the proper format, and also one dataset can be used in any of the three algorithms of ML, NLP, or DL.

Collection sources of the raw data must be authentic for accurate and efficient data processing. The data can then be imported to the Jupyter Notebook. Next, data preparation steps follows, such as filling all the missing spaces, encoding the data in a machine-readable format, splitting the dataset into two parts, feature scaling, and refining the data for further processing. All these steps are discussed in detail below.

The data thus processed can be applied to make various predictions, such as whether a person of a certain age and income group and living in a particular country would purchase a product or not.

1) **Importing the Libraries**

This step is the most important as in this the libraries are imported with initials for easy identification and processing. The initials are added following the "as" keyword.

▾ Importing the libraries

```
[ ]  import numpy as np
     import matplotlib.pyplot as plt
     import pandas as pd
```

In these commands, NumPy, Pandas, and Matplotlib.pyplot are imported.

2) **Importing the Dataset**

In this step, the file that contains data is imported in a tabular form. Here the file has an extension of .csv.

```
[ ]  dataset = pd.read_csv('Data.csv')
     x = dataset.iloc[:, :-1].values
     y = dataset.iloc[:, -1].values
```

pd.read_csv = helps to read the csv file present in the working directory folder.

x = variable is used to store the independent variables (these are the ones which one inputs to predict something out of them).

y = variable is used to store the dependent variable (they contain the value that is dependent on independent variable).

iloc, values = method that helps to index columns in a given table and values helps to get the data present in the table.

After this print x and y to check if the data is imported correctly.

```
[ ]  print(x)
```

```
[→   [['France' 44.0 72000.0]
      ['Spain' 27.0 48000.0]
      ['Germany' 30.0 54000.0]
      ['Spain' 38.0 61000.0]
      ['Germany' 40.0 nan]
      ['France' 35.0 58000.0]
      ['Spain' nan 52000.0]
      ['France' 48.0 79000.0]
      ['Germany' 50.0 83000.0]
      ['France' 37.0 67000.0]]
```

```
[ ]  print(y)
```

```
[→   ['No' 'Yes' 'No' 'No' 'Yes' 'Yes' 'No' 'Yes' 'No' 'Yes']
```

3) Taking Care of Missing Data

As in x, two values have nan as their values, which means there is no data in the Data.csv in those cells. This is the missing data that needs to be treated because any of the dependent columns having the missing data can create a great difference in the output predictions.

This missing data can be replaced using many methods like the mean, the median value of the column, or the most frequent value from the column. Below the mean method is used.

```
[ ] from sklearn.impute import SimpleImputer
    imputer = SimpleImputer(missing_values=np.nan, strategy='mean')
    imputer.fit(x[:, 1:3])
    x[:, 1:3] = imputer.transform(x[:, 1:3])
```

```
[ ] print(x)
```

```
[→ [['France' 44.0 72000.0]
    ['Spain' 27.0 48000.0]
    ['Germany' 30.0 54000.0]
    ['Spain' 38.0 61000.0]
    ['Germany' 40.0 63777.77777777778]
    ['France' 35.0 58000.0]
    ['Spain' 38.77777777777778 52000.0]
    ['France' 48.0 79000.0]
    ['Germany' 50.0 83000.0]
    ['France' 37.0 67000.0]]
```

In the above commands, SimpleImputer is used and where it is defined which all values need to be replaced by what value. Then the "fit" method is used to retrieve the missing value cells from the table and also the mean for each of the columns of age and salary. Further "transform" method is used to make changes in the table. Print(x) command shows the output after missing values are replaced in both the columns.

4) Encoding Categorical Data

This is a step where the data is made in machine-readable forms, like country and purchase columns.

a.) Encoding the Independent Variable

The country column has three countries—France, Spain, and Germany—and each country is given a particular code of 0,1,2 and made in a machine-readable form.

```
[ ] from sklearn.compose import ColumnTransformer
    from sklearn.preprocessing import OneHotEncoder
    ct = ColumnTransformer(transformers =[('encoder' , OneHotEncoder(), [0])], remainder ='passthrough')
    x = np.array(ct.fit_transform(x))
```

```
[ ] print(x)
```

```
[→ [[0.0 1.0 0.0 0.0 44.0 72000.0]
    [1.0 0.0 0.0 1.0 27.0 48000.0]
    [1.0 0.0 1.0 0.0 30.0 54000.0]
    [1.0 0.0 0.0 1.0 38.0 61000.0]
    [1.0 0.0 1.0 0.0 40.0 63777.77777777778]
    [0.0 1.0 0.0 0.0 35.0 58000.0]
    [1.0 0.0 0.0 1.0 38.77777777777778 52000.0]
    [0.0 1.0 0.0 0.0 48.0 79000.0]
    [1.0 0.0 1.0 0.0 50.0 83000.0]
    [0.0 1.0 0.0 0.0 37.0 67000.0]]
```

In the above code, the fit_transform method is called from OneHotEncoder class. It transforms all the strings to integers and assigns them to separate columns in the binary format of 0 and 1.

b.) **Encoding the Dependent Variable**

The purchase column has the value as yes and no and so the machine-readable format will be in 0,1.

```
[ ]  from sklearn.preprocessing import LabelEncoder
     le = LabelEncoder()
     y = le.fit_transform(y)


[ ]  print(y)

 ⟶  [0 1 0 0 1 1 0 1 0 1]
```

In the above code, the fit_transform method is called from LabelEncode class. It transforms all the strings to integers, thus assigning the value of 1 and 0 to yes and no, respectively.

5) **Splitting the Dataset into Test and Training Sets**

The step to split the dataset into the training set and the test set is almost the same in all the model-building techniques.

```
[ ]  from sklearn.model_selection import train_test_split
     x_train, x_test, y_train, y_test = train_test_split(x, y, test_size = 0.2, random_state = 1)


[ ]  print(x_train)

 ⟶  [[0.0 0.0 1.0 38.77777777777778 52000.0]
     [0.0 1.0 0.0 40.0 63777.77777777778]
     [1.0 0.0 0.0 44.0 72000.0]
     [0.0 0.0 1.0 38.0 61000.0]
     [0.0 0.0 1.0 27.0 48000.0]
     [1.0 0.0 0.0 48.0 79000.0]
     [0.0 1.0 0.0 50.0 83000.0]
     [1.0 0.0 0.0 35.0 58000.0]]


[ ]  print(x_test)

 ⟶  [[0.0 1.0 0.0 30.0 54000.0]
     [1.0 0.0 0.0 37.0 67000.0]]


[ ]  print(y_train)

 ⟶  [0 1 0 0 1 1 0 1]


[ ]  print(y_test)

 ⟶  [0 1]
```

In the above command, the train_test_split method is used that takes into account four arguments, namely dependent and independent variables, test_size, and random_state

Dependent and independent variables are already defined.

Test_size is the size that one wants to use; the suggested size is 20% of the total data.

Random_state is by which one defines whether they want to split data sequentially or in random manner; 1 means true and 0 means false.

x_test, x_train, y_test, and y_train are the variables where the value obtained after train_test_split is stored in the form of matrices.

6) **Feature Scaling of the Data**

Feature scaling is the method to define a range for each and every attribute in a dataset, mostly training set is defined which is why splitting of data must be done before feature scaling of data. The range is usually between −3 to +3. This can be done using normalization, or standardization which is used mostly.

In our data, age and salary are the attributes that need to undergo this step. We do not do feature scaling of encoded attributes unless they are in the range of 0–3 or unless they are in the form of 0 and 1, so the country column does not need to undergo this process.

```
[28]  from sklearn.preprocessing import StandardScaler
      sc = StandardScaler()
      x_train = sc.fit_transform(x_train[:, 3:])
      x_test = sc.transform(x_test[:, 3:])
```

```
[29]  print(x_train)
```

```
[>  [[-0.19159184 -1.07812594]
    [-0.01411729 -0.07013168]
    [ 0.56670851  0.63356243]
    [-0.30453019 -0.30786617]
    [-1.90180114 -1.42046362]
    [ 1.14753431  1.23265336]
    [ 1.43794721  1.57499104]
    [-0.74014954 -0.56461943]]
```

```
   print(x_test)
```

```
[>  [[-1.46618179 -0.9069571 ]
    [-0.44973664  0.20564034]]
```

In the above code, StandardScaler is used to perform standardization on the indexed column of x_train and y_test data. Using fit_transform, we can convert the values to the desired range and transform them in our actual dataset.

2.6 TYPES OF MACHINE LEARNING ON THE BASIS OF OUTPUT TO BE PREDICTED

2.6.1 REGRESSION

This is also a type of supervised learning. In this, the output predicted are in a continuous form rather than in a discrete form [16]. The graph formed is linear. Further, regression is divided into many methods such as decision tree, Bayesian tree, and random forest.

This method has a real-world and continuous numerical value as its output such as salary, age, and stock price. The method uses linear and nonlinear datasets and consists of many ways:

I. Simple Linear Regression [17]

- This is a method that performs regression, where a target variable is predicted using an independent variable.
- The equation for a simple linear regression model is as follows:

$$y = b_0 + b_1 * x_1$$

where

  y is the dependent variable

  b_0 is the constant

  b_1 is the coefficient of x

  x_1 is the independent variable which is input as training data

- In the above equation, x_1 has power 1, indicating that the prediction of the dependent variable is made using only one variable.
- In Figure 2.1, the grey crosses indicate the numeric values present in the x_1 variable and the black line is drawn using the simple linear equation on the y-axis, where the dependent variable is indicated.
- The more the points on the black line, the more accurate the prediction of the test data.
- The following is the code block with the output for the simple linear regression model.

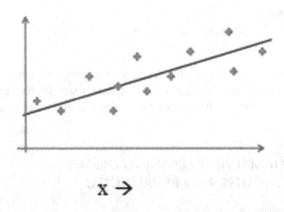

$$x \rightarrow$$

FIGURE 2.1 This figure represents the linear regression between x and y.

- Importing the libraries

```
[ ] import numpy as np
    import matplotlib.pyplot as plt
    import pandas as pd
```

- Importing the dataset

```
[ ] dataset = pd.read_csv('Salary_Data.csv')
    X = dataset.iloc[:, :-1].values
    y = dataset.iloc[:, -1].values
```

- Splitting the dataset into the Training set and Test set

```
[ ] from sklearn.model_selection import train_test_split
    X_train, X_test, y_train, y_test = train_test_split(X, y, test_size = 1/3, random_state = 0)
```

This block will remain the same as that in data preprocessing, except that the output file is now Salary_Data.csv, which contains 30 samples of salary based on years of experience. In this test, the data size is 30% of the total dataset.

- Training the Simple Linear Regression model on the Training set

```
[ ] from sklearn.linear_model import LinearRegression
    regressor = LinearRegression()
    regressor.fit(X_train, y_train)
```

```
LinearRegression(copy_X=True, fit_intercept=True, n_jobs=None, normalize=False)
```

- Predicting the Test set results

```
[ ] y_pred = regressor.predict(X_test)
```

In this code, the LinearRegression method is used on training data to train it in a model.

After that the prediction of test results is done using predict method in the regressor variable.

- Visualising the Training set results

```
[ ] plt.scatter(X_train, y_train, color = 'red')
    plt.plot(X_train, regressor.predict(X_train), color = 'blue')
    plt.title('Salary vs Experience (Training set)')
    plt.xlabel('Years of Experience')
    plt.ylabel('Salary')
    plt.show()
```

First, visualization of the training data is made to get an idea of whether the model is applied correctly or not. For this, Matplotlib is used with scatter, plot, show, and label methods (Figure 2.2).

▾ Visualising the Test set results

```
[ ]  plt.scatter(X_test, y_test, color = 'red')
     plt.plot(X_train, regressor.predict(X_train), color = 'blue')
     plt.title('Salary vs Experience (Test set)')
     plt.xlabel('Years of Experience')
     plt.ylabel('Salary')
     plt.show()
```

Finally the test set is visualized using the Matplotlib library alone.
- Both the graphs having almost similar lines show that the simple linear regression model is formed successfully and is now predicting the data accurately. In this way, by using the LinearRegression method, one can easily make a simple linear regression model using a single variable (Figure 2.3).

II. **Multiple Linear Regression [18]**
- The second type of the linear regression model is the multiple linear model where one target value is predicted using two or more variables.
- The equation for this model is as follows:

$$y = b_0 + b_1 * x_1 + b_2 * x_2 + b_3 * x_3 + \cdots + b_n * x_n$$

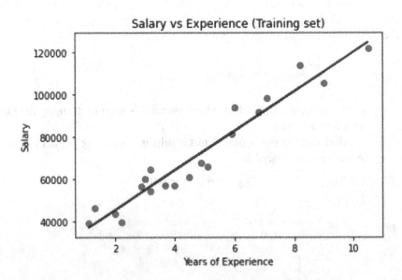

FIGURE 2.2 This figure represents the straight line between Salary vs Experience in Training set.

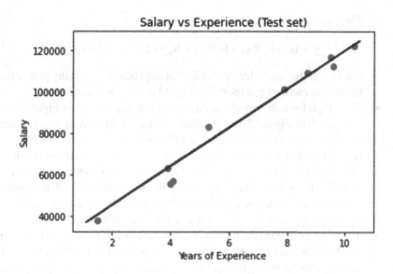

FIGURE 2.3 This figure represents the straight line between salary vs experience in testing set.

where y is the target variable that depends on all the feature variables, x_1, x_2, x_3, ..., x_n, and b_0 is the constant while all the others are coefficients.

- The x or the dependent variable can be anything—a numeric value or a categorical data. If it is a categorical data, then it should be encoded beforehand by the steps shown in data preprocessing. But once the data is encoded, it cannot be considered as a single unit; therefore each category must be considered as a separate unit and then must be computed using the equation.
- Multiple linear regression is performed in the same manner as that of simple linear regression with the LinearRegression method having training and test data.
- There are a few things that need to be checked or assumed beforehand while performing MLR, such as whether a linear relationship exists between the response variable and the feature variable, whether the residuals follow normal distributions, and whether least or no correlation exists between all the dependent variables.
- This method is used in the stock market to predict the profit or loss percentage; it can also be used in detecting pollutants from vehicles and in many other real-world situations where the output is a numeric value and is dependent on many changing, continuous, or categorical variables.

III. **Polynomial Linear Regression [19]**
- This is a type of nonlinear regression where the graph obtained is curvilinear instead of a straight line. It is because the line obtained is based on the data type and not on the mean of the data points.

- The equation for PLM is

$$y = b_0 + b_1 * x_1 + b_2 * x_1^2 + b_3 * x_1^3 + \cdots + b_n * x_1^n$$

where y is the dependent variable that depends on x_1 having power that shows the increasing exponentially and not in the same format.
- The graph for polynomial linear regression is as shown in Figure 2.4: The graph in Figure 2.4 shows that the line passes through all the data points of a single feature variable following the equation of PLM.
- It is still called linear because this is considered as an advanced model of multiple linear regression which gives the prediction more accuracy. This similarity exists due to similarity in the equation of both the models where x has a different exponent values but have the same coefficients. So, it is a type of linear model that implements a nonlinear dataset.
- Therefore, one can say that in a polynomial model, the features or the independent variables are first converted into polynomial features with certain change in degree and then linear regression is used to model this dataset.
- This model is created using the same code as that of simple linear regression using the LinearRegression method and then the output is predicted again in the same way by the predict method.
- Finally, this method can increase the accuracy and efficiency of nonlinear data in regression, and can decrease errors.

IV. **Decision Tree Regression [20]**
- This is again a regression model that deals with a nonlinear dataset. It can be a part of both regression and classification, but here it only involves regression.
- It is also called CART (Classification and Regression Tree).

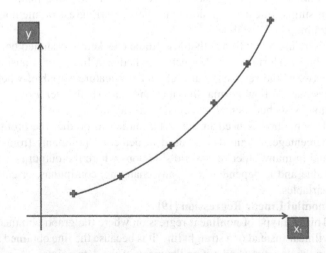

FIGURE 2.4   This figure represents the line between data points.

- In DecisionTreeRegression (DTR), there is no equation involved in forming a model; instead, all the datapoints of variables are marked on a 3D graph, with the dependent variables on the z-coordinate.
- Once all the data points are marked, using certain random parameters the graph is then spilt into various sections where each section's mean is calculated and assigned to that split block.
- Following this, one tree is formed where each node is a test condition and after passing all the nodes, the test value is assigned a split. The result of that prediction is the mean of that particular block where its data point lies.
- Figure 2.5 shows the graph of decision tree regression:

In the graph of Figure 2.5, x_1 and x_2 are the two features or independent variables whose data points are marked on the graph in black. On one side of the graph is the three-dimensional graph showing y or the dependent variable coming out of the plane.

There are four split blocks that are formed one by one on the graph. And the mean for each split is written inside the block.

- Figure 2.6 shows the graph of the tree based on the test condition fulfilling the split markings.

If value is passed in test variable then first it will go to the root node; which will be considered as a yes, then another node in one direction or if the value is not passes that is no will stem in another direction the value is checked further below at every condition in the same pattern until it reaches the final prediction value.

- The code for building a decision tree regression model is as follows:

First the import commands are executed using steps similar to those applied for data preprocessing, which helps us to import all the required libraries and dataset files whose data is saved using different variables as dependent and independent variables.

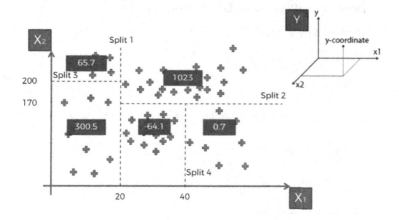

FIGURE 2.5 This figure represents the relation between dependent and independent variables.

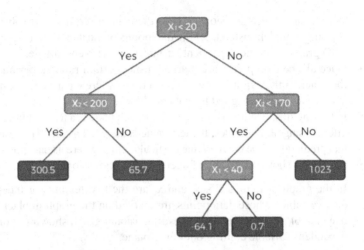

FIGURE 2.6   This figure represents the decision tree of test conditions.

▾ Training the Decision Tree Regression model on the whole dataset

```
from sklearn.tree import DecisionTreeRegressor
regressor = DecisionTreeRegressor(random_state = 0)
regressor.fit(X, y)
```

```
DecisionTreeRegressor(ccp_alpha=0.0, criterion='mse', max_depth=None,
                      max_features=None, max_leaf_nodes=None,
                      min_impurity_decrease=0.0, min_impurity_split=None,
                      min_samples_leaf=1, min_samples_split=2,
                      min_weight_fraction_leaf=0.0, presort='deprecated',
                      random_state=0, splitter='best')
```

As no categorical data is taken into consideration, there is no need to run the encoding block. So, the model is directly made using the DecisionTreeRegression class with two variables.

▾ Predicting a new result

```
[ ] regressor.predict([[6.5]])
```

```
array([150000.])
```

▾ Visualising the Decision Tree Regression results (higher resolution)

```
[ ] X_grid = np.arange(min(X), max(X), 0.01)
    X_grid = X_grid.reshape((len(X_grid), 1))
    plt.scatter(X, y, color = 'red')
    plt.plot(X_grid, regressor.predict(X_grid), color = 'blue')
    plt.title('Truth or Bluff (Decision Tree Regression)')
    plt.xlabel('Position level')
    plt.ylabel('Salary')
    plt.show()
```

In DTR, one does not need to perform the splitting of training and test datasets because their value can be input manually. If more than one feature variable is involved or more than one value is to be predicted, then the input can be easily fed into the predict method.

Prediction is made using the predict method, while visualization is done using the Matplotlib library. In the above block of code, visualization must be performed in high resolution, meaning a grid is used to visualize the output; otherwise, the graph would not be accurate, so one cannot know the range of each test condition Figure 2.7 shows a high-resolution graph for easy visualization.

- This is how a decision tree regression model works. It is efficient and easy to use when the data has a precise and clearly defined range.
- Real-world examples are flight selection for travel, ordering food online, etc.

V. **Random Forest Regression (RFR) [21]**
- This type of model is present in both regression and classification and works on nonlinear data.
- This technique is a simple yet efficient one as it combines n number of decision tree to give one output and so is called the ensemble model.
- The ensemble model that is used to perform RFR is bagging.
- RFR is required because one decision tree is good for one particular type of data having a particular range; if the range varies by a large percentage or if the attributes change, then decision tree gives garbage output. So, one can achieve accuracy and efficiency in predictions using

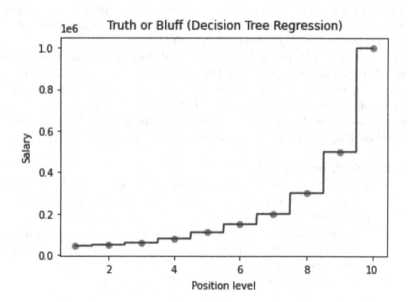

FIGURE 2.7   This graph represents the decision tree regression between x and y variables.

RFR, which combines n trees, and then the test case has to pass each decision tree, and every tree gives a separate mean value. Then the aggregate average of these values is calculated and finally one output is predicted.

- All the steps in RFR are similar to those of decision tree, except the class used is RandomForestRegressor that contains the code for building the model. This class is part of the ensemble package in the sklearn library. It also takes input of few arguments. After the model is made, one can again visualize the predicted data by Matplotlib and the prediction is done using the predict method only.
- RFR can handle a large number of inputs without any deletion and it also gives unbiased results, which makes it one of the best algorithms to be used. It is highly accurate as it can handle missing data very effectively.
- One of the drawbacks of RFR is that it causes overfitting of the data, giving noisy results.

These are the available regression models that help one to create a model for continuous data. These models can be further checked and evaluated based on their error rates. Also, score is calculated using the score method available in the sklearn. metrices package.

2.6.2 CLASSIFICATION

In this type of ML, the input data is used to divide the dataset into different classes. This is a type of supervised learning because it uses trained datasets. An example of classification is categorizing mails into spam and not spam. Further classifications include various parts such as Logistic, KNN, SVM.

Classification is a type of algorithm used to build Machine Learning models. It uses finite and discrete values for predicting a category of data and gives one of two outputs: positive or negative. For example, it shows two aspects of a prediction such as pass/fail or yes/no, or it predicts gender based on the handwriting, house price, etc. The dependent variable need not be a real-world value while using classification [22]. There are many different algorithms present in classification, which are discussed below.

I. **Logistic Regression [28]**
- The first algorithm of classification is logistic regression. As the name suggests, it uses the equation of regression with different functions to give probability of any test value.
- But as LR is a part of classification, it works to predict a category of the value, so it gives the value either 0 or 1. If the condition is fulfilled, then the value is 1; if it is not, then 0.
- LR follows a sigmoid equation to predict its output.

$$1/(1+e^{-\text{value}})$$

This equation gives a sigmoid line, which is similar to a simple regression line, but its value is restricted only between 0 and 1, meaning the range coverage is between 0 and 1 for any attribute.

- The final equation of LR is:

$$y = e^{(b0+b1*x)} / (1 + e^{(b0+b1*x)})$$

where y is the dependent variable and x is the independent variable; b is a constant.

- This equation predicts the probability of any value and then it defines a mid-range for a particular factor. Once the mid-range of this factor is defined, the probability value above that range is considered to be 1 i.e., yes, and the value below that range is treated as 0, i.e., no.
- Now implementation of logistic regression is shown below.

▾ Importing the libraries

```
[14] import numpy as np
     import matplotlib.pyplot as plt
     import pandas as pd
```

▾ Importing the dataset

```
[15] dataset = pd.read_csv('Social_Network_Ads.csv')
     X = dataset.iloc[:, [2, 3]].values
     y = dataset.iloc[:, 4].values
```

▾ Splitting the dataset into the Training set and Test set

```
[16] from sklearn.model_selection import train_test_split
     X_train, X_test, y_train, y_test = train_test_split(X, y, test_size = 0.25, random_state = 0)
```

▾ Feature Scaling

```
[21] from sklearn.preprocessing import StandardScaler
     sc = StandardScaler()
     X_train = sc.fit_transform(X_train)
     X_test = sc.transform(X_test)
```

```
[22] print(X_train)
```

```
[  0.08648817  1.05583366]
 [-0.11157634 -0.3648304 ]
 [-1.20093113  0.07006676]
 [-0.30964085 -1.3505973 ]
 [ 1.57107107  1.11281005]
```

This code shows the basic import of libraries and dataset. And once the data is imported, it is split into test and training data. Thereafter, all the four components will be printed using the print function, which shows all the columns separately. Then feature scaling is also performed.

▾ Training the Logistic Regression model on the Training set

```
[24] from sklearn.linear_model import LogisticRegression
     classifier = LogisticRegression(random_state = 0)
     classifier.fit(X_train, y_train)
```

```
⊡  LogisticRegression(C=1.0, class_weight=None, dual=False, fit_intercept=True,
                      intercept_scaling=1, l1_ratio=None, max_iter=100,
                      multi_class='auto', n_jobs=None, penalty='l2',
                      random_state=0, solver='lbfgs', tol=0.0001, verbose=0,
                      warm_start=False)
```

This block of code shows how the data is trained using LogisticRegression class and how the model is formed. This class is present in the sklearn. linear_model package.

▾ Predicting a new result

```
[25] print(classifier.predict(sc.transform([[30,87000]])))
```

```
⊡  [0]
```

▾ Predicting the Test set results

```
[26] y_pred = classifier.predict(X_test)
     print(np.concatenate((y_pred.reshape(len(y_pred),1), y_test.reshape(len(y_test),1)),1))
```

```
⊡  [0 0]
     [0 1]
     [1 1]
     [0 0]
     [0 0]
     [0 0]
```

This block shows the predict method by which the value is predicted. The first shows the prediction of a new value, and the next shows the prediction of the test result.

▾ Making the Confusion Matrix

```
[27] from sklearn.metrics import confusion_matrix, accuracy_score
     cm = confusion_matrix(y_test, y_pred)
     print(cm)
     accuracy_score(y_test, y_pred)
```

```
⊡  [[65  3]
     [ 8 24]]
     0.89
```

This block is used to create a confusion matrix, which is built using confusion_metrices of the sklearn.metrices package. This is performed to determine which of the prediction is correct and which one incorrect.

▾ Visualising the Training set results

```
[28] from matplotlib.colors import ListedColormap
     X_set, y_set = sc.inverse_transform(X_train), y_train
     X1, X2 = np.meshgrid(np.arange(start = X_set[:, 0].min() - 10, stop = X_set[:, 0].max() + 10, step = 0.25),
                          np.arange(start = X_set[:, 1].min() - 1000, stop = X_set[:, 1].max() + 1000, step = 0.25))
     plt.contourf(X1, X2, classifier.predict(sc.transform(np.array([X1.ravel(), X2.ravel()]).T)).reshape(X1.shape),
                  alpha = 0.75, cmap = ListedColormap(('red', 'green')))
     plt.xlim(X1.min(), X1.max())
     plt.ylim(X2.min(), X2.max())
     for i, j in enumerate(np.unique(y_set)):
         plt.scatter(X_set[y_set == j, 0], X_set[y_set == j, 1], c = ListedColormap(('red', 'green'))(i), label = j)
     plt.title('Logistic Regression (Training set)')
     plt.xlabel('Age')
     plt.ylabel('Estimated Salary')
     plt.legend()
     plt.show()
```

⊳ 'c' argument looks like a single numeric RGB or RGBA sequence, which should be avoided as value-mapping will have
   'c' argument looks like a single numeric RGB or RGBA sequence, which should be avoided as value-mapping will have

Then one can visualize the output for the training dataset and the test dataset. The graph shows a light grey zone indicating people belonging to a certain age and income group will not buy an SUV and the dark grey zone shows that they will buy. There is a distinct line between these two zones formed using sigmoid function, but we also see that a few points lie on this line and are not clear as to which region they belong. These are the points which we can identify using the confusion matrix as incorrect values. A few points are also present between the zones that can help us in calculating the error rate of this method (Figure 2.8).

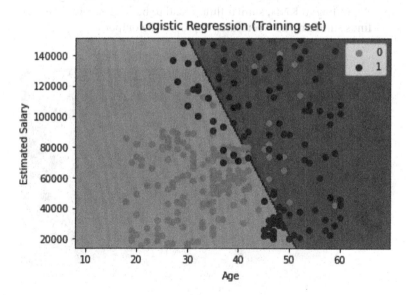

FIGURE 2.8 This picture represents the logistics regression beween age and salary in training set.

▾ Visualising the Test set results

```
[29] from matplotlib.colors import ListedColormap
     X_set, y_set = sc.inverse_transform(X_test), y_test
     X1, X2 = np.meshgrid(np.arange(start = X_set[:, 0].min() - 10, stop = X_set[:, 0].max() + 10, step = 0.25),
                          np.arange(start = X_set[:, 1].min() - 1000, stop = X_set[:, 1].max() + 1000, step = 0.25))
     plt.contourf(X1, X2, classifier.predict(sc.transform(np.array([X1.ravel(), X2.ravel()]).T)).reshape(X1.shape),
                  alpha = 0.75, cmap = ListedColormap(('red', 'green')))
     plt.xlim(X1.min(), X1.max())
     plt.ylim(X2.min(), X2.max())
     for i, j in enumerate(np.unique(y_set)):
         plt.scatter(X_set[y_set == j, 0], X_set[y_set == j, 1], c = ListedColormap(('red', 'green'))(i), label = j)
     plt.title('Logistic Regression (Test set)')
     plt.xlabel('Age')
     plt.ylabel('Estimated Salary')
     plt.legend()
     plt.show()
```

```
⊑→ 'c' argument looks like a single numeric RGB or RGBA sequence, which should be avoided as value-mapping will have
   'c' argument looks like a single numeric RGB or RGBA sequence, which should be avoided as value-mapping will have
```

Then a graph obtained using the test dataset can help to determine if the result is correct. The starting point and the ending point of the line dividing the zones can be different, but this graph should contain a less number of incorrect values than the training data as machine has learned to identify almost everything. So, using this, one can get the desired result in a presentable manner (Figure 2.9).

- This is how a logistic regression model works. It is efficient and accurate because it does not require scaling and uses least amount of resources. Its simplicity makes it easy to use and so this algorithm is used widely.

II. K-Nearest Neighbor (KNN) [24]

- This is another type of classification for supervised learning.
- According to KNN, similar things tend to be in close proximity; i.e., it finds similarity between cases to predict the output.

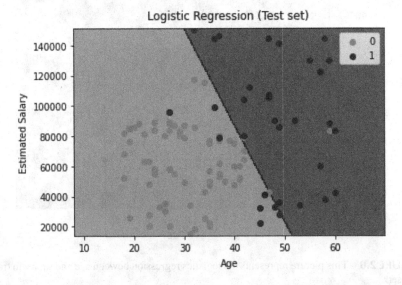

FIGURE 2.9 This picture represents the logistics regression beween age and salary in testing set.

- KNN works on the Euclidean distance equation.
  Figure 2.10 shows the distance between two points A and B.
- In KNN also, two or more categories are made, as shown in Figure 2.11. Then a place for the test data value is selected by following the below steps.
- In KNN, first a K value is assigned, which indicates the number of neighbors, and then Euclidean distance of these K numbers of points is calculated for each of the test data value. Thereafter, the total number of data points nearest to the test value is checked in both the categories. Once this is done, the category which has the maximum number of data points is selected as the predicted output.
- Code for K-nearest neighbor is pretty much similar to logistic regression except that feature scaling is done before the training data is trained by

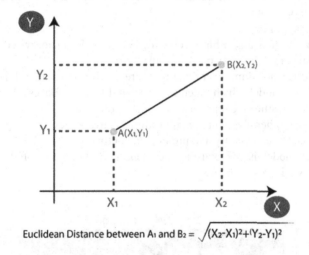

Euclidean Distance between A_1 and $B_2 = \sqrt{(X_2-X_1)^2+(Y_2-Y_1)^2}$

FIGURE 2.10   The graph shows the distance between two points A and B through a straight line.

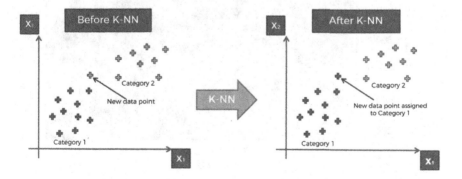

FIGURE 2.11   The figure shows how a data point is assigned to a cluster after KNN is done.

the K-nearest classifier method. This method takes the value of K as one of its argument. Once this is done, one can visualize the output in the graphical form similar to that of logistic regression.

- Feature scaling is an important step in this model if the values of an attribute are in a wide range, because later it will be difficult to judge the minimum distance between them.
- The graph visualized in KNN is different from that of logistic regression as this graph does not contain a straight line between the light grey and the dark grey zones, but it contains a random yet distinct line separating the two zones (Figure 2.12).
- This way KNN is an important algorithm because it is easy to implement and very effective on large training data. But it is difficult to decide a K-value beforehand, and calculating Euclidean distance is very costly. On the other hand, KNN's robustness makes it efficient to use for noisy data.

III. **Naive Bayes [25]**
- It is another algorithm of classification based on supervised Machine Learning that works on Bayes' theorem.
- In this algorithm, several methods are combined together. It is a probabilistic model which calculates probability from Bayes' theorem and then classifies the data based on each probability.
- Unlike other classification algorithms, Naive Bayes gives equal importance to each quality and predicts the output.
- The model is made using the GaussianNB method of the sklearn. Naive_Bayes package.

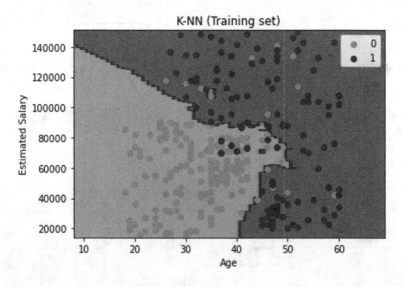

FIGURE 2.12 This picture represents K-NN effects on age and salary with training set.

▾ Training the Naive Bayes model on the Training set

```
[ ] from sklearn.naive_bayes import GaussianNB
    classifier = GaussianNB()
    classifier.fit(X_train, y_train)
```

- The graph obtained shows a distinct line, but it is made by vertical and horizontal groups, thus making it different from the other two classification techniques.
- All the steps are similar to those of other classification techniques.

IV. **Decision Tree Classification [26]**
- This algorithm is a supervised algorithm part of classification.
- As described previously, decision tree is also a part of regression; the difference between the two is that in classification the end node represents a category instead of a mean numeric value.
- In decision tree, there are two types of nodes: decision node and leaf node. Decision nodes are those where test cases are assigned a category and passed on further to be identified in another split; leaf node is the last node on each decision node that tells us the final category a test value belongs to.
- Splits formed in decision tree classification is not done randomly; instead, it is done on the basis of category: in one split only one type of data attribute is present and can be dark grey or light grey.
- As seen in the graph, all splits are categorized before only (Figure 2.13).
- This way a decision tree is made using the DecisionTreeClassifier (DTC) method in which certain arguments are taken to build an accurate model. The rest of the steps are similar to those of other classification models (Figure 2.14).

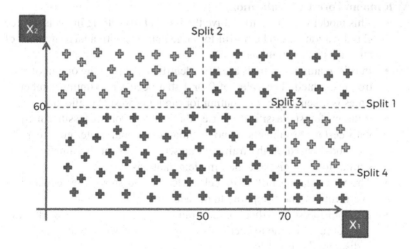

FIGURE 2.13 Splits are distinct for 2*2 cases.

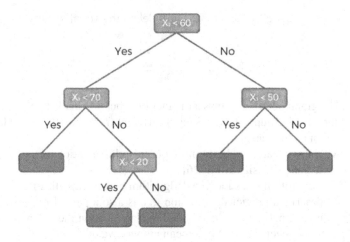

FIGURE 2.14   This figure represents the decision tree of the dataset.

- Visualization is also done in a similar way but the graph formed does not have a clear line between the light grey and the dark grey zone. Rather, it is spread unevenly between the two zones. This is because in DTC, overfitting is done and the model tries to include each and every dataset possible. But one should also notice that the graph below has only horizontal and vertical lines that separate the light grey and dark grey boxes, showing how splitting is done in DTC.
- Therefore, this model works similarly to how a human takes a decision and is very useful to take decisions that can have a lot of outcomes. It also needs lesser cleaning of data than other models (Figure 2.15).

V. **Random Forest Classification[27]**
- This model was made to resolve the issue of overfitting in decision tree classification and to be useful for large datasets with a large number of attributes and variations.
- In this, n number of trees are first identified and then the output of each tree is counted. The value of 0 or 1 that occurs maximum number of times is taken as the final output for random forest classification.
- Random forest classification uses the RandomForestClassifier method with certain arguments as no_estimator, random_state, etc., to build the model based on the training dataset. The rest of the functioning is similar to other classification implementations.
- The visualization in this model is clearer and shows the reduction is overfitting to that compared to decision tree classification.
- Random forest classification and random forest regression work similarly, except that the former's data is continuous, while that of the latter is discrete (Figure 2.16).
- It is efficient for high-dimensional large datasets and is used widely.

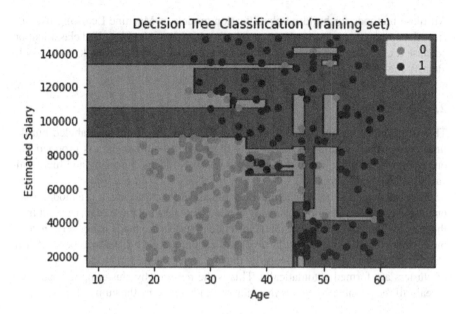

FIGURE 2.15 Decision tree classification of training set between age and salary.

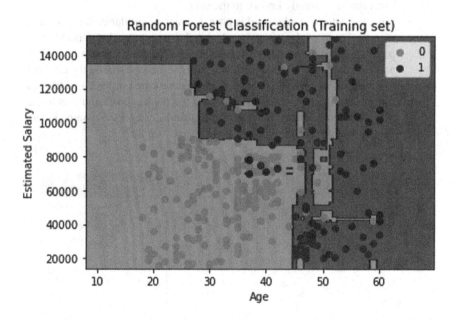

FIGURE 2.16 Random forest classification of training set between age and salary.

All these methods for building classification models of Machine Learning use discrete data to give a categorized output. That's why this method is called classification because it classifies any amount of data into particular parts, thus making it easy to identify the characteristics of a group.

2.6.3 CLUSTERING

This is a type of unsupervised learning. In this, the data used is unlabeled but the final prediction is similar to that of classification, i.e., similar data is grouped into one cluster by keeping in mind a few parameters. K-means clustering and hierarchical clustering are its types.

Another method to build Machine Learning model is clustering. It is a model based on the unsupervised Machine Learning method that takes unlabeled data as input from the user. As the name implies, small clusters of datasets are made using certain common features. Clustering is similar to classification, the only difference being that in classification, prior groups are made by the user only, whereas in clustering n number of clusters are formed automatically. This is the reason why clustering is used, as it reveals all the possible outcomes that cannot be identified by the human brain [29].

I. **K-Means Clustering [30]**
  - It is a method of clustering that is similar to K-nearest neighbor.
  - In this method clusters are made using Euclidean distance and the features that are already known to the user.
  - First, the dataset is taken and is placed alongside similar data points, and then the mean of these two is calculated and a centroid is formed for a particular cluster. Similarly, each dataset is placed near its similar cluster and then the mean is calculated. Next, this new mean will be the centroid of this circle or cluster. This way all the datasets are arranged and trained into various clusters. Once this is done, a test point is taken and kept to the mean or centroid that is most similar to it and a category is assigned to it.
  - Figure 2.17 shows the graph of how clusters are formed.

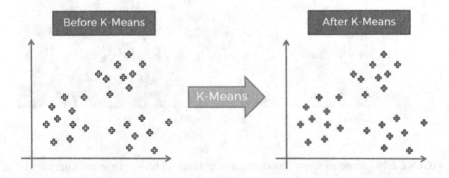

FIGURE 2.17   This picture represents the K-NN effect on various points.

- Now the code for K-means clustering is as follows:

▾ Importing the libraries

```
[4]  import numpy as np
     import matplotlib.pyplot as plt
     import pandas as pd
```

▾ Importing the dataset

```
[5]  dataset = pd.read_csv('Mall_Customers.csv')
     X = dataset.iloc[:, [2, 3]].values
```

First the data and libraries are imported as usual.

▾ Using the elbow method to find the optimal number of clusters

```
[6]  from sklearn.cluster import KMeans
     wcss = []
     for i in range(1, 11):
         kmeans = KMeans(n_clusters = i, init = 'k-means++', random_state = 42)
         kmeans.fit(X)
         wcss.append(kmeans.inertia_)
     plt.plot(range(1, 11), wcss)
     plt.title('The Elbow Method')
     plt.xlabel('Number of clusters')
     plt.ylabel('WCSS')
     plt.show()
```

Then using the K-means method and the append method, the optimal number of clusters is calculated and the dataset is trained using the same method. The elbow method is used, which means a point where an elbow or knee shape is formed is taken as the optimum number of K (Figure 2.18).

▾ Training the K-Means model on the dataset

```
[ ]  kmeans = KMeans(n_clusters = 5, init = 'k-means++', random_state = 42)
     y_kmeans = kmeans.fit_predict(X)
```

In this one need not split the data in training and test data as it is a part of unsupervised learning.

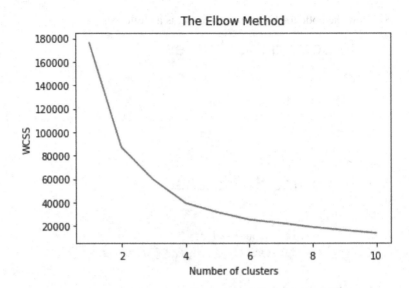

FIGURE 2.18   This graph represents the Elbow method of two points.

▾ Visualising the clusters

```
[ ]  plt.scatter(X[y_kmeans == 0, 0], X[y_kmeans == 0, 1], s = 100, c = 'red', label = 'Cluster 1')
     plt.scatter(X[y_kmeans == 1, 0], X[y_kmeans == 1, 1], s = 100, c = 'blue', label = 'Cluster 2')
     plt.scatter(X[y_kmeans == 2, 0], X[y_kmeans == 2, 1], s = 100, c = 'green', label = 'Cluster 3')
     plt.scatter(X[y_kmeans == 3, 0], X[y_kmeans == 3, 1], s = 100, c = 'cyan', label = 'Cluster 4')
     plt.scatter(X[y_kmeans == 4, 0], X[y_kmeans == 4, 1], s = 100, c = 'magenta', label = 'Cluster 5')
     plt.scatter(kmeans.cluster_centers_[:, 0], kmeans.cluster_centers_[:, 1], s = 300, c = 'yellow', label = 'Centroids')
     plt.title('Clusters of customers')
     plt.xlabel('Annual Income (k$)')
     plt.ylabel('Spending Score (1-100)')
     plt.legend()
     plt.show()
```

Finally, the dataset is visualized in the form of clusters showing the centroid value of each cluster. This is done using the Matplotlib library (Figure 2.19).

- This way K-means is a very important algorithm that helps in building a model for unsupervised learning and it can categorize data into several categories more than a human brain can see.
- As the clusters formed in K-means clustering are not spherical, the result cannot be trusted to be accurate and a slight variation in the dataset can create a huge difference in the clusters. So it is not so much efficient to use.

II. **Hierarchical Clustering [31]**

- Another type of clustering is hierarchical clustering. It works just like a hierarchy tree that has many nodes with one root node.
- This clustering is divided into two parts:
  1. *Agglomerative:* In this, each data point is treated as separate unit in starting and then all separate units are combined into a single unit.

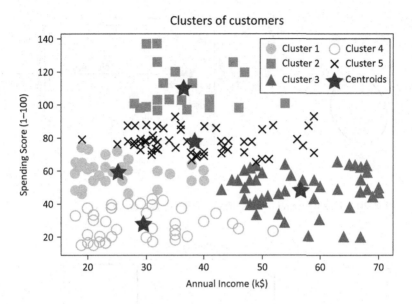

FIGURE 2.19 This figure represents the clusters of customers.

2. *Divisive:* In this, first the whole data is considered as a single data point and then the values are broken down one by one.

- As divisive clustering is not used much in the real world, one has to focus more on agglomerative clustering. And the steps are as follows:

  First two data points are taken and the mean is calculated.

  Then another data point is taken and this forms a cluster again with the nearest mean present to the cluster.

  This way, each cluster starts from two points and addition of a similar data point changes its mean and the clusters with similar properties are formed.

- This method uses a dendrogram to make the number of clusters. A dendrogram is made from a big cluster. It separates the big cluster into two parts and a point value is considered in graph above in which 22 clusters are considered. Similarly, as the line moves below the dendrogram, clusters are defined and each data point is part of any one cluster. The graph in Figure 2.20 can be used to explain how a line is drawn to decide a cluster.

- Code for hierarchical clustering is again similar to that of K-means clustering, except that instead of k-means, first dendrogram class is used to decide the optimal number of clusters. The dendrogram formed is shown in Figure 2.21.

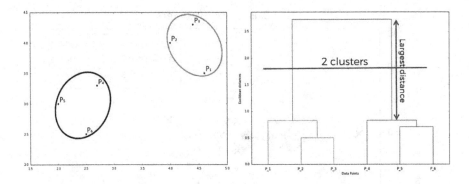

FIGURE 2.20   This figure represents the clustering of two data points.

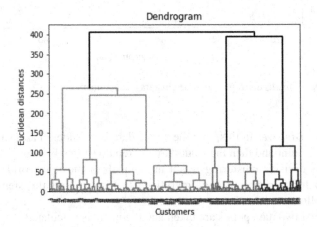

FIGURE 2.21   This figure represents the Euclidian distances between x and y axis..

- Using the dendrogram to find the optimal number of clusters

```
[3]  import scipy.cluster.hierarchy as sch
     dendrogram = sch.dendrogram(sch.linkage(X, method = 'ward'))
     plt.title('Dendrogram')
     plt.xlabel('Customers')
     plt.ylabel('Euclidean distances')
     plt.show()
```

- Then the agglomerative clustering method is used to train the dataset.

- Training the Hierarchical Clustering model on the dataset

```
[4]  from sklearn.cluster import AgglomerativeClustering
     hc = AgglomerativeClustering(n_clusters = 5, affinity = 'euclidean', linkage = 'ward')
     y_hc = hc.fit_predict(X)
```

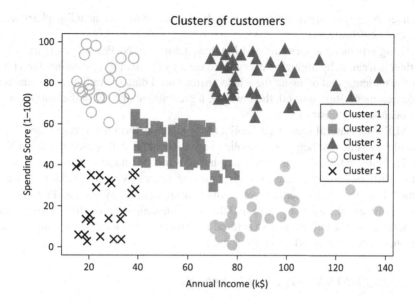

FIGURE 2.22 This figure represents the cluster of customers based on annual income..

- Visualization of clusters in the graphical form is shown in Figure 2.22.
- This is how hierarchical clustering works. It is a popular and easy way to cluster data.

These two methods make clustering an efficient method to categorize discrete unlabeled data. These two methods are the only ones which can help in training unsupervised data efficiently because clustering involves minimal human interventions once the data is fed to the machine (Figure 2.22).

This way Machine Learning is used to make different models to make it easy and fast to use a huge amount of data. These topics will help further to train real-world data and make it useful in one way or the other.

2.7 NATURAL LANGUAGE PROCESSING FOR BIG DATA

It is a form of Artificial Intelligence that helps machines in reading text data just the way a human reads it. It aids in several domains like statistics, linguistics, semantics and machine learning by helping to define relationships between entities and to understand texts that are either verbal or written. Tasks such as automatic summary, translation, named entity recognition, relationship extraction, sentiment analysis, speech recognition, and topic segmentation can be performed using NLP [32].

Natural language processing is in trend nowadays because every field has a large amount of text data that have to be interpreted for useful reports and analyses. All this humongous data is big data and NLP deals with it in a very smooth and subtle manner. NLP finds application in various biomedical domains including pharmaceutics and healthcare.

Using advanced algorithms and Machine Learning, NLP can change the way a patient is treated, by digitizing every word used by the doctor, by making fixed plans for the patients, and by using the whole unstructured data to predict results and provide treatment. Rest assured, there will be a great usage of NLP in the near future in the healthcare industry [33].

NLP uses Natural Language Toolkit (NLTK) to perform text recognition. NLTK is a library suite that helps in symbolic and statistical NLP. It is used mostly in NLP. NLTK helps in tokenization (punctuations are removed and sentences are converted into words or clauses), stemming (grouping of related words to a common stem), removal of stop words (removal of words that are commonly used and do not have any significance), and many more. All the functions help in converting verbal reports from doctors and patients into structured documents for quick reference and in making such reports more effective and generic [34].

2.8 BIG DATA WITH DEEP LEARNING

Deep learning is a subfield of Machine Learning; it helps machines mimic the human brain in performing tasks such as speech recognition, processing data, detecting entities and their relationships, and analyses and making decisions. But we know that Machine Learning does the same kind of work, so why do we need deep learning? Unlike Machine Learning where the machine learns on its own using algorithms, deep learning performs these tasks by structuring algorithms and making artificial neural networks. Deep learning has a major impact on big data as it helps to extract relevant information from huge amounts of unstructured, unlabeled big data [35].

Deep learning uses artificial neural networks to do the programming. Artificial neural networks are a web-like structure which has nodes equivalent to synapses of the human brain. These neural networks work in a hierarchical pattern while in Machine Learning the algorithms are run in a linear fashion; hence it is said that deep learning is an advancement of Machine Learning. There are three components of a neural network: input layer, output layer, and middle layer that undergo entire processing to make the raw data provided in the input layer into relevant output. Neural networks are built in Python language and use libraries like Tensorflow and pyTorch to build the model. The advantage of neural networks over Machine Learning algorithm is that it helps to get the data as a whole without the need to remove the undesired data or consider the missing data. They also provide a solution to the problem of overfitting as it processes the data in a stepwise manner [36].

In the healthcare industry, deep learning is used in image recognition and chatbots that interact with patients in an easy manner. Medical imaging feature is the one that is most used in treating patients with cancer as it recognizes the patterns that are developed and also compares the cancer data with the already present data. It can also easily inform us of the unusual pattern or the new one, thus making the job easy for doctors and efficient for the medical system. This is just the starting stage of deep learning and AI in the healthcare field. According to experts, deep learning has great potential in making medical systems more relevant and easy for doctors. More and more clinical functions can be performed by deep learning that helps in patient analysis, e.g., in radiology or administration interference to review patients' details, etc. [37].

2.9 HOW MACHINE LEARNING CAN BE APPLIED TO BIG DATA

So far we have looked at all the algorithms that can be performed in Machine Learning. Let us see how big data can be applied to these algorithms to predict a pattern or a solution from unorganized data [38].

1. **Applying K-Nearest Neighbors to Data**
   - Classification, which is a supervised form of Machine Learning, explains the intuition of K-nearest neighbors algorithm. In this section, we're going to apply a simple example of the algorithm using Scikit-Learn, and then in the subsequent sections we'll build our own algorithm to learn more about how it works under the hood.
   - To exemplify classification, we're going to use a Breast Cancer Dataset, which is a dataset donated to the University of California, Irvine (UCI) collection from the University of Wisconsin-Madison. UCI has a large Machine Learning repository. The datasets present are organized by types of Machine Learning often used for them, such as data types, attribute types, topic areas, and a few others. It is very useful for both educational uses and development of Machine Learning algorithms. From the Breast Cancer Dataset page, choose the Data Folder link. From there, grab breast-cancer-wisconsin.data and breast-cancerwisconsin.names. These may not download automatically, but may instead display in the browser. Right click to save, if this is the case for you.
   - After downloading, open the breast-cancer-wisconsin.names file. Scrolling down the file just after line 100, we can get the names of the attributes (columns). With this information, we can manually add these labels to the breast-cancer-wisconsin.data file.
       Open that, and enter a new first line:
       - Id,
       - clump_thickness,
       - uniform_cell_size,
       - uniform_cell_shape,
       - marginal_adhesion,
       - single_epi_cell_size,
       - bare_nuclei,
       - bland_chromation,
       - normal_nucleoli,
       - mitoses,
       - class.

You might wonder what these features and labels are. What we're attempting is to classify things so that we have a list of attributes indicating either a benign or a malignant tumor. Also, most of these columns appear to be of use, but the question is whether they are similar to the others or they might be useless? Absolutely, this ID column is not something we actually want to feed into the classifier.

- *Missing/bad data*

  This dataset also has some missing data in it, which we're going to need to clean! Let's start off with our imports, pulling in the data, and do some cleaning:

```
import numpy as np
from sklearn import preprocessing, cross_validation, neighbors
import pandas as pd

df = pd.read_csv('breast-cancer-wisconsin.data.txt')
df.replace('?',-99999, inplace=True)
df.drop(['id'], 1, inplace=True)
```

After feeding in the data, we take note that there are some columns with missing data. These columns have a "?" filled in. The .names file informed us of this, but we would have discovered this eventually via an error if we attempted to feed this information to a classifier. In this case, we're choosing to fill in a −99,999 value for any missing data. You can choose how you want to handle missing data, but, in the real world, you may find that 50% or more of your rows contain missing data in one of the columns, especially if you are collecting data with extensive attributes. The value −99999 isn't perfect, but it works well enough. Next, we're dropping the IDcolumn. When we are done, we'll comment out the dropping of the id column just to see what sort of impact it might have to include it.

- Next, we define our features (X) and labels (y):

```
X = np.array(df.drop(['class'], 1))
y = np.array(df['class'])
```

The features X are everything except for the class. Doing df.drop returns a new dataframe with our chosen column(s) dropped. The label y is just the class column.

- Now we create training and testing samples using Scikit-Learn Learns cross_validation.train_test_split:

```
X_train, X_test, y_train, y_test =
cross_validation.train_test_split(X, y, test_size=0.2)
```

- Define the classifier:

```
clf = neighbors.KNeighborsClassifier()
```

In this case, we're using the K-nearest neighbors classifier from Sklearn.

- Train the classifier:

```
clf.fit(X_train, y_train)
```

- Test:

```
accuracy = clf.score(X_test, y_test)
print(accuracy)
```

The result should be about 95%, and that's out of the box without any tweaking. Very cool! Let's show what happens when we do indeed include truly meaningless and misleading data by commenting out the dropping of the id column:

```
import numpy as np
from sklearn import preprocessing, cross_validation, neighbors
import pandas as pd

df = pd.read_csv('breast-cancer-wisconsin.data.txt')
df.replace('?',-99999, inplace=True)
```

```
#df.drop(['id'], 1, inplace=True)

X = np.array(df.drop(['class'], 1))
y = np.array(df['class'])

X_train, X_test, y_train, y_test =
cross_validation.train_test_split(X, y, test_size=0.2)

clf = neighbors.KNeighborsClassifier()
clf.fit(X_train, y_train)
accuracy = clf.score(X_test, y_test)
print(accuracy)
```

The impact is staggering, where accuracy drops from ~95% to ~60% on average. In the future, when AI rules the planet, note that you just need to feed it meaningless attributes to outsmart it! Interestingly enough, adding noise can be a way to help or hurt your algorithm. When combatting your robot overlords, being able to distinguish between helpful noise and malicious noise may save your life!

- Next, you can probably guess how we'll be predicting if you followed the regression tutorial that used Scikit-Learn. First, we need some sample data. We can just make it up. For example, I will look at one of the lines in the sample file and make something similar by merely shifting some of the values. You can also just add noise to do further testing, provided the standard deviation is not outrageous. Doing this is relatively safe as well, since you're not actually training on the falsified data but merely testing. I will just manually do this by making up a line:

```
example_measures = np.array([4,2,1,1,1,2,3,2,1])
```

Feel free to search the document for that list of features. It doesn't exist.
Now you can do:

```
prediction = clf.predict(example_measures)
print(prediction)
```

... or depending on when you are watching this, you might not be able
to! When doing that, I get a warning:

```
DeprecationWarning: Passing 1d arrays as data is deprecated in
0.17 and will raise ValueError in 0.19. Reshape your data
either using X.reshape(-1, 1) if your data has a single
feature or X.reshape(1, -1) if it contains a single sample.
```

Okay, no problem. Do we have a single feature? Nope. Do we have a
single example? Yes! So we will use X.reshape(1, −1):

```
example_measures = np.array([4,2,1,1,1,2,3,2,1])
example_measures = example_measures.reshape(1, -1)
prediction = clf.predict(example_measures)
```

```
print(prediction)
```

Output:

$$0.95$$
$$[2]$$

The output here is first the accuracy (95%) and then the prediction (2),
and this is what we expected to model from our fake data.
- What if we had two samples?

```
example_measures =
np.array([[4,2,1,1,1,2,3,2,1],[4,2,1,1,1,2,3,2,1]])
example_measures = example_measures.reshape(2, -1)
prediction = clf.predict(example_measures)
print(prediction)
```

- What if we don't know how many samples?!

```
example_measures =
np.array([[4,2,1,1,1,2,3,2,1],[4,2,1,1,1,2,3,2,1]])
example_measures =
example_measures.reshape(len(example_measures), -1)
prediction = clf.predict(example_measures)
print(prediction)
```

As you can see, implementing K-nearest neighbors is not only easy but
also extremely accurate in this case. In the next section, we're going to
build our own K-nearest neighbors algorithm from scratch, rather than
using Scikit-Learn, in an attempt to learn more about the algorithm,
understand how it works, and, most importantly, learn one of its pitfalls.

2. **The CART Training Algorithm**

Scikit-Learn uses the *Classification And Regression Tree* (CART) algorithm to train decision trees (also called "growing" trees). The idea is really quite simple: the algorithm first splits the training set into two subsets using a single feature k and a threshold tk (e.g., "petal length $\leq$ 2.45 cm"). How does it choose k and tk? It searches for the pair (k, tk) that produces the purest subsets (weighted by their size). The cost function that the algorithm tries to minimize is given by the following equation:

$$J\left(k, t_k\right) = \frac{m_{\text{left}}}{m} G_{\text{left}} + \frac{m_{\text{right}}}{m} G_{\text{right}}$$

where $\begin{cases} G_{\text{left/right}} \text{ measures the impurity of the left/right subset} \\ m_{\text{left/right}} \text{ is the number of instances of the left/right subset} \end{cases}$

Once it has successfully split the training set into two, it splits the subsets using the same logic into sub-subsets, and so on, recursively. It stops recursing once it reaches the maximum depth (defined by the max_depth hyperparameter), or if it cannot find a split that will reduce impurity. A few other hyperparameters (described in a moment) control additional stopping conditions (min_samples_split, min_samples_leaf, min_weight_fraction_leaf, and max_leaf_nodes).

Algorithm

We will use the Scikit-Learn library to build the decision tree model. We will be using the iris dataset to build a DecisionTreeClassifier. The dataset contains information of three classes—Iris Setosa, Iris Versicolour, and Iris Virginica—of the iris plant with the following attributes:

- Sepal length
- Sepal width
- Petal length
- Petal width

The task is to predict which class do the iris plant belong to based on the attributes.

```
#Importing required libraries
import pandas as pd
import numpy as np
from sklearn.datasets import load_iris
from sklearn.tree import DecisionTreeClassifier
from sklearn.model_selection import train_test_split

#Loading the iris data
data = load_iris()
print('Classes to predict: ', data.target_names)
```

```
#Extracting data attributes
X = data.data
### Extracting target/ class labels
y = data.target

print('Number of examples in the data:', X.shape[0])

#First four rows in the variable 'X'
X[:4]

#Output
Out: array([[5.1, 3.5, 1.4, 0.2],
            [4.9, 3. , 1.4, 0.2],
            [4.7, 3.2, 1.3, 0.2],
            [4.6, 3.1, 1.5, 0.2]])
```

```
#Using the train_test_split to create train and test sets.
X_train, X_test, y_train, y_test = train_test_split(X, y, random_state = 47,
test_size = 0.25)
```

```
#Importing the Decision tree classifier from the sklearn library.
from sklearn.tree import DecisionTreeClassifier
clf = DecisionTreeClassifier(criterion = 'entropy')
```

```
#Training the decision tree classifier.
clf.fit(X_train, y_train)
```

```
#Output:
Out:DecisionTreeClassifier(class_weight=None, criterion='entropy', max_depth=None,
            max_features=None, max_leaf_nodes=None,
            min_impurity_decrease=0.0, min_impurity_split=None,
            min_samples_leaf=1, min_samples_split=2,
            min_weight_fraction_leaf=0.0, presort=False, random_state=None,
            splitter='best')
```

```
#Predicting labels on the test set.
y_pred =  clf.predict(X_test)
```

```
#Importing the accuracy metric from sklearn.metrics library

from sklearn.metrics import accuracy_score
print('Accuracy Score on train data: ', accuracy_score(y_true=y_train,
y_pred=clf.predict(X_train)))
print('Accuracy Score on test data: ', accuracy_score(y_true=y_test, y_pred=y_pred))
```

```
#Output:
Out: Accuracy Score on train data:  1.0
     Accuracy Score on test data:  0.9473684210526315
```

```
clf = DecisionTreeClassifier(criterion='entropy', min_samples_split=50)
clf.fit(X_train, y_train)
print('Accuracy Score on train data: ', accuracy_score(y_true=y_train,
y_pred=clf.predict(X_train)))
print('Accuracy Score on the test data: ', accuracy_score(y_true=y_test,
y_pred=clf.predict(X_test)))

#Output:
Out: Accuracy Score on train data:  0.9553571428571429
     Accuracy Score on test data:   0.9736842105263158
```

```
from sklearn.externals.six import StringIO
from IPython.display import Image
from sklearn.tree import export_graphviz
import pydotplus
dot_data =StringIO()
export_graphviz(dtree, out_file=dot_data, filled=True, rounded=True)
graph = pydotplus.graph_from_dot_data(dot_data.getvalue())
Image(graph.create_png())
```

Decision Tree (Figure 2.23).

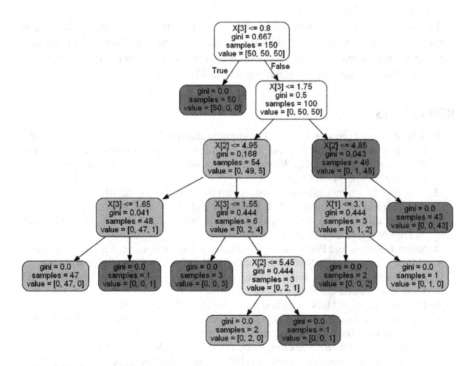

FIGURE 2.23 This figure represents the decision tree of the dataset.

2.10 MACHINE LEARNING IN HEALTHCARE

We now know what Machine Learning means and how it works on big data and biological data. Let us see in brief what its uses are in today's world. In healthcare, Machine Learning and Artificial Intelligence have played a great role as they have made it easy for patients to interact with the system as well as for doctors to diagnose patients and analyze their medical profiles. Not only this, Machine Learning has made it easy and fast to do researches on biological data as it is always large in amount and is always present in an unstructured form [39].

The collaboration between big data and artificial intelligence had helped in analyzing and deriving conclusions out of humongous data available. Currently, a large number of companies are able to understand their customers better using machine learning.

Not only this, Machine Learning helps in cost-reduction for research work and medicinal formulation and also helps in detecting the root cause of disease in large numbers of patients at a time. With reduction in paper work and manual input of data, Machine Learning has helped in saving time as well, and also diagnostics results can be generated faster than it used to be. Better treatment plans can be made on a more generic level. Interaction between community and doctors can be made easy and fast. All this tells us that usage of Machine Learning, Artificial Intelligence, deep learning, and natural language processing is going to increase in future as the amount of data collected day to day is increasing

In future the usage of machine learning, artificial intelligence, deep learning and natural language processing is going to enhance exponentially keeping abreast with the enormous amount of data generated on a daily basis due to the ease of easy-to-use algorithms and no human interference. [40, 41]

REFERENCES

1. John R. Koza, Forrest H. Bennett, David Andre and Martin A. Keane (1996). *Automated Design of Both the Topology and Sizing of Analog Electrical Circuits Using Genetic Programming. Artificial Intelligence in Design '96* (Dordrecht: Springer), pp. 151–170. doi: 10.1007/978-94-009-0279-4_9.
2. "Machine Learning textbook". www.cs.cmu.edu. Retrieved 2020-05-28.
3. A. L'Heureux, K. Grolinger, H. F. Elyamany and M. A. M. Capretz (2017). Machine learning with big data: Challenges and approaches. *IEEE Access* 5: 7776–7797. doi: 10.1109/ACCESS.2017.2696365.
4. Stuart J. Russell and Peter Norvig (2009). *Artificial Intelligence: A Modern Approach* (3rd ed.). Upper Saddle River, NJ: Prentice Hall. ISBN 978-0-13-604259-4.
5. John Haugeland (1985). *Artificial Intelligence: The Very Idea*, Cambridge, MA: MIT Press. ISBN 0-262-08153-9.
6. David Poole, Alan Mackworth and Randy Goebel (1998). *Computational Intelligence: A Logical Approach.* New York: Oxford University Press. ISBN 978-0-19-510270-3. Archived from the original on 26 July 2020. Retrieved 22 August 2020.
7. Dr. John Kelly III (2015). "Computing, cognition and the future of knowing" (PDF). *IBM Research: Cognitive Computing.* IBM Corporation. Retrieved February 9, 2016.
8. MIT Encyclopedia of Cognitive Science Archived 19 July 2008 at the Wayback Machine (quoted in "AITopics").

9. Sergio Alejandro Gómez, Carlos Iván Chesñevar and Guillermo Ricardo Simari (2010). Reasoning with inconsistent ontologies through argumentation. *Applied Artificial Intelligence* 24 (1–2): 102–148. doi: 10.1080/08839510903448692.

10. Y. C. Huei (2014). "Benefits and introduction to python programming for freshmore students using inexpensive robots," *2014* IEEE International Conference on Teaching, Assessment and Learning for Engineering (TALE), *Wellington*, 12–17. doi: 10.1109/TALE.2014.7062611.

11. Sebastian Raschka, Joshua Patterson and Corey Nolet (2020). Machine learning in python: Main developments and technology trends in data science, machine learning, and artificial intelligence. *Information* 11: 193. doi: 10.3390/info11040193.

12. Stuart J. Russell and Peter Norvig (2010). *Artificial Intelligence: A Modern Approach* (3rd ed.). Upper Saddle River, NJ: Prentice Hall.

13. Victor Roman (2019). Unsupervised machine learning: Clustering analysis. *Medium*. Retrieved: 2019–10-01.

14. Leslie P. Kaelbling, Michael L. Littman and Andrew W. Moore (1996). Reinforcement learning: A survey. *Journal of Artificial Intelligence Research* 4: 237–285. arXiv:cs/9605103. doi: 10.1613/jair.301.

15. Y. Reddy, Viswanath Pulabaigari and B. Eswara (2018). Semi-supervised learning: A brief review. *International Journal of Engineering & Technology* 7: 81. doi: 10.14419/ijet.v7i1.8.9977.

16. David A. Freedman (2009). *Statistical Models: Theory and Practice*. Cambridge University Press.

17. Naomi Altman and Martin Krzywinski (2015). Simple linear regression. *Nature Methods* 12 (11): 999–1000. doi: 10.1038/nmeth.3627.

18. https://www.investopedia.com/terms/m/mlr.asp.

19. Yin-Wen Chang, Cho-Jui Hsieh, Kai-Wei Chang, Michael Ringgaard, Chih-Jen Lin (2010). Training and testing low-degree polynomial data mappings via linear SVM. *Journal of Machine Learning Research* 11: 1471–1490.

20. Lingjian Yang, Songsong Liu, Sophia Tsoka and Lazaros Papageorgiou (2017). A regression tree approach using mathematical programming. *Expert Systems with Applications* 78: 347–357. doi: 10.1016/j.eswa.2017.02.013.

21. Adele Cutler, David Cutler and John Stevens (2011). "Random Forests," in Zhang, C. and Ma, Y.Q. (eds.), *Ensemble Machine Learning*, Springer, New York, 157–175. http://dx.doi.org/10.1007/978-1-4419-9326-7_5.

22. Sotiris Kotsiantis, I. Zaharakis and P. Pintelas (2006). Machine learning: A review of classification and combining techniques. *Artificial Intelligence Review* 26: 159–190. Doi: 10.1007/s10462-007-9052-3.

23. Maher Maalouf (2011). Logistic regression in data analysis: An overview. *International Journal of Data Analysis Techniques and Strategies* 3: 281–299. doi: 10.1504/IJDATS.2011.041335.

24. Youguo Li and Haiyan Wu (2012). A clustering method based on K-Means algorithm. *Physics Procedia* 25: 1104–1109. doi: 10.1016/j.phpro.2012.03.206.

25. Irina Rish (2001). "An empirical study of the Naïve Bayes Classifier," in IJCAI 2001 Workshop on Empirical Methods in Artificial Intelligence, vol. 3.

26. Harsh Patel and Purvi Prajapati (2018). Study and analysis of decision tree based classification algorithms. *International Journal of Computer Sciences and Engineering* 6: 74–78. doi: 10.26438/ijcse/v6i10.7478.

27. Qiong Ren, Hui Cheng and Hai Han (2017). Research on machine learning framework based on random forest algorithm. *AIP Conference Proceedings* 1820: 080020. doi: 10.1063/1.4977376.

28. O. Simeone (2018). "A Very Brief Introduction to Machine Learning With Applications to Communication Systems," in *IEEE Transactions on Cognitive Communications and Networking* (vol. 4, no. 4, pp. 648–664). doi: 10.1109/TCCN.2018.2881442.

29. Alauddin Al-Omary and Mohammad Jamil (2006). A new approach of clustering based machine-learning algorithm. *Knowledge-Based Systems* 19: 248–258. doi: 10.1016/j.knosys.2005.10.011.

30. Youguo Li and Haiyan Wu (2012). A clustering method based on K-Means algorithm. *Physics Procedia* 25: 1104–1109. doi: 10.1016/j.phpro.2012.03.206.

31. Fionn Murtagh and Pedro Contreras (2011). Methods of hierarchical clustering. Computing Research Repository - CORR. doi: 10.1007/978-3-642-04898-2_288.

32. Diksha Khurana, Aditya Koli, Kiran Khatter and Sukhdev Singh (2017). Natural Language Processing: State of The Art, Current Trends and Challenges. Cornell University.

33. Sumithra Velupillai, Hanna Suominen, Maria Liakata, Angus Roberts, Anoop Shah, Katherine Morley, David Osborn, Joseph Hayes, Robert Stewart, Johnny Downs, Wendy Chapman and Rina Dutta (2018). Using clinical natural language processing for health outcomes research: Overview and actionable Suggestions for future advances. *Journal of Biomedical Informatics* 88: 11–19. doi: 10.1016/j.jbi.2018.10.005.

34. S. Mohagaonkar, A. Rawlani and A. Saxena (2019). "Efficient decision tree using machine learning tools for acute ailments," in *2019* 6th International Conference on Computing for Sustainable Global Development (INDIACom), New Delhi, India, pp. 691–697.

35. A. Saxena, N. Kushik, A. Chaurasia and N. Kaushik (2020). "Predicting the outcome of an election results using sentiment analysis of machine learning," in *International Conference on Innovative Computing and Communications. Advances in Intelligent Systems and Computing*, vol. 1087 (Singapore: Springer), pp. 503–516.

36. S. Mohanty, A. Mishra and A. Saxena (2020). "Medical data analysis using machine learning with KNN," in Gupta D., Khanna A., Bhattacharyya S., Hassanien A., Anand S. and Jaiswal A. (eds.), International Conference on Innovative Computing and Communications. *Advances in Intelligent Systems and Computing*, vol 1166 (Singapore: Springer). doi: 10.1007/978-981-15-5148-2_42.

37. Riccardo Miotto, Fei Wang, Shuang Wang and Xiaoqian Jiang (2017). Deep learning for healthcare: Review, opportunities and challenges. *Briefings in Bioinformatics* 19, pp. 1236–1246. doi: 10.1093/bib/bbx044.

38. A. Agarwal and A. Saxena (2018). Malignant tumor detection using machine learning through Scikit-learn. *International Journal of Pure and Applied Mathematics* 119(15): 2863–2874.

39. K. Shailaja, B. Seetharamulu and M. A. Jabbar (2018). "Machine learning in healthcare: A review," *2018* Second International Conference on Electronics, Communication and Aerospace Technology (ICECA), *Coimbatore*, pp. 910–914. doi: 10.1109/ICECA.2018.8474918.

40. A. Agarwal and A. Saxena (2020). "Comparing machine learning algorithms to predict diabetes in women and visualize factors affecting it the most—A step toward better health care for women," in *International Conference on Innovative Computing and Communications. Advances in Intelligent Systems and Computing*, vol 1087. (Singapore: Springer), pp. 339–350.

41. A. Agarwal and A. Saxena (2019). "Analysis of Machine Learning Algorithms and Obtaining Highest Accuracy for Prediction of Diabetes in Women," in *2019* 6th International Conference on Computing for Sustainable Global Development (INDIACom), New Delhi, India, pp. 686–690.

Part II

Application

3 Machine Learning in Clinical Trials
A New Era

Shazia Rashid and Neha Kathuria

CONTENTS

3.1 INTRODUCTION

Artificial Intelligence (AI) and Machine Learning (ML) have been the most important technological innovations of the modern world. AI generally infers the use of a computer to ideal intelligent behavior with minor human interference (Hamet and Tremblay 2017). AI uses specific algorithms that help the computer system to think in terms of human intelligent behavior (Park et al. 2019). The term "Artificial Intelligence" was first coined by John McCarthy in 1956 during a computer science conference held at Dartmouth College (Shortliffe 2019). ML is a branch of AI that utilizes computer calculations to recognize designs in enormous informational collections and can consistently improve with extra information (Waljee 2010). AI has a wide range of applications in the healthcare sector and has revolutionized several patient management programs. The first clinical experiment using computer research and artificial neural networks (ANN) was carried out by Nathanial Rochester at International Business Machines (IBM) and by Bernard Widrow and Marcian Hoff at Stanford in 1950 (Miller and Brown 2017). ANN are simple mathematical designs which comprise various algorithms that help in determining the relationships within large analytical datasets (Miller and Brown 2017). The ANN used in the brain model is one of the most interesting areas in AI. ANN operate on the principle of the biological neural network, where the neurons are interconnected to and coordinate with each other (Renganathan 2019). Hence, the application of AI is very useful in the area of medicine and healthcare. For example, AI-based programs, methods, and algorithms are used in cardiology to examine advanced imaging technologies, EHR (electronic health records), biobanks, clinical trials, clinical sensors, genomics, and other molecular profiling techniques (Shameer et al. 2018). The simple repetitive task of maintaining clinical records can be quickly performed using AI applications (Park et al. 2019). ML is based on a simple process of making computer programs access data followed by learning from it, which can also be incorporated through deep learning algorithms and simple decision-making trees such as if-then, for-while, do-while, etc. (Dhillon et al. 2019). Algorithms like ANN, support vector machines (SVM), and decision trees are the most used in ML (Waljee and Higgins 2010). The ML algorithm methods are of two types: the supervised method and the unsupervised method (Sidey-Gibbons et al. 2019). Both the algorithms of ML have been used for developing different devices and for examining clinical results. As of late, managed learning was utilized to build up a psychological ML-based classifier machine to recognize the constrictive pericarditis and prohibitive cardiomyopathy (Shameer et al. 2018), where both unsupervised learning and supervised learning are used in ANN (Lavrač 1999). Apart from AI and ML, big data, which is an extension of these technologies, has also played an important part in the healthcare industry. Big data is referred to as managing enormous collections of data which cannot be managed through traditional ways. The basic application of big data analytics is associated with functions like improving patient-based services, detecting the spread of disease, analyzing the mode of action of certain diseases, providing better healthcare services as well as maintenance and monitoring the quality of treatment of medical institutions (Ristevski and Chen 2018).

3.2 ML-BASED ALGORITHMS AND METHODS

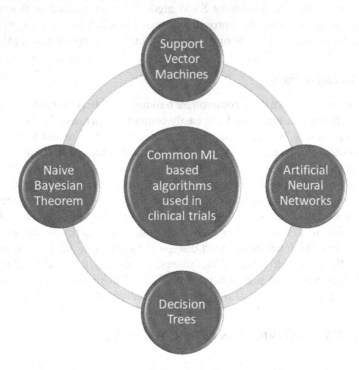

FIGURE 3.1 Some common ML-based algorithms used in clinical trials.

An algorithm is defined as the set of well-defined sequences and mathematical equations put together to resolve a problem that applies to the computer. Machine learning algorithms in the medical sector are designed in such a way that they can predict results after reading the data entries. So far, various algorithms like SVM, supervised, unsupervised, ANN, decision trees, K-means, and Naive Bayes' theorem have been developed and implemented successfully. Here some of these algorithms will be discussed in detail (Figure 3.1).

3.2.1 SUPPORT VECTOR MACHINE

In 1992, Boser, Guyon, and Vapnik introduced SVMs in COLT-92 (Weston 2013). Starting from 1962, SVMs have gained pace, and the first SVM algorithm and method was published in 1996 with the "Generalised Portrait" method for pattern recognition. Further, methods like "The Kuhn–Tucker Theorem," "Searching for Coefficients Instead of Coordinates," "Optimum (Largest Margin) Hyperplane," and "Lagrangian Dual Function" came into existence and are used till date in almost all the algorithms (Chervonenkis 1970). SVMs to date have shown enormous uses in the medical sector and have always been up to the mark in their performance. The major areas of the SVM application are chemistry, biotechnology, molecular biology, and further ahead to bioinformatics (Liang et al. 2011). For example, Battineni et al. (2019) experimented on validating SVM algorithm performance in determining dementia through a statistical approach and reported reliable results for predicting dementia. SVM is considered as one of the most important algorithms in ML.

3.2.2 DECISION TREES

Decision trees are known to be common for building classification models that easily understand human reasoning and can easily combine sequences of tests (Kotsiantis 2011). Decision tree, as the name suggests, uses a tree-like model to predict the probable outcomes and chances of events. These models are formed based on conditional statements like do-while, for, and do-until used while coding the algorithms. In medical sciences, decision trees help in making decisions based on the probability of managing and organizing many patient data on the system. Decision trees often help in the classification and diagnosis of certain diseases (Podgorelec 2002). For instance, Shouman et al. (2011) concluded through an experiment the usefulness of decision trees in determining heart disease risks with specificity, reliability, and efficiency. Since early detection of liver diseases is not easy, Abdar et al. (2017) used the multilayer perceptron neural network (MLPNN) algorithm, which is based on decision trees, and was successful in the early detection of liver diseases.

3.3   ML-BASED DEVICES IN CLINICAL TRIALS

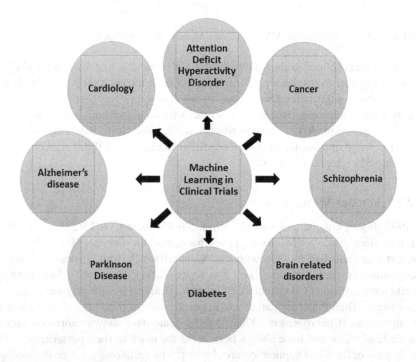

FIGURE 3.2   Applications of Machine Learning in clinical trial.

The evolution of ML-based algorithms and methods have further given rise to healthcare devices. ML-based devices are used for either detection of a disease or analyzing its status followed by monitoring its transmission. Their main applications are in clinical trials, imaging and radiology laboratories, protein engineering, genetic engineering, pharmaceuticals, bioinformatics, and biotechnology. Below are some recently developed ML-based devices along with their uses in different clinical trials.

3.3.1 ML-BASED CLASSIFIERS AND SENSOR DATA TO DIAGNOSE NEUROLOGICAL ISSUES IN STROKE PATIENTS

The most common issue that arises after brain-related strokes in patients is that of motor movements. The brain, which is the controller of all activities, alters the muscles and results in motor weakness or their complete loss. Thus, to test this weakness in patients, a pronator drift test (PDT) is performed by the neurological examiners. Park et al. (2017) used the ML-based classifiers and successfully identified the causes of the stroke using sensors and signaling based on proximal arm weakness. Thus, ML-based classifiers could help in monitoring stroke patients in the future.

3.3.2 DETECTION OF SEVERE WOUNDS AND THE RISK OF INFECTION

The maintenance of chronic wounds after surgery is a tedious task and requires proper treatment, care, and changing bandages from time to time to avoid any type of infection. Hsu et al. (2019) developed an ML-based hands-on app for automatically detecting any type of wound-related infection, which could help in immediate response to infection and prevent complications in diagnosis and treatment.

3.3.3 BONE AGE ANALYSIS

The study of bone age and its assessment is important especially for older people and orthopedics to identify different types of diseases and bone-related disorders. But it is a time-consuming task and is mostly carried out through wrist and hand radiographs. Dallora et al. (2019) presented the research studies on bone age analysis using machine learning techniques and included a total of 26 studies that all discussed on the use of ML-based techniques for diagnosis.

3.3.4 SMART WATCH AND SHOULDER PHYSIOTHERAPY

One of the friendliest and widely used ML applications in gadgets has been in a smart watch. Smart watches, being extremely handy and easy to carry, have gained attention all over the world. Burns et al. (2018) developed a home-performing shoulder physiotherapy monitoring system using the easily available smart watch. Algorithms like activity recognition chain (ARC) framework, supervised learning, k-nearest neighbor (k-NN), random forest (RF), support vector machine classifier (SVC), and a convolutional recurrent neural network (CRNN) were used to develop this system. Thus, the smart watch and SVM algorithm are efficient tools that could help manage home-adherent physiotherapy.

3.4　MACHINE LEARNING IN THE HEALTHCARE SECTOR

Healthcare is the system that is involved in providing better medical services and treatment facilities to patients (Dhillon et al. 2018). The development of vaccines, antibiotics, and advanced devices for monitoring and management of patients in the healthcare sector is one of the fastest-growing sectors in AI (Bhardwaj et al. 2017). In broad terms, ML is the ability of the computer system to learn from experience, which means the processing of the current acquired information (Mintz 2019). ML in healthcare helps to determine the patient's existing medical condition and then predict the future needs and requirements of the patient for the improvement of the health along with proper management of medical records in the technical system (Dhillon et al. 2018). For instance, a recent study indicated the role of ML in diagnosing various types of cancers, along with suggesting the type of symptoms as well as causes for each type (Hafeez and Ahmed 2019). The most common algorithm used in ML is the one used in the Naive Bayesian Classifier (Kononenko 2001). The Naive Bayesian Classifier works on the simple Bayle's Theorem, named after the Reverend Thomas Bayes. This is a collection of algorithms that works on the principle of probability and treating each entry as independent of another (Kononenko 2001). For example, if we feed the data as patient "A" having flu with symptoms like fever, cold, cough, and tiredness, the algorithm will process each of these entries independent of the probability that the disease is flu, regardless of any relation between symptoms. ML has also helped in developing techniques for biologists and scientists. For example, Benevolent Bio is used for applying technology in biosciences industries, and was discovered by Ken Mulvany (founder of Proximagen) in 2013 (Bhardwaj et al. 2017). Technologies like Butterfly Network, Flatiron Health, iCarbonX, Pathway Genomics, and AliveCor are currently changing the face of medicine (Bhardwaj et al. 2017). ML applications have also been used in diagnostic, imaging and radiology laboratories and have revolutionized patient care (Lynch and Liston 2018).

3.5　MACHINE LEARNING IN CLINICAL TRIALS

The application of ML algorithms and their methods has given rise to advances in clinical trials and associated research areas. ML-based techniques have proved reliable as well as efficient. Dhungana et al. experimented on validating supervised machine learning methods for producing fast, reliable, and efficient results in data abstraction of sepsis and septic shock alternative to manual chart review. The results revealed that the sensitivity-specificity was 100%–100% for the validation cohort for both sepsis and septic shock (Dhungana et al. 2019). ML has also been applied in biotechnology companies and associated research laboratories (Shah et al. 2019). Some of these sectors include pharmaceutical industries for advancement in drug development, imagining, and diagnostic laboratories using pattern recognition and segmentation techniques and in deep learning techniques for analysis of genomic and clinical data. ML in clinical trials has gained pace and is showing promising results. Various clinical trials have succeeded in improving the treatment outcome of patients. DNA profiling, RNA sequencing, proteomics, and preclinical datasets are also emerging through various ML applications (Shah et al. 2019). The application of ML in clinical trials for some of the diseases is explained in more detail below (Figure 3.2).

3.5.1 ALZHEIMER'S DISEASE (AD)

AD is a very common disease in elderly people that distorts the memory and mental functions of an individual. Thus, AD requires the diagnosis of the mild cognitive impairment (MCI) stage in the brain that is associated with impairment in the brain resulting in a memory loss which is different from dementia. The need to identify the MCI stage is important for the development of a disease-modifying drug for AD. However, conducting AD clinical trials is a tedious task and requires a lot of attention. ML can help to identify biomarkers and data patterns for fast monitoring using ML-based CT scans and analysis of the disease by reducing the need for a larger sample size for analysis. A study carried out by Escudero applied four ML classifiers that decreased the sample size of CT by using SVM as well as for MCI subjects (Escudero et al. 2011). Mirzaei et al. reviewed various imaging techniques for AD; however, the sensitivity of images depends on the specificity of biomarkers detection. ML-based methods and algorithms like ANN, logistic regression classification, probabilistic methods, K-means clustering (hard clustering), fuzzy clustering, and atlas-guided approaches have been successfully used for AD (Mirzaei et al. 2016).

3.5.2 PARKINSON'S DISEASE (PD)

PD is the disorder of the central nervous system which affects bodily movement, often resulting in tremors. Zhan et al. used ML in smartphones to determine PD severity, symptom fluctuations, and response to dopaminergic therapy (Zhan et al. 2018). This study evaluated individuals suffering from PD for five tasks such as voice, finger tapping, gait, balance, and reaction time and developed an ML-based mobile Parkinson score (mPDS) derived from smartphones. The mPDS could detect symptom fluctuations and compare them with the PD symptoms and respond to the dopaminergic medication. Another innovation of ML is the recent large-scale "wearable, sensor-based, quantitative, objective, and easy-to-use systems for quantifying PD signs for large numbers of participants over extended durations" (Kubota et al. 2016). This technology is ML based that can improve clinical diagnosis as well as management in PD for conducting clinical trials.

3.5.3 ATTENTION-DEFICIT HYPERACTIVITY DISORDER (ADHD)

ADHD is a very common neurodevelopment disorder, which is marked by an ongoing pattern of inattention, hyperactivity, and impulsiveness. An 8-week open-laboratory trial was carried out in 83 ADHD youths to predict methylphenidate response using ML (Kim et al. 2015). The results reported 84.6% accuracy of SVMs for analyzing methylphenidate response, supporting the development of SVMs, which could help estimate treatment response in ADHD. Yasumura et al. reported an independent biomarker for ADHD using ML algorithms (Yasumura et al. 2017). The use of SVM showed results with 88.7% sensitivity and 83.78% specificity while the result of the discrimination rate was 86.25%, establishing the importance of SVM for diagnosing ADHD among children.

3.5.4 Cancer

Cancer is the abnormal and uncontrollable spread of cells and tissues in the body and one of the leading causes of death in the world, with the prevalence of >10 million mortalities annually. ML-based solutions have the potential to revolutionize medicine by performing complex tasks that are currently assigned to specialists to improve diagnostic accuracy, increase the efficiency of throughputs, improve clinical work process, decline human asset costs, and improve treatment decisions. A clinical trial was reported to identify the status of genetic lesions in the tumor of cancer patients. The ML method used consisted of two steps: first was to distinguish gene entities from that of non-gene entities, and second was to identify and analyze the genetic lesion associated with the identified gene entity. The results were reported with 83.7% accuracy, while the results for real-world cancer trial annotation showed 89.8% accuracy, establishing the role of ML-based methods in gene-associated clinical trials (Wu et al. 2012). ML was also applied to predict the possibility of prostate cancer among the patients (Jovic et al. 2017). ML can be used to carry out probability-based experiments and three different ML-based methods were used in this study, out of which the ELM model showed the most accurate results, and can be used in the future for carrying out predictions related to different cancers.

3.5.5 Heart and the Circulatory System Disorders

The most common heart-related problems are cardiac arrest, atrial fibrillation, acute myocardial infarction, and cardiovascular diseases. The major limitation in the treatment of heart-related disease is that most of the time it remains undiagnosed unless complications arise. Since the ML-based approaches and methods are not restricted, they provide a wide scope for understanding cardiology better. Than et al. (2019) performed a clinical trial using an ML algorithm (myocardial-ischemic-injury-index [MI^3]) incorporating their age, sex, and concentrations of cardiac troponin I. The algorithm provided detailed and elaborated information about diagnosing the risks of myocardial infarction along with a profile of low-risk and high-risk patients. Kartal and Balaban (2018) conducted an experiment to identify the cardiac risk assessment on patients' pre- or postsurgery, which would predict the mortality rates in patients. A C4.5 tree decision model was used for the same process, which showed the highest performance. The use of ML-based models and algorithms for predicting and diagnosing various diseases could be beneficial to both doctors and patients.

3.6 CHALLENGES AND FUTURE SCOPE IN CLINICAL TRIALS WITH MACHINE LEARNING

Although ML has modernized the area of clinical trials, some major challenges need to be addressed. The major issues with ML are the complexity of the methods and complicated language to be learned and applied. ML algorithms are completely independent systems and require no manual assistance, which could lead to the replacement of clinical staff and technicians and hence could be responsible for seizing several jobs (Weins et al. 2020). The second problem is that most clinical reasoning for different diseases is collected from various institutions, while, contrary to this, ML-based models are developed using data from a single institute, which creates the problem of limited data generalization (Sendak et al. 2019). Third, biologists and scientists interested in ML-based research in medicine should be ready to spend a large amount of money in setting up an ML-based environment which is both expensive and time-consuming (Sendak et al. 2019). The fourth issue reported on ML is the lack of privacy, confidentiality, and misuse of data. However, it is nearly challenging to protect this data due to the "black box" approach in most of the algorithms. "Black Box" is a direct approach where data is created directly from ML-based algorithms. Since data is linked to the electronic systems, the threat to the personal information of patients as well as doctors increases as many medical identity thefts have been reported (Mothkur and Poornima 2018). Thus, access permission to this data should be assigned to the concerned authorities.

3.6.1 FUTURE SCOPE

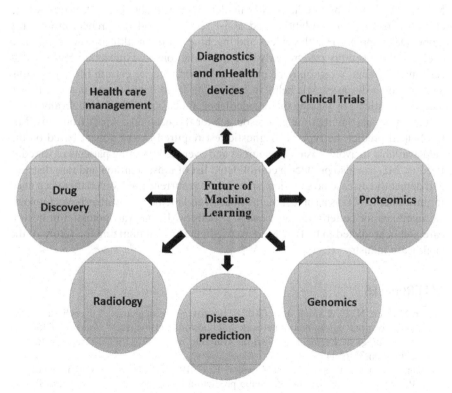

FIGURE 3.3 Applications of Machine Learning in various fields of health science.

The clinical development of drug innovation has not changed much for the past 30 years due to unknown and unproved technologies of AI and ML (Shah et al. 2019). The need to improve the efficiency of clinical trials is also increasing as carrying out these trials is expensive in terms of both time and money (Zhang et al. 2018). ML-based application has a huge potential for advancement not only in clinical trials which involve identifying meaningful clinical patterns but also in the diagnosis of diseases, radiology, and imaging in healthcare along with providing a strong basis for the healthcare system (Handelman 2018). ML is potentially a technology of choice for future that can help to improve the prognosis system, automate image analysis which should reduce the time considerably compared to manual interpretation, and quicker patient test result prediction, thus reducing the overuse of testing and wasting of resources (Obermeyer and Emanuel 2016). ML has scope for the development of next-generation antibiotics and personalized medicine (Shah et al. 2019). The power of prediction in ML-based algorithms could help to understand and predict the pathways of disease development and response to drugs, which can be very useful for their clinical trials (Savage 2012) (Figure 3.3).

3.7 CONCLUSION

ML offers algorithms, methods, and models with valuable characteristics, which can provide long-term solutions and assist scientists and researchers around the globe. Developing mHealth devices and machines in the healthcare sector can help decrease the mortality rate by early disease predictions and quick and efficient disease management, which may be of utmost importance for certain life-threatening and unknown diseases. ML helps in organizing large datasets and medical health records of patients by placing them under labels for easy access to the data anywhere and anytime and saving time and resources for the hospitals. Apart from this, ML has helped predict the type of diagnostic test required by the patient based on the data available to avoid waste of resources and overuse by testing patients repeatedly. Further, ML can also produce a consolidated list of most common and rare diseases and depict the disease progression, spread, and recurrence. However, there is a need for introducing ML as a subject in universities and medical as well as biotechnological institutes for better awareness and knowledge. ML has vast potential in healthcare and is predicted to be the "Modern Medicine" revolutionizing the future of the healthcare industry.

REFERENCES

Abdar, M., Yen, N. Y., & Hung, J. C. (2017). "Improving the diagnosis of liver disease using multilayer perceptron neural network and boosted decision trees". *Journal of Medical and Biological Engineering*, 38 (3). Available from: https://www.researchgate.net/publication/321653455.

Battineni, G., Chintalapudi, N., & Amenta, F. (2019). "Machine learning in medicine: Performance calculation of dementia prediction by support vector machines (SVM)". *Informatics in Medicine Unlocked*, 16, 100200. doi: 10.1016/j.imu.2019.100200.

Bhardwaj, R., et al. (2017). "A Study of Machine Learning in Healthcare". Available from https://www.researchgate.net/publication/319634446_A_Study_of_Machine_Learning_in_Healthcare.

Burns, D., Leung, N., Hardisty, M., Whyne, C., Henry, P., & McLachlin, S. (2018, July 23). "Shoulder physiotherapy exercise recognition: Machine learning the inertial signals from a smartwatch". *Physiological Measurement*, 39 (7), 075007. Available from https://www.ncbi.nlm.nih.gov/pubmed/29952759.

Chervonenkis, A. (1970). "Early history of support vector machines". In *Empirical Inference 2013* (pp. 13–20). Berlin, Heidelberg: Springer. Available from https://link.springer.com/chapter/10.1007/978-3-642-41136-6_3.

Dhillon, A. (2019). "Machine learning for Internet of Things data analysis". *Journal of Biology and Today,s World*, 2018 Jan; 8 (2), 1–10. Available from https://www.researchgate.net/publication/320393191_Machine_learning_for_Internet_of_Things_data_analysis_A_survey.

Dhungana, P., Serafim, L. P., Ruiz, A. L., Bruns, D., Weister, T. J., Smichney, N. J., & Kashyap, R. (2019). "Machine learning in data abstraction: A computable phenotype for sepsis and septic shock diagnosis in the intensive care unit". *World Journal of Critical Care Medicine*, 8 (7), 120–126. doi:10.5492/wjccm.v8.i7.120.

Escudero, J., Zajicek, J. P., & Ifeachor, E. (2011). "Machine Learning classification of MRI features of Alzheimer's disease and mild cognitive impairment subjects to reduce the sample size in clinical trials", in Annual International Conference of the IEEE Engineering in Medicine and Biology Society. doi:10.1109/iembs.2011.6091962.

Hafeez, K., & Ahmed, Q. (2019). "Applications of machine learning in education and health sector: An empirical study". *Journal of Software Engineering and Intelligent Systems*, 3. Journal of Software Engineering & Intelligent Systems ISSN 2518-8739 31st December 2019, Volume 4, Issue 3, JSEIS, CAOMEI

Handelman, G., Kok, H., Chandra, R., Razavi, A., Lee, M., & Asadi, H. (2018, December). *Edoctor: Machine learning and the future of medicine.* Retrieved from https://www.ncbi.nlm.nih.gov/pubmed/30102808

Hamet, P., & Tremblay, J. (2017). "Artificial intelligence in medicine". *Metabolism*, 69. doi: 10.1016/j.metabol.2017.01.011.

Hsu, J., Chen, Y., Ho, T., Tai, H., Wu, J., Sun, H., Lai, F. (2019). "Chronic Wound Assessment and Infection Detection Method". *BMC Medical Informatics and Decision Making*, 19 (1), 99. Available from: https://www.ncbi.nlm.nih.gov/pubmed/31126274.

Jović, S., Miljković, M., Ivanović, M., Šaranović, M., & Arsić, M. (2017). "Prostate cancer probability prediction by machine learning technique". *Cancer Investigation*, 35 (10), 647–651. doi: 10.1080/07357907.2017.1406496.

Kartal, E., & Balaban, M. E. (2018). "Machine learning techniques in cardiac risk assessment". *The Turkish Journal of Thoracic and Cardiovascular Surgery*, 26 (3), 394–401. doi: 10.5606/tgkdc.dergisi.2018.15559.

Kim, J., Sharma, V., & Ryan, N. D. (2015). "Predicting methylphenidate response in ADHD using machine learning approaches". *International Journal of Neuropsychopharmacology*, 18 (11), 1–7. doi: 10.1093/ijnp/pyv052.

Kononenko, I. (2001). "Machine learning for medical diagnosis: History, state of the art and perspective". *Artificial Intelligence in Medicine*, 23 (1), 89–109. doi: 10.1016/s0933-3657(01)00077-x.

Kotsiantis, S. B. (2011). "Decision trees: A recent overview." *Artificial Intelligence Review*, 39 (4), 261–283. doi: 10.1007/s10462-011-9272-4.

Kubota, K. J., Chen, J. A., & Little, M. A. (2016). "Machine learning for large-scale wearable sensor data in Parkinson's disease: Concepts, promises, pitfalls, and futures". *Movement Disorders*, 31 (9), 1314–1326. doi: 10.1002/mds.26693.

Lavrač, N. (1999). "Machine Learning for Data Mining in Medicine", 47–62. doi: 10.1007/3-540-48720-4_4.

Liang, Y., Xu, Q., Li, H., & Cao, D. (2011). "Support Vector Machines and Their Application in Chemistry and Biotechnology". Available from https://www.worldcat.org/title/supp ort-vector-machines-and-their-application-in-chemistry-and-biotechnology/oclc/72 9371391.

Lynch, C. J., & Liston, C. (2018). "New machine-learning technologies for computer-aided diagnosis". *Nature Medicine*, 24 (9), 1304–1305. doi: 10.1038/s41591-018-0178-4.

Miller, D. D., & Brown, E. W. (2018). "Artificial intelligence in medical practice: The question to the answer?" *The American Journal of Medicine*, 131 (2), 129–133. doi: 10.1016/j. amjmed.2017.10.035.

Mirzaei, G., Adeli, A., & Adeli, H. (2016). "Imaging and machine learning techniques for diagnosis of Alzheimer's disease". *Reviews in the Neurosciences*, 27 (8), 857–870. doi: 10.1515/revneuro-2016-0029.

Mintz, Y., & Brodie, R. (2019). *Introduction to artificial intelligence in medicine*. Retrieved from https://www.tandfonline.com/doi/abs/10.1080/13645706.2019.1575882

Mothkur, R., & Poornima, K. (2018). "Machine Learning will Transfigure Medical Sector: A Survey", in International Conference on Current Trends towards Converging Technologies (ICCTCT). doi:10.1109/icctct.2018.8551134.

Obermeyer, Z., & Emanuel, E. J. (2016). "Predicting the future — Big data, machine learning, and clinical medicine". *New England Journal of Medicine*, 375 (13), 1216–1219. doi: 10.1056/nejmp1606181.

Park, E., Chang, H., & Nam, H. (2017, April 18). "Use of Machine Learning Classifiers and Sensor Data to Detect Neurological Deficit in Stroke Patients". Available from https:// www.ncbi.nlm.nih.gov/pubmed/28420599.

Park, S. H., Do, K., Kim, S., Park, J. H., & Lim, Y. (2019). "What should medical students know about artificial intelligence in medicine?" *Journal of Educational Evaluation for Health Professions*, 16, 18. doi:10.3352/jeehp.2019.16.18.

Podgorelec, V., Kokol, P., Stiglic, B., & Rozman, I. (2002). *(PDF) decision Trees: An overview and their use in medicine*. Retrieved from https://www.researchgate.net/public ation/11205595_Decision_Trees_An_Overview_and_Their_Use_in_Medicine

Renganathan, V. (2019). "Overview of artificial neural network models in the biomedical domain". *Bratislava Medical Journal*, 120 (07), 536–540. doi: 10.4149/bll_2019_087.

Ristevski, B., & Chen, M. (2018). "Big data analytics in medicine and healthcare". *Journal of Integrative Bioinformatics*, 15 (3). doi: 10.1515/jib-2017-0030.

Savage, N. (2012). "Better medicine through machine learning". *Communications of the ACM*, 55 (1), 17–19. doi: 10.1145/2063176.206182.

Sendak, M., Gao, M., Nichols, M., Lin, A., & Balu, S. (2019). "Machine learning in health care: A critical appraisal of challenges and opportunities". *EGEMs (Generating Evidence & Methods to Improve Patient Outcomes)*, 7 (1), 1. doi:10.5334/egems.287.

Shah, P., Kendall, F., Khozin, S., Goosen, R., Hu, J., Laramie, J., & Schork, N. (2019). "Artificial intelligence and machine learning in clinical development: A translational perspective". *NPJ Digital Medicine*, 2 (1). doi: 10.1038/s41746-019-0148-3.

Shameer, K., Johnson, K. W., Glicksberg, B. S., Dudley, J. T., & Sengupta, P. P. (2018). "Machine learning in cardiovascular medicine: Are we there yet?" *Heart*, 104 (14): 1156–1164. doi: 10.1136/heartjnl-2017-311198.

Shortliffe, E. (2019). "Artificial intelligence in medicine: Weighing the accomplishments, hype, and promise". *Yearbook of Medical Informatics*, 28 (01), 257–262. doi: 10.1055/s-0039-1677891.

Shouman, M., Turner, T., & Stocker, R. (2011). "Using Decision Tree for Diagnosing Heart Disease". Available from: https://www.researchgate.net/publication/262321354.

Sidey-Gibbons, J., & Sidey-Gibbons, C. (2019). "Machine learning in medicine: A practical introduction". *BMC Medical Research Methodology*, 19 (1).

Than, M., Pickering, J., Sandoval, Y., Shah, A., Tsanas, A., & Apple, F. (2019). "Machine learning to predict the likelihood of acute myocardial infarction". *MI3 Collaborative*. Available from https://www.ncbi.nlm.nih.gov/pmc/articles/PMC6749969/.

Waljee, A. K., & Higgins, P. D. (2010). "Machine learning in medicine: A primer for physicians". *American Journal of Gastroenterology*, 105 (6), 1224–1226. doi: 10.1038/ajg.2010.173.

Weston, J. (2013). "Support Vector Machine - Columbia University". Available from http://www.cs.columbia.edu/~kathy/cs4701/documents/jason_svm_tutorial.pdf.

Wiens, J., Saria, S., Sendak, M., Ghassemi, M., Liu, V. X., Doshi-Velez, F., & Goldenberg, A. (2019). "Do no harm: A roadmap for responsible machine learning for health care". *Nature Medicine*, 25 (9), 1337–1340. doi:10.1038/s41591-019-0548-6.

Wu, Y., Levy, M. A., Micheel, C. M., Yeh, P., Tang, B., Cantrell, M. J., & Xu, H (2012). "Identifying the status of genetic lesions in cancer clinical trial documents using machine learning". *BMC Genomics*, 13 (Suppl 8). doi:10.1186/1471-2164-13-s8-s21.

Yasumura, A., Omori, M., Fukuda, A., Takahashi, J., Yasumura, Y., Nakagawa, E., & Inagaki, M. (2017). "Applied machine learning method to predict children with ADHD using prefrontal cortex activity: A multicenter study in Japan". *Journal of Attention Disorders*, 108705471774063. doi: 10.1177/1087054717740632.

Zhan, A., Mohan, S., Tarolli, C., Schneider, R. B., Adams, J. L., Sharma, S., & Saria, S. (2018). "Using smartphones and machine learning to quantify Parkinson disease severity". *JAMA Neurology*, 75 (7), 876. doi: 10.1001/jamaneurol.2018.0809.

4 Deep Learning and Its Biological and Biomedical Applications

Bhawna Rathi and Aditya Narayan Sarangi

CONTENTS

4.1 INTRODUCTION

Advancement in newer-generation sequencing technology led to the increased availability of omics data in the public domain at a brisk pace. These voluminous and highly divergent omics data (genomics, transcriptomics, proteomics, epigenomic, metagenomics, metabolomics, etc.) directed biological and biomedical research toward the big data era. The data generated post sequencing requires efficient analysis as it addresses various biological queries and paves the way for revolutionizing health and medical sciences. The memory usage and execution times of the algorithms used to analyze the big data scale linearly with the depth of the reads demand high-computing power in terms of memory, which is actually challenging for a small-scale research lab. Biological and bio-medical big data analytics demands development of advanced and efficient computational algorithms to gain insights into these data not only to get detailed information regarding diseases but also to improve diagnosis and develop personalized medicines. Machine Learning (ML) algorithms have become one of the most promising methods to address such issues.

Machine Learning methods can broadly be divided into two categories: supervised learning and unsupervised learning. Supervised learning algorithms are based on the theory of inductive inference, i.e., prediction based on prior observation. Examples of supervised Machine Learning approaches are decision tree, support vector machine (SVM), and neural network. Unsupervised learning algorithms help to deduce previously undetected patterns from data without any preexisting labels. Two popular unsupervised methods that are used to detect patterns in high-dimensional biological and bio-medical data are clustering and principal component analysis. Methods and algorithm in the ML do classification, regression, and clustering, which have been proven beneficial for solving biological research questions related to gene patterns, functional genomics, genotype-phenotype associations, and gene-protein interactions. A major constraint of ML methods is that they cannot handle proficiently natural data in their raw form.

Deep learning (DL), a subcategory of the Machine Learning method, can be both supervised and unsupervised, and uses reinforcement learning models to train a class of large neural networks. Deep learning has been successfully applied to create predictive models and deduce information from much complex and heterogeneous omics and clinical data. Deep learning has been widely used in big data analytics these days (Najafabadi et al., 2015). DL has enormous uses in voice, signal processing, machine vision, text and sequence prediction, and computational biology areas, altogether shaping the productive Artificial Intelligence (AI) fields (Bengio and LeCun, 2007; Zhang et al., 2016; Esteva et al., 2017; Ching et al., 2018). Deep learning has several application models such as artificial neural network, hierarchical learning, and deep structured learning, which generally apply a class of structured networks (Ditzler et al., 2015; Liang et al., 2015; Xu et al., 2016; Giorgi and Bader, 2018).

DL has also proven to provide models with higher precision that are efficient at discovering patterns in high-dimensional data, making them applicable to a variety of areas (Koumakis, 2020). In the case of DL, the amount of training data is more demanding as compared to ML, because there are many parameters in a deep learning algorithm which can drastically affect the predicting value of the trained model.

The graph in Figure 4.1 reflects the number of published papers in Pubmed in the last decade, which clearly depicts an exponential growth of the usage of these techniques in biological research.

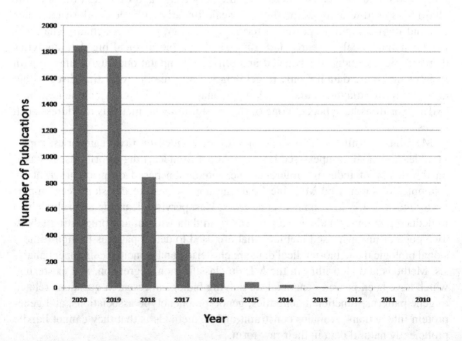

FIGURE 4.1   Deep learning searches by years in PubMed.

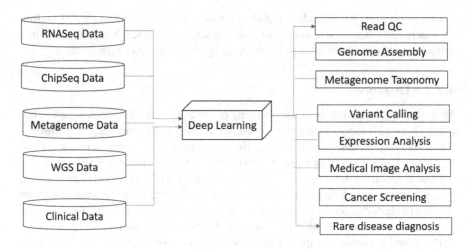

FIGURE 4.2 Biological and biomedical application of deep learning.

This chapter depicts various methods and tools to discuss Machine Learning and deep learning, a subfield that emerged from Machine Learning, for the NGS data analytics.

4.1.1 (I) Application of Deep Learning in Biological Data Analysis

The overview of the potential biological and biomedical applications of deep learning is shown in Figure 4.2.

4.2 READ QUALITY CONTROL ANALYSIS

In the NGS data, the read specifies a single uninterrupted series of nucleotides representing the sequence of the template. Advanced sequencing technologies can generate an enormous number of sequence reads in a single experiment. However, no sequencing technology is flawless, and each instrument may generate different types and numbers of errors. Therefore, it is necessary to understand, identify, and exclude the errors that may impact the interpretation of experiment. Sequence quality control is therefore an essential first step in the NGS analysis. Catching errors early saves time later on. Mentioned below are the methods developed using deep learning for read quality control analysis.

4.2.1 MiniScrub: De Novo Nanopore Read Quality Improvement Using Deep Learning

Oxford Nanopore long read sequencing technology significantly reduces the complexity of de novo assembly. The tool MiniScrub is developed on a convolutional neural network (CNN) based method, which identifies and subsequently removes low-quality Nanopore read segments to minimize their interference in the downstream assembly process. MiniScrub is found to robustly improve read quality of Oxford Nanopore reads, especially in the metagenome setting. MiniScrub is an open-source software and is available at https://bitbucket.org/berkeleylab/jgi-miniscrub.

4.2.2 DEEPBINNER

Multiplexing, the simultaneous sequencing of multiple barcoded DNA samples, has made Oxford Nanopore sequencing cost-effective for small genomes. Deepbinner is a tool for Oxford Nanopore demultiplexing that uses a deep neural network (DNN) to classify reads. Deepbinner had the lowest rate of unclassified reads (7.8%) and the highest demultiplexing precision (98.5% of classified reads were correctly assigned in comparison with Albacore and Porechop). It can be used alone (to maximize the number of classified reads) or in conjunction with other demultiplexers (to maximize precision and minimize false positive classifications). Deepbinner is open source (GPLv3) and available at https://github.com/rrwick/Deepbinner.

4.3 GENOME ASSEMBLY

Genome assembly refers to the process of putting nucleotide sequences into the correct order. To assemble the read obtained by the sequencing experiment, various methods and programs are used. This segment refers to the deep learning method used for genome assembly.

4.3.1 CONNET: ACCURATE GENOME CONSENSUS IN ASSEMBLING NANOPORE SEQUENCING DATA VIA DEEP LEARNING

To have a high-quality consensus from long reads is important and can be achieved by spatial relationship of alignment pileup. CONNET is a deep-learning-based consensus tool based on partial order alignment. It has been tested using a 90× dataset of *E. coli* and a 37× human dataset. The tool has the capability of delivering phased diploid genome consensus.

4.4 APPLICATION IN METAGENOMICS

Metagenomics is the technique of retrieving microbial genome directly from the environmental samples regardless of the nature of the sample and abundance of microbial entities (Oulas et al., 2015). The analysis explores the entire genetic composition of the microbial communities by sequencing and subsequently doing data analysis. It also plays a role in understanding the biochemical part of the microbes in the atypical environments as well as their interactions with other environmental factors (Thomas et al., 2012). A metagenomic analysis comprises the isolation of metagenomic DNA from the samples, followed by 16S rRNA gene amplification and shotgun metagenome sequencing, analysis of amplicon reads, analysis of metagenomic reads, and finally the determination of microbial community diversity using the databases (Sarangi et al., 2019). This section reviews some tools developed on the basis of the deep learning algorithms for metagenome analysis.

4.4.1 DeepARG: A Deep Learning Approach for Predicting Antibiotic Resistance Genes (ARGs) from Metagenomic Data

Due to the increasing antibiotic resistance, there is a need to identify the antibiotic-resistant genes, their hot spots or gene hubs, and the several pathways where these genes are playing a pivotal role. ARGs can be predicted by considering the similarity search of the whole metagenomic gene pool with the databases, but the approach leads to a lot of false negatives. To address this limitation, deep learning approach takes into account a dissimilarity matrix created using all known categories and parameters of ARGs. Evaluation of the deep learning models over 30 antibiotic resistance categories demonstrates that the DeepARG models can predict ARGs with both high precision (>0.97) and recall (>0.90).

4.4.2 NanoARG: A Web Service for Detecting and Contextualizing Antimicrobial Resistance Genes from Nanopore-Derived Metagenomes

Indirect and direct pressures enforced by antibiotics, along with horizontal gene transfer and co-selective agents, are the primary reasons for evolution as well as spread of antibiotic resistance. The various tools in existence just help to identify the ARGs, but this information is limited to the mobile genetic elements (MGEs) and the co-selective pressure; for example, metal-resistant genes have not been identified. Second, various methods and web servers consider the short reads in assembling the NGS data, whereas NanoARG takes advantage of the long reads produced by nanopore sequencing technology. These long nanopore reads help to identify not only the ARGs but also the genes in the vicinity with the mobile genetic elements as well as other co-selectives. NanoARG is publicly available and freely accessible at https://bench.cs.vt.edu/nanoarg.

4.4.3 DeepBGC: A Deep Learning Genome-Mining Strategy for Biosynthetic Gene Cluster (BGC) Prediction

Natural products represent a rich pool of small-molecule drug candidates. These molecules are microbial secondary metabolites synthesized by co-localized genes termed Biosynthetic Gene Clusters (BGCs). A deep learning strategy—DeepBGC—proposes reduced false positive rates in BGC identification and an enhanced ability to extrapolate and identify novel BGC classes compared to present Machine Learning tools. DeepBGC has been supplemented with random forest classifiers that accurately predict BGC product classes and potential chemical activity. Application of DeepBGC to bacterial genomes uncovered earlier untraceable putative BGCs that may code for natural products with novel biologic activities.

4.4.4 MetaPheno: A Critical Evaluation of Deep Learning and Machine Learning in Metagenome-Based Disease Prediction

Revolutions in sequencing technology have led to a swift surge in publicly available sequencing data. This leads to growing efforts to predict disease status from metagenomic sequencing data, with utilization of new approaches. Deeper analysis of type 2 diabetes and obesity datasets that have eluded improved results was performed using a variety of Machine Learning and feature extraction methods. This study concluded by offering perspectives on study design considerations that may impact results and future. The scripts and extracted features for the analyses conducted in this chapter are available at GitHub:https://github.com/nlapier2/met apheno.

4.4.5 MetagenomicDC

Metagenomic Data Classifier based on deep learning models uses a deep learning approach for taxonomic classification of metagenomic data, which can be employed for both whole genome shotgun (WGS) and amplicon (AMP). The data from both WGS and AMP short reads were simulated using the tool called Grinder (Angly et al., 2012). k-mer representation was adopted to map sequences as vectors into a numerical space. Finally, two different deep learning architectures, i.e., convolutional neural network and deep belief network (DBN), were used to train models for each taxon. MetagenomicDC pipeline was found to outperform the RDP classifier at each taxonomic level with both architectures. For instance, at the genus level, both CNN and DBN reached 91.3% of accuracy with AMP short reads, whereas RDP classifier obtained 83.8% with the same data.

4.4.6 DEEPre: Sequence-Based Enzyme Commission (EC) Number Prediction by Deep Learning

Annotation of enzyme function has a broad range of applications, from metagenomics to diagnosis to industrial biotechnology. Computational enzyme function prediction has become quite important. This approach determines the enzyme function by predicting the Enzyme Commission number. The method proposes an end-to-end feature selection and classification model training approach, as well as an automatic and robust feature dimensionality uniformization method. In spite of extracting the enzyme sequence manually, the model takes the raw sequence encoding as inputs, extracting convolutional and sequential features from the raw encoding based on the classification result to directly improve the prediction performance. In addition, the server is shown to outperform the other programs in determining the main class of enzymes on a separate low-homology dataset. Two case studies demonstrate DEEPre's ability to capture the functional difference of enzyme isoforms. The server could be accessed freely at http://www.cbrc.kaust.edu.sa/DEEPre.

4.4.7 DEEPMASED: EVALUATING THE QUALITY OF METAGENOMIC ASSEMBLIES

DeepMAsED is a deep learning approach for identifying misassembled contigs without the need for reference genomes. Moreover, the tool provides an in silico pipeline for generating large-scale, realistic metagenome assemblies for comprehensive model training and testing. DeepMAsED accuracy substantially exceeds the state of the art when applied to large and complex metagenome assemblies. DeepMAsED accurately identifies misassemblies in metagenome-assembled contigs from a broad diversity of bacteria and archaea without the need for reference genomes or strong modeling assumptions. DeepMAsED is available from GitHub at https://github.com/leylabmpi/DeepMAsED.

4.4.8 DEEPMICROBES: TAXONOMIC CLASSIFICATION FOR METAGENOMICS WITH DEEP LEARNING

DeepMicrobes trained on genomes reconstructed from gut microbiomes has helped discover potential novel signatures in inflammatory bowel diseases. DeepMicrobes facilitates effective investigations into the uncharacterized roles of metagenomic species.

4.4.9 META-MFDL: GENE PREDICTION IN METAGENOMIC FRAGMENTS WITH DEEP LEARNING

Accurately identifying genes from metagenomics fragments is one of the most fundamental challenges in metagenomics. This tool combines multifeatures (i.e., monocodon usage, monoamino acid usage, ORF length coverage, and Z-curve features) and, using deep stacking networks learning model, presents a novel method (called Meta-MFDL) to predict the metagenomic genes. Meta-MFDL is a powerful tool for identifying genes from metagenomic fragments.

4.4.10 IDMIL

The tool articulates the problem of predicting human disease from whole-metagenomic data using multiple instance learning (MIL), a popular supervised learning technique. This method proposes an alignment-free approach that provides higher accuracy in prediction by harnessing the capability of deep CNN within a MIL framework and provides interpretability via neural attention mechanism. The approach does not rely on alignment, assembly, and reference sequence databases, thus making it fast and scalable for large-scale metagenomic data. IDMIL is available at https://github.com/mrahma23/IDMIL.

4.5 VARIANT CALLING FROM NGS DATA

Variant calling is the process by which we identify variants from sequence data. Variant analysis is the study of the genetic differences (variants) between healthy and diseased tissue, between individuals of a population, or between strains of an organism. It can provide mechanistic insight into disease processes and the natural function of affected genes. This section specifies the various models of deep learning employed for variant calling.

4.5.1 GARFIELD-NGS: Genomic vARiants FILtering by dEep Learning moDels in NGS

Exome sequencing is a widely used approach in clinical research as it helps identify the genomic variants. However, a substantial number of genomic variants identified may be false positive. This new tool GARFIELD-NGS relies on deep learning models to predict false and true variants in exome sequencing experiments performed with the help of Illumina or ION platforms. GARFIELD-NGS depicted strong performances for both SNP (single-nucleotide polymorphism) and INDEL variants (AUC 0.71-0.98). Thus, it can be easily integrated into existing analysis pipeline. GARFIELD-NGS is available at https://github.com/gedoardo83/GARFIELD-NGS.

4.5.2 DeepSVR: A Deep Learning Approach to Automate Refinement of Somatic Variant Calling from Cancer Sequencing Data

Cancer sequencing data requires in-depth analysis to accurately identify the somatic variations. After the automatic processing of the data, manual review of the data is required, though this is time-consuming, more expensive, non-reproducible, and even standardization is required. DeepSVR (https://github.com/griffithlab/DeepSVR) has been developed using the Machine Learning approach for standardizing the somatic variation refinement. The final model incorporates 41,000 variants from 440 sequencing cases. The model improves on manual somatic refinement by reducing bias on calls otherwise subject to high inter-reviewer variability.

4.5.3 DeepVariant: A Universal SNP and Small-Indel Variant Caller Using Deep Neural Networks

In spite of the high-end sequencing technologies, calling the genomic variants accurately still remains a big challenge. A deep convolutional neural network can call genetic variation in aligned next-generation sequencing read data by learning statistical relationships between images of read pileups around putative variant and true genotype calls. DeepVariant can learn to call variants in a variety of sequencing technologies and experimental designs, including deep whole genomes from 10X Genomics and Ion Ampliseq exomes, highlighting the benefits of using more automated and generalizable techniques for variant calling.

4.5.4 CLAIRVOYANTE: A MULTI-TASK CONVOLUTIONAL DEEP NEURAL NETWORK FOR VARIANT CALLING IN SINGLE-MOLECULE SEQUENCING

For a single-molecule sequencing, it is a challenging task to identify DNA sequence variants. Clairvoyante is a multitask five-layer convolutional neural network model for predicting variant type (SNP or indel), alternative allele, zygosity, and indel length from aligned reads. Clairvoyante finds variants in less than 2 hours on a standard server. Clairvoyante is available open-source (https://github. com/aquaskyline/Clairvoyante), with modules to train, utilize, and visualize the model.

4.6 SNP EFFECT PREDICTION

Single-nucleotide polymorphisms, frequently called SNPs (pronounced "snips"), are the most general type of genetic variation among individuals. These can act as biological markers, helping researchers to locate genes that are associated with disease. When SNPs occur within a gene or in any regulatory region near a gene, they might play a more important role in disease by affecting the gene's function. The methods below states the deep learning methods used for SNP predictions.

4.6.1 DEEPSEA: PREDICTING EFFECTS OF NON-CODING VARIANTS WITH DEEP-LEARNING-BASED SEQUENCE MODEL

In human genetics, it is a challenging task to identify the functional effect in the non-coding region. A deep-learning-based algorithmic framework, DeepSEA (http://deepsea.princeton.edu/), directly learns a regulatory sequence code from large-scale chromatin-profiling data, enabling prediction of chromatin effects of sequence alterations with single-nucleotide sensitivity. This approach is further used to improve the identification of the functional variants.

4.6.2 DANN: A DEEP LEARNING APPROACH FOR ANNOTATING THE PATHOGENICITY OF GENETIC VARIANTS

Combined annotation-dependent depletion (CADD) is an algorithm designed to annotate both coding and non-coding variants. CADD trains a linear kernel support vector machine to differentiate evolutionarily derived, likely benign alleles from simulated, likely deleterious variants. However, SVMs cannot capture non-linear relationships among the features, which can be captured by a deep learning approach. DANN uses the same feature set and training data as CADD to train a deep neural network. DNNs can capture non-linear relationships among features and are better suited than SVMs for problems with a large number of samples and features. All data and source code are available at https://cbcl.ics.uci.edu/public_data/DANN/.

4.6.3 DEEPMAsED

Functional interpretation of genetic variants using deep learning predicts impact on chromatin accessibility and histone modification.

DeepMAsED is a deep learning approach for identifying misassembled contigs without the requirement for any reference genomes. It provides an in silico pipeline for generating large-scale, realistic metagenome assemblies for comprehensive model training and testing. Executing DeepMAsED is simple. DeepMAsED is a flexible misassembly classifier that can be applied to a wide range of metagenome assembly projects.

DeepMAsED is available from GitHub at https://github.com/leylabmpi/Deep MAsED.

4.6.4 DeFine

Deep convolutional neural networks accurately quantify intensities of transcription factor (TF)-DNA binding and facilitate evaluation of functional non-coding variants.

The tool DeFine (deep-learning-based functional impact of non-coding variants evaluator) has improved performance of assessing the functional impact of non-coding variants, including SNPs and indels. DeFine accurately identifies the causal functional non-coding variants from disease-associated variants in Genome Wide Association Studies (GWAS). DeFine is an effective and easy-to-use tool that facilities systematic prioritization of functional non-coding variants.

4.7 GENE EXPRESSION ANALYSIS (BULK RNASEQ, SINGLE-CELL RNASEQ)

Gene expression analyses study the formation of a gene product from its coding gene. It is an important indicator of biological activity wherein changes in gene expression patterns are reflected in changes in biological processes. Gene expression profiling goes beyond the information of the genome sequence into a functional view of an organism's biology and is a widely used approach in research, clinical, and pharmaceutical settings to better understand individual genes, gene pathways, or greater gene activity profiles. This section states the various deep learning approaches used for gene expression analyses with huge precision and accuracy.

4.7.1 Decode

Deep learning decodes the principles of differential gene expression (DE).

Differential gene expression analysis is a very important way to study the molecular mechanism. These studies are quite popular in health as well as diagnostics. A model called Decode utilizes the deep learning approach to predict differential gene expression based on genome-wide binding sites on RNAs and promoters. To identify influential molecular mechanisms for any human expression data, researchers can freely utilize Decode available at www.differentialexpression.org.

4.7.2 DESC

Deep learning enables accurate clustering with batch effect removal in single-cell RNA-seq analysis.

DESC is an unsupervised deep embedding algorithm that clusters single-cell RNA-seq data by iteratively optimizing a clustering function. Comprehensive evaluations show that DESC offers a proper balance of clustering accuracy and stability both. DESC is an important tool for the researchers to solve the complex cellular problems.

4.7.3 SCANCLUSTER: INTEGRATING DEEP-SUPERVISED, SELF-SUPERVISED, AND UNSUPERVISED LEARNING FOR SINGLE-CELL RNA-SEQ CLUSTERING AND ANNOTATION

scAnCluster combines deep-supervised learning, self-supervised learning, and unsupervised learning techniques together, and it outperforms other customized scRNA-seq annotation methods (CellAssign, Garnett, SingleR, scANVI-semi-supervised deep generative model) in both simulation and real data. The method performs efficiently on the challenging task of discovering novel cell types that are absent in the reference data.

4.7.4 DIGITALDLSORTER: DEEP-LEARNING ON SCRNA-SEQ TO DECONVOLUTE GENE EXPRESSION DATA

The approach makes use of a Deep Neural Network model that allows quantification of lymphocytes and also of specific CD8+, CD4Tmem, CD4Th, and CD4Tregs subpopulations, as well as B-cells and stromal content. This method was applied to synthetic bulk RNA-Seq and to samples from the TCGA project, yielding very accurate results in terms of quantification and survival prediction.

4.8 TRANSCRIPTION FACTOR/ENHANCER (CHIPSEQ)

Transcription factor (or sequence-specific DNA-binding factor) is a protein that controls the rate of transcription of genetic information from DNA to messenger RNA, by binding to a specific DNA sequence. The method below discusses the various deep learning models to identify the transcription factors/enhancers.

4.8.1 ENHANCER RECOGNITION AND PREDICTION DURING SPERMATOGENESIS BASED ON DEEP CONVOLUTIONAL NEURAL NETWORKS

The development of ChIP-Chip and ChIP-Seq sequencing technology has enabled the researchers to focus on the relationship between enhancers and DNA sequences and histone protein modifications. This study proposed a convolutional neural network model to predict enhancers that can regulate gene expression during spermatogenesis. Finally, it compared the CNN algorithm with the gkmSVM algorithm.

It is well proven that CNN has better performance than the gkmSVM algorithm, especially in the generalization ability. The work demonstrated their strong learning ability and the low CPU requirements for the experiment, with a small number of convolution layers and simple network structure, while avoiding overfitting the training data.

4.8.2 DeepEnhancer: Predicting enhancers with deep convolutional neural networks

Experimental methods are both time-consuming and expensive for the large-scale identification of enhancers. DeepEnhancer is a tool to distinguish enhancers from background genomic sequences. The method purely relies on DNA sequences to predict enhancers in an end-to-end manner by using a deep convolutional neural network. The method proves to be quite efficient in the classification of the enhancers against the random sequences.

4.8.3 DeepHistone: A Deep Learning Approach to Predict Histone Modifications

Identification of the histone modification has proved to be very successful in understanding the biological processes such as DNA damage and chromosome packing. DeepHistone demonstrated the possibility of using a deep learning framework to link DNA sequence and experimental data for predicting epigenomic signals. With the state-of-the-art performance, DeepHistone was expected to ease out the study of epigenomic. DeepHistone is freely available at https://github.com/QijinYin/DeepHistone.

4.8.4 An Integrative Framework for Combining Sequence and Epigenomic Data to Predict Transcription Factor Binding Sites (TFBSs) Using Deep Learning

TFBS is essential for understanding the underlying binding mechanisms and follow-up cellular functions. Convolutional neural networks have outperformed the traditional methods in predicting TFBSs from the primary DNA sequence. This CNN model integrates data like histone modifications and chromatin accessibility for predicting TFBSs. Moreover, the integrative CNN framework is superior to traditional Machine Learning methods with significant improvements.

4.9 RNA PROTEIN INTERACTION PREDICTION

RNA-protein interactions (RPIs) play important roles in an extensive variety of cellular processes, ranging from transcriptional and posttranscriptional regulation of gene expression to host defense against pathogens. High-throughput experiments to identify RNA-protein interactions are beginning to provide valuable information about the complexity of RNA-protein interaction networks, but are expensive and time-consuming. Hence, there is a need for reliable computational methods for predicting RNA-protein interactions. The following section states few deep learning methods for RNA-protein interactions.

4.9.1 RECENT METHODOLOGY PROGRESS OF DEEP LEARNING FOR RNA-PROTEIN INTERACTION PREDICTION

Interactions between RNAs and proteins play a pivotal role in many important biological processes. The advances in next-generation sequencing technologies have hugely benefitted researchers to identify hundreds of RNA-binding proteins (RBP) and their associated RNAs, which enables the large-scale prediction of RNA-protein interactions using Machine Learning approaches. This chapter provides an overview of the successful implementation of various deep learning approaches for predicting RNA-protein interactions, mainly focusing on the prediction of RNA-protein interaction pairs and RBP-binding sites on RNAs. It also discusses the advantages and disadvantages of these approaches, and highlights future perspectives on how to design better deep learning models. Finally, it provides deep insights into the future directions of computational tasks in the study of RNA-protein interactions, especially the interactions between non-coding RNAs and proteins.

4.9.2 iDEEP: RNA-PROTEIN BINDING MOTIFS MINING WITH A NEW HYBRID DEEP-LEARNING-BASED CROSS-DOMAIN KNOWLEDGE INTEGRATION APPROACH

RNA-binding proteins and their binding motifs enable crucial understanding of the posttranscriptional regulation of RNAs. Machine-Learning-based algorithms are widely acknowledged to be capable of speeding up this process. We propose a deep learning-based framework (iDeep) by using a novel hybrid convolutional neural network and deep belief network to predict the RBP interaction sites and motifs on RNAs. This new protocol transforms the original observed data into a high-level abstraction feature space using multiple layers of learning blocks. The iDeep framework can not only achieve promising performance than the state-of-the-art predictors, but also easily capture interpretable binding motifs. iDeep is available at http://www.csbio.sjtu.edu.cn/bioinf/iDeep.

4.9.3 iDEEPS: PREDICTION OF RNA-PROTEIN SEQUENCE AND STRUCTURE BINDING PREFERENCES USING DEEP CONVOLUTIONAL AND RECURRENT NEURAL NETWORKS

A deep-learning-based method, iDeepS simultaneously identifies the binding sequence and structure motifs from RNA sequences using convolutional neural networks and a bidirectional long short-term memory network (BLSTM). It first performs encoding for both the sequence and predicted secondary structure. CNNs are applied to reveal the hidden binding knowledge from the observed sequences. Considering the close relationship between sequence and predicted structures, the BLSTM is used to capture possible long-range dependencies between binding sequence and structure motifs identified by the CNNs. Finally, the learned weighted representations are fed into a classification layer to predict the RBP-binding sites. It has been evaluated on verified RBP-binding sites derived from large-scale representative CLIP-seq datasets. The iDeepS method identifies the sequence and structure motifs to accurately predict

RBP-binding sites. iDeepS is available at https://github.com/xypan1232/iDeepS.

4.9.4 APPLICATIONS OF DEEP LEARNING IN BIOMEDICAL RESEARCH

An overview of applications of deep learning in biomedical research is shown in Figure 4.3.

Advances in biological and medical areas are resulting in explosive volumes of biological data like genomic and proteomic sequences, medical images, and lots of physiological data. Learning from these data simplifies the understanding of human

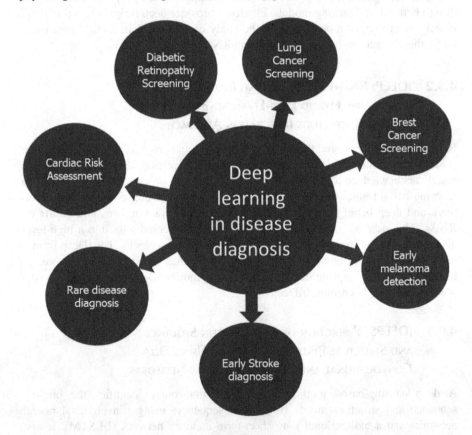

FIGURE 4.3 Deep learning in disease diagnosis.

health and diagnosis of disease. Deep-learning-based algorithms show revolutionary results in fetching features and learning patterns from complex datasets. This section aims to provide an insight into deep learning techniques and some of the state-of-the-art applications in the biomedical field.

4.10 DEEP LEARNING IN DISEASE DIAGNOSIS

Deep learning has largely been employed in radiology as well as in other diagnosis practices because of the sustained growth of computing power and storage technologies, decreasing cost of hardware, increasing cost of healthcare, the scarcity of healthcare workers, and a plenty of medical datasets to train the models.

4.10.1 BREAST CANCER SCREENING

According to the World Health Organization (WHO) survey analysis, breast cancer is the most common cancer among women that leads to around 627,000 deaths annually. To save lives, many countries have introduced screening programs targeting to spot the cancer at an early stage. In the very beginning of 2020, Google's Artificial Intelligence division DeepMind introduced a deep learning model that reportedly improved results of an average radiologist by 11.5%.

Commercially Available Solutions

Breast Health Solutions by iCAD (based in New Hampshire, USA, FDA-cleared, CE-marked): The AI suite applies deep learning algorithms to 2D mammography, 3D mammography (digital breast tomosynthesis or DBT), and breast density assessment. Its ProFound AI technology became the first Artificial Intelligence solution for 3D mammography approved by the FDA.

Transpara by ScreenPoint Medical (based in the Netherlands, FDA-cleared, CE-marked): Trained on over a million mammograms, Transpara deep learning algorithm helps radiologists analyze both 2D and 3D mammograms. The solution is already in use in many countries.

4.10.2 EARLY MELANOMA DETECTION

Skin diseases are the fourth most frequent cause of disability worldwide, while skin cancer is the world's most common malignancy, hitting 20% of people by age 70. At this place, AI can play a promising role. Similar to radiologists, dermatologists largely rely on visual pattern identification. In 2017, computer scientists from Stanford University created a convolutional neural network model that was trained on over 130,000 clinical images of skin pathologies to spot cancer. The algorithm reached the accuracy demonstrated by dermatologists. Finally, in March 2020, the *Journal of Investigative Dermatology* published the study by researchers from Seoul National University. Their CNN model learned from over 220,000 images to predict malignancy and classify 134 skin disorders.

Commercially Available Solutions

SkinVision (based in the Netherlands, CE-marked): The app is designed for assessing the risk of cancer based on photos of suspicious moles or other marks. Its AI algorithm was trained to spot warning signs on 3.5 million pictures. SkinVision has already contributed to the diagnosing of over 40,000 cases of skin cancer.

skinScan by TeleSkin ApS (based in Denmark, CE-marked): The iOS app available for downloading in Scandinavia, New Zealand, and Australia uses an AI algorithm for distinguishing a typical mole from an atypical one.

4.10.3 Lung Cancer Screening

Lung cancer is one of the world's deadliest cancers. It leads the list of cancer-related mortality and is second only to skin cancer in the prevalence rate. As with other malignancies, early detection may always be lifesaving.

The 2019 research by Google showed a promising result: a deep learning model created in collaboration with Northwestern Medicine and trained on 42,000 chest CT scans was way better at diagnosing lung cancer than radiologists with eight years of expertise. The algorithm was able to find malignant lung modes 5–9.5% more often than human specialists. Earlier, another CNN model proved its ability to spot chronic obstructive pulmonary disease (COPD) which often develops into cancer.

Commercially Available Solutions

Veye Chest by Aidense (based in the Netherlands, CE-marked): The AI solution automatically detects suspicious nodules in the lungs from low-dose CT scans, measures them, and compares them with previous images to identify the growth rate.

Veye Chest by ClariPi (based in South Korea, FDA-cleared): This solution does not detect cancer, but denoises low-dose and ultra-low-dose CT scans, thus improving the confidence of radiologists. The CNN model was trained on over a million images of different parts of the body, but ClariPi accentuates lung cancer screening as a key application of their algorithm.

4.10.4 Diabetic Retinopathy Screening

In the field of ophthalmology, AI is mostly used for retina image analysis—and specifically for diabetic retinopathy (DR) detection. This eye complication can cause blindness and strikes one in three patients with diabetes, amounting to 422 million globally. Early detection prevents the risk of vision loss.

IBM's deep learning technology launched in 2017 reached an accuracy score of 86% in detecting DR and classifying its severity—from mild to proliferative.

This result was outperformed by Google. In collaboration with its sister organization, Verily, the tech giant had been training a deep neural network for three years, using a dataset of 128,000 retinal images. In 2018, Google's AI Eye Doctor demonstrated 98.6% accuracy, on par with human experts. Now the algorithm serves to help doctors at Aravind Eye Hospital in India.

Commercially Available Solutions

IDx-DR by IDx (based in Iowa, USA, FDA-cleared, CE-marked): Known as the first AI system for DR diagnosis approved by FDA, IDx-DR software can be paired only with a particular retinal camera called Topcon. The deep learning algorithm provides one of two results:

1) Visit an ophthalmologist (for more than mild DR spotted)
2) Rescreen in 12 months (for mild and negative results)

IRIS (based in Florida, USA, FDA-cleared): Intelligent Retinal Imaging Systems can work with different cameras as it automatically enhances the quality of original images. The company benefits from Microsoft's Azure Machine Learning Package for Computer Vision.

4.10.5   CARDIAC RISK ASSESSMENT FROM ELECTROCARDIOGRAMS (ECGs)

Heart disease is the number one cause of death among men and women in the United States and worldwide. Timely risk assessment based on ECGs—the quickest and simplest test of heart activity—may significantly decrease mortality and prevent heart attacks.

With more than 300 million ECGs preformed globally each year, algorithms obtain a huge data pool for learning. Multiple studies show that AI already not only spots current abnormalities from ECGs but predicts future risks as well. For example, RiskCardio technology developed in 2019 at MIT assesses the likelihood of cardiovascular death within 30–365 days for patients who have already survived acute coronary syndrome (ACS).

Commercially Available Solution

KardiaMobile by AliveCor (based in California, USA, FDA-cleared, CE-marked): The personal ECG solution consists of a small recording device that captures an ECG in 30 seconds and a mobile app that utilizes a deep neural network to detect slow and fast heart rhythms (bradycardia and tachycardia), atrial fibrillation (AF), and normal rhythms. Once taken, ECG recording can be sent to a clinician for further analysis.

4.10.6   EARLY STROKE DIAGNOSIS FROM HEAD CT SCANS

Stroke or the sudden death of brain cells due to lack of oxygen is the second major cause of death and the third leading cause of long-term disability globally. This dangerous condition requires immediate diagnosis and treatment. Statistics show that patients who receive professional help within 3 hours after the first symptoms typically make a better and faster recovery.

Commercially Available Solutions

Viz LVO and Viz-ICH by Viz.ai (based in California, USA, and Israel, FDA-cleared, CE-marked): The deep learning algorithms analyze CT scans to detect suspected ICH and LVO strokes. The system automatically alerts specialists, saving precious time and brain cells.

AI Stroke by Aidoc (based in Israel, FDA-cleared, CE-marked): AI Stroke package covers two types of stroke—ICH and LVO. The system automatically flags suspected cases, enabling radiologists to quickly decide on the course of action.

e-Stroke suite by Brainomix (based in UK, CE-marked): This AI-driven imaging software automatically assesses CT scans of stroke patients. Currently, the algorithm identifies only the ischemic stroke that amounts to 85% of all cases.

4.11 DEEP LEARNING IN DIAGNOSIS OF RARE DISEASES

Diseases that affect fewer than 5 patients per 10,000 are defined as rare in Europe. With more than 6000 known rare diseases, their joint global health burden is large, and recent estimates report a population occurrence of at least 3.5–5.9%. According to a study from 2013, it takes, on average, more than five years, eight physicians, and two to three misdiagnoses until a rare disease patient obtains the correct diagnosis. Once appropriately diagnosed, the challenges remain: due to the small patient numbers, commercials for developing medications are often low. Furthermore, the pathophysiological mechanisms underlying rare diseases are often not well understood. As a consequence, many rare diseases lack adequate treatment options.

One of the most extensive knowledge bases for rare diseases is Orphanet, which provides data about disease epidemiology, linked genes, inheritance types, disease onsets, or bibliography to terminologies, as well as links to expert centers, patient organizations, and other resources. Another European ventures include RD-Connect, which combines archives, biobanks, and genetic datasets with bioinformatics tools to provide a central resource for research on rare diseases; the European Reference Networks (ERNs), which also provides an IT infrastructure that allows healthcare professionals to collaborate on virtual panels to exchange knowledge and decide on optimal treatments; and the European Joint Programme on Rare Diseases (EJP RD), a multinational cooperation aiming to create an ecosystem that facilitates research, care, and medical innovation in the field of rare diseases. In the United States, the Undiagnosed Diseases Network (UDN) brings together experts to diagnose and treat patients with rare conditions.

In addition to these collaborative efforts and international platforms, another important factor that can improve the condition for rare disease patients are improvements in information technology—particularly in the field of deep learning and Artificial Intelligence. DL and AI classically use large, multivariate datasets to "train" models and algorithms, which are then used to make predictions on new data (for example, by classifying tumors in radiological images as benign or malignant). Importantly, the computations by which these models generate their output are not explicitly coded by a programmer, but instead they are implicitly "learned" by the algorithm from example data (hence the term "Machine Learning" or "deep learning"). DL and AI and are progressively applied in medicine and healthcare and, in some areas, are beginning to achieve (and sometimes even surpass) human-level performance and precisions.

4.12 CONCLUSIONS

In this chapter, we have comprehensively summarized all the fundamental but essential concepts, methods, and tools of deep learning extensively used for the processing and analysis of the next-generation sequencing data. By reviewing these deep learning and Machine Learning methods—from quality control analysis of the reads to their assembly, followed by metagenomics analysis, variant analysis, SNP detection, gene expression analysis, identification of transcriptomics factors, RNA-protein interaction predictions—we highlighted and explored all the important analysis parameters of next-generation sequencing data which would help to gain knowledge from the biological data.

Second, the successful application of deep learning and Artificial Intelligence in the field of medical research and diagnostics has been discussed. Deep learning algorithms, in particular convolutional networks, have rapidly become a methodology of choice for analyzing medical images. Concise overviews are provided for studies per application area: neuro, retinal, pulmonary, melanoma detection, breast, cardiac, stroke, and rare disease diagnosis. We have ended with a summary of the current state-of-the-art approach and open challenges and directions for future research.

Deep learning is a big-data-driven approach, which has made it unique from conventional statistical approaches, as statistical methods rely on the assumptions of the generated data, deep learning. Statistics can deliver clear interpretations through fitting a definite probability model when adequate data are collected from well-designed studies, whereas deep learning is involved with the creation of questions and application of algorithms which improvise with training datasets. Many deep learning approaches can derive models for pattern recognition, classification, and prediction from existing data and do not rely on strict assumptions about the data-generating systems, which makes them more efficient in some complicated applications. Finally, deep learning can be integrated with the existing conventional methods and algorithms to tackle the complicated biological data analysis.

BIBLIOGRAPHY

Ainscough, B.J., Barnell, E.K., Ronning, P., Campbell, K.M., Wagner, A.H., Fehniger, T.A., Dunn, G.P., Uppaluri, R., Govindan, R., Rohan, T.E., and Griffith, M. "A deep learning approach to automate refinement of somatic variant calling from cancer sequencing data." *Nature Genetics* 50 (12): 1735–1743.

Angly, F.E., Willner, D., Rohwer, F., Hugenholtz, P., Tyson, G.W. (2012) "Grinder: A versatile amplicon and shotgun sequence simulator." *Nucleic Acids Research* 40 (12): e94.

Arango-Argoty, G., Garner, E., Pruden, A., Heath, L.S., Vikesland, P., and Zhang, L. (2018) "DeepARG: A deep learning approach for predicting antibiotic resistance genes from metagenomic data." *Microbiome* 6 (1): 23.

Arango-Argoty, G.A., Dai, D., Pruden, A., Vikesland, P., Heath, L.S., and Zhang, L. (2019) "NanoARG: A web service for detecting and contextualizing antimicrobial resistance genes from nanopore-derived metagenomes." *Microbiome* 7 (1): 88.

Bengio, Y. and LeCun, Y. (2007) "Scaling learning algorithms toward AI," in *Large-Scale Kernel Machines*, edited by L. Bottou, O. Chapelle, D. DeCoste, and J. Weston (Cambridge, MA: The MIT Press).

Chen, L., Zhai, Y., He, Q., Wang, W., and Deng, M. (2020) "Integrating deep supervised, self-supervised and unsupervised learning for single-cell RNA-seq clustering and annotation." *Genes (Basel)* 11 (7): 792.

Ching, T., Himmelstein, D. S., Beaulieu-Jones, B. K., Kalinin, A. A., Do, B. T., Way, G. P., et al. (2018) "Opportunities and obstacles for deep learning in biology and medicine". *Journal of the Royal Society Interface* 15: 20170387. doi: 10.1098/rsif.2017.0387.

Ditzler, G., Polikar, R., Member, S., Rosen G., and Member, S. (2015) "Multi-layer and recursive neural networks for metagenomic classification". *IEEE* Transactions *on NanoBioscience* 14: 608. doi: 10.1109/TNB.2015.2461219.

Esteva, A., Kuprel, B., Novoa, R.A., Ko, J., Swetter, S.M., Blau, H.M., and Thrun, S. (2017) "Dermatologist-level classification of skin cancer with deep neural networks". *Nature* 542: 115–118. doi: 10.1038/nature21056.

European Commission. (n.d.) https://ec.europa.eu/info/research-and-innovation/research-a rea/health-research-and-innovation/rare-diseases_en. Accessed 16 Apr 2020.

European Joint Programme on Rare Diseases. (n.d.) https://www.ejprarediseases.org. Accessed 16 Apr 2020.

European Reference Networks. (n.d.) https://ec.europa.eu/health/ern_en. Accessed 16 Apr 2020.

EURORDIS. (n.d.) https://www.eurordis.org/about-rare-diseases. Accessed 16 Apr 2020.

Fiannaca, A., La Paglia, L., La Rosa, M., Renda, G., Rizzo, R., Gaglio, S., and Urso, A. (2018) "Deep learning models for bacteria taxonomic classification of metagenomic data." *BMC Bioinformatics* 19 (Suppl 7): 198.

Giorgi, J.M. and Bader, G.D. (2018) "Transfer learning for biomedical named entity recognition with neural networks". *Bioinformatics* 34: 4087–4094. doi: 10.1093/bioinformatics/bty449.

Hannigan, G.D., Prihoda, D., Palicka, A., Soukup, J., Klempir, O., Rampula, L., Durcak, J., Wurst, M., Kotowski, J., Chang, D., and Wang, R. (2019) "A deep learning genome-mining strategy for biosynthetic gene cluster prediction." *Nucleic Acids Research* 47 (18): e110.

Jing, F., Zhang, S., Cao, Z., and Zhang, S.. (2019) "An integrative framework for combining sequence and epigenomic data to predict transcription factor binding sites using deep learning." *IEEE/ACM Transactions on Computational Biology Bioinformatics* (18): 355–364.

Korvigo, I., Afanasyev, A., Romashchenko, N., and Skoblov, M. (2018) "Generalising better: Applying deep learning to integrate deleteriousness prediction scores for whole-exome SNV studies." *PLoS One* 13 (3): e0192829.

Koumakis, L. (2020) "Deep learning models in genomics; are we there yet?" *Computational and Structural Biotechnology Journal* 18: 1466–1473.

LaPierre, N., Egan, R., Wang, W., and Wang, Z. (2019) "De novo Nanopore read quality improvement using deep learning". *BMC Bioinformatics* 20 (1): 552.

LaPierre, N., Ju, C.J.T., Zhou, G., and Wang, W. (2019) "MetaPheno: A critical evaluation of deep learning and machine learning in metagenome-based disease prediction." *Methods* 166: 74–82.

Li, X., Wang, K., Lyu, Y., Pan, H., Zhang, J., Stambolian, D., Susztak, K., Reilly, M.P., Hu, G., and Li, M. (2020) "Deep learning enables accurate clustering with batch effect removal in single-cell RNA-seq analysis." *Nature Communications* 11 (1): 2338.

Li, Y., Wang, S., Umarov, R., Xie, B., Fan, M., Li, L., and Gao, X. (2018) "DEEPre: Sequence-based enzyme EC number prediction by deep learning." *Bioinformatics* 34 (5): 760–769.

Liang, M., Li, Z., Chen, T., and Zeng, J. (2015) "Integrative data analysis of multi-platform cancer data with a multimodal deep learning approach". *IEEE/ACM Transactions on Computational Biology and Bioinformatics* 12: 928–937. doi: 10.1109/TCBB.2014. 2377729.

Liang, Q., Bible, P.W., Liu, Y., Zou, B., and Wei, L. (2020) "DeepMicrobes: Taxonomic classification for metagenomics with deep learning." *NAR Genomics and Bioinformatics* 2 (1): lqaa009.

Libbrecht, M.W. and Noble, W.S. (2015) "Machine learning applications in genetics and genomics". Nature Reviews Genetics 16: 321–322. doi: 10.1038/nrg3920.

Luo, R., Sedlazeck, F.J., Lam, T.W. and Schatz, M.C. (2019) "A multi-task convolutional deep neural network for variant calling in single molecule sequencing." *Nature Communications* 10 (1): 998.

Min, X., Zeng, W., Chen, S., Chen, N., Chen, T., and Jiang, R. (2017) "Predicting enhancers with deep convolutional neural networks." *BMC Bioinformatics* 18 (Suppl 13): 478.

Mineeva, O., Rojas-Carulla, M., Ley, R.E., Schölkopf, B., and Youngblut, N.D. (2020) "DeepMAsED: Evaluating the quality of metagenomic assemblies." *Bioinformatics* 36 (10): 3011–3017.

Mineeva, O., Rojas-Carulla, M., Ley, R.E., Schölkopf, B., and Youngblut, N.D. (2020) "DeepMAsED: Evaluating the quality of metagenomic assemblies." *Bioinformatics* 36 (10): 3011–3017.

Najafabadi, M.M., Villanustre, F., Khoshgoftaar, T.M., Seliya, N., Wald, R., and Muharemagic, E. (2015) "Deep learning applications and challenges in big data analytics". *Journal of Big Data* 2: 1. doi: 10.1186/s40537-014-0007-7.

Orphanet. (n.d.) http://www.orpha.net. Accessed 16 Apr 2020.

Pan, X. and Shen, H. (2017) "RNA-protein binding motifs mining with a new hybrid deep learning based cross-domain knowledge integration approach." *BMC Bioinformatics* 18 (1): 136.

Pan, X., Rijnbeek, P., Yan, J., and Shen, H.B. (2018) "Prediction of RNA-protein sequence and structure binding preferences using deep convolutional and recurrent neural networks." *BMC Genomics* 19 (1): 511.

Pan, X., Yang, Y., Xia, C.Q., Mirza, A.H., and Shen, H.B. (2019) "Recent methodology progress of deep learning for RNA-protein interaction prediction." *Wiley Interdisciplinary Reviews: RNA* 10 (6): e1544.

Poplin, R., Chang, P.C., Alexander, D., Schwartz, S., Colthurst, T., Ku, A., Newburger, D., Dijamco, J., Nguyen, N., Afshar, P.T., and Gross, S.S. (2018) "A universal SNP and small-indel variant caller using deep neural networks." *Nature Biotechnology* 36 (10): 983–987.

Quang, D., Chen, Y., and Xie, X. (2015) "DANN: A deep learning approach for annotating the pathogenicity of genetic variants." *Bioinformatics* 31 (5): 761.

Rahman, M.A., and Rangwala, H. (2020) "IDMIL: An alignment-free Interpretable Deep Multiple Instance Learning (MIL) for predicting disease from whole-metagenomic data." *Bioinformatics* 36 (Supplement_1): i139–i47.

Ramoni, R.B., Mulvihill, J.J., Adams, D.R., Allard, P., Ashley, E.A., Bernstein, J.A., et al. (2017) "The undiagnosed diseases network: Accelerating discovery about health and disease." *American Journal of Human Genetics* 100: 185–192.

Ravasio, V., Ritelli, M., Legati, A., and Giacopuzzi, E. (2018) "GARFIELD-NGS: Genomic vARiants FIltering by dEep Learning moDels in NGS." *Bioinformatics* 34 (17): 3038–3040.

Sarangi, A.N., Goel, A., and Aggarwal, R. (2019) "Methods for studying gut microbiota: A primer for physicians." *Journal of Clinical and Experimental Hepatology* 9 (1): 62–73. doi: 10.1016/j.jceh.2018.04.016.

Shire, Rare Disease Impact Report. (n.d.) https://globalgenes.org/wp-content/uploads/2013 /04/ShireReport-1.pdf. Accessed 16 Apr 2020.

Sun, C., Zhang, N., Yu, P., Wu, X., Li, Q., Li, T., Li, H., Xiao, X., Shalmani, A., Li, L., and Che, D. (2020) "Enhancer recognition and prediction during spermatogenesis based on deep convolutional neural networks." *Molecular Omics* 16: 308–321.

Tasaki, S., Gaiteri, C., Mostafavi, S., and Wang, Y. (2020) "Deep learning decodes the principles of differential gene expression." *Nature Machine Intelligence* 2 (7): 376–386.

Telenti, A., Lippert, C., Chang, P.C., and DePristo, M. (2018) "Deep learning of genomic variation and regulatory network data." *Human Molecular Genetics* 27 (R1): R63–R71.

Thompson, R., Johnston, L., Taruscio, D., Monaco, L., Béroud, C., Gut, I.G., et al. (2014) "RD-connect: An integrated platform connecting databases, registries, biobanks and clinical bioinformatics for rare disease research." *Journal of General Internal Medicine* 29 (Suppl 3): S780– S787.

Torroja, C., and Sanchez-Cabo, F. (2019) "Digitaldlsorter: Deep-learning on scRNA-Seq to deconvolute gene expression data." *Frontiers in Genetics* 10: 978.

Wakap, S.N., Lambert, D.M., Olry, A., Rodwell, C., Gueydan, C., Lanneau, V., et al. (2020) "Estimating cumulative point prevalence of rare diseases: Analysis of the Orphanet database." *European Journal of Human Genetics* 28: 165–173.

Wang, M., Tai, C., Weinan, E., and Wei, L. (2018) "DeFine: Deep convolutional neural networks accurately quantify intensities of transcription factor-DNA binding and facilitate evaluation of functional non-coding variants." *Nucleic Acids Research* 46 (11): e69.

Wick, R.R., Judd, L.M., and Holt, K.E. (2018) "Deepbinner: Demultiplexing barcoded Oxford Nanopore reads with deep convolutional neural networks." *PLOS Computational Biology* 14 (11): e1006583.

Xu, J., Xiang, L., Liu, Q., Gilmore, H., Wu, J., Tang, J., and Madabhushi, A. (2016) "Stacked sparse autoencoder (SSAE) for nuclei detection on breast cancer histopathology images". *IEEE Transactions on Medical Imaging* 35: 119–130. doi: 10.1109/TMI.2015.2458702.

Yin, Q., Wu, M., Liu, Q., Lv, H., and Jiang, R.. (2019) "DeepHistone: A deep learning approach to predicting histone modifications." *BMC Genomics* 20 (Suppl 2): 193.

Zhang, S., Zhou, J., Hu, H., Gong, H., Chen, L., Cheng, C., and Zeng, J. (2016) "A deep learning framework for modeling structural features of RNA-binding protein targets". *Nucleic Acids Research* 44: e32. doi: 10.1093/nar/gkv1025.

Zhang, S.W., Jin, X.Y., and Zhang, T. (2017) "Gene prediction in metagenomic fragments with deep learning". *BioMed Research International* (9).

Zhang, Y., Liu, C.M., Leung, H.C., Luo, R., and Lam, T.W. (2020) "Nanopore sequencing data via deep learning." *iScience* 23 (5): 101128.

Zhou, J. and Troyanskaya, O.G. (2015) "Predicting effects of noncoding variants with deep learning-based sequence model." *Nature Methods* 12 (10): 931–934.

5 Applications of Machine Learning Algorithms to Cancer Data

Suba Suseela, Nita Parekh

CONTENTS

5.1 INTRODUCTION

Classification of cancer types/subtypes has become more important with increasing incidence rates, and cancer remains the leading cause of death globally. Identification of novel classes (subtypes) in cancer can help in planning more effective treatment strategies, reduce toxicity, and improve survival rates of patients. Traditionally, tumors have been classified based on tissue types, primary sites of occurrence, and/ or their morphology, which can often be very subjective. Moreover, treatment therapies based on tumor histology alone are not very effective as different tumors may respond differently to the same drug therapy. A promising alternative approach is the classification of tumors based on expression levels of multiple genes involved in the disease. Even though the human genome has approximately 20,000 protein coding genes, all of them would not be active/expressed in any single biological process, including cell growth, metabolism, tumorigenesis, etc. This requires identifying relevant genes that may be responsible for the proliferation of malignant cells. Most research in this area has focused on selecting a subset of genes in cancer samples for classification purposes using expression data. The advances in gene profiling technologies like high-throughput sequencing have generated huge amounts of genomic data. Large-scale cancer studies initiated by various consortia, viz., TCGA, ICGC, ENCODE project, etc., have generated thousands of samples from over hundreds of different types of cancer. However, the scale of data generation has made it highly challenging to integrate and model this complex, noisy, high-dimensional data. Classification approaches based on supervised/unsupervised learning, viz., support vector machines (SVM), decision trees, or neural networks for identifying genetic features for binary or multi-class classification of tumors and tumor subtypes have been proposed. These approaches help in revealing relationships between the features in the data and exhibit improved performance compared to other alternative approaches.

In this chapter, an attempt has been made to provide an overview of the evolution of Machine Learning (ML) algorithms in analyzing gene expression data over the past two decades. A brief review of some widely used algorithms for feature selection and subtype classification is also provided. Cancer datasets are of different types based on the data type (e.g., gene expression, copy number variation [CNV], DNA methylation), experimental techniques (e.g., microarray, RNASeq), microarray platforms (e.g., Agilent, Affymetrix, Illumina), data formats (e.g., text, XML, JSON, TSV), etc. The two most common platforms generating gene expression data are microarrays and RNA sequencing. The data types are very different in the two cases and require very different preprocessing and analysis pipelines; in microarray data, it is intensity values while in RNASeq data it is represented as read counts. Typically, in any experiment, the number of features (genes) is considerably higher than the number of samples available. This makes it difficult to select the optimal number of features for classifying various cancers and subtypes. Machine Learning algorithms can be useful to some extent in dealing with such problems and can be broadly classified as supervised, unsupervised, and semisupervised approaches (Ang et al., 2016). Numerous methods have been proposed in each category based on how the model is generated. In this chapter, some of these algorithms for gene selection in prediction/classification of binary/multiclass cancers, classification of benign/malign tumor cells, different grades of cancers, prognosis/survival of cancer patients, etc., are reviewed. Graph-based algorithms to associate the features selected with various pathways involved in cancer are also briefly discussed.

Feature selection is a major preprocessing step in ML applications to gene expression data analysis of tumor samples. Other challenges include limited access to data, integration of data from different experimental platforms/techniques, and lack of reproducibility in modeling high-dimensional data in the case of limited samples. A raw gene expression file may contain expression values of more than 20,000 genes. Majority of these genes are irrelevant in tumor progression and many others, though relevant, are redundant, resulting in noisy signals or in overfitting of data when used for training in an ML algorithm. Thus, there clearly is a need for feature selection in reducing dimensionality of the data. With reduced sets of features, ML algorithms have been successfully applied to classify samples into appropriate categories (Zhang and Deng, 2007), predict the prognosis of patients (Gevaert et al., 2006), or identify suitable therapy (Tabl et al., 2018). Various methods proposed for feature selection or feature transformation are principal component analysis, linear discriminant analysis, singular value decomposition (SVD), information gain, chi-square test, fisher score, etc. The objective in the classification problem is to identify genes that are significant to a particular type/subtype of cancer. Numerous classes of ML approaches have been used for this purpose, e.g., random forests, support vector machines, regression, and neural networks.

5.2 OVERVIEW OF FEATURE SELECTION APPROACHES

Methods for feature selection have been applied in various domains over the past 50 years. These are categorized into filter, wrapper, and embedded methods based on the evaluation metrics used to score the feature subsets. In filter-based methods, feature selection is based on the score of a feature in a statistical test for their correlation with the outcome variable, e.g., Pearson's correlation, chi-square test, or linear discriminant analysis. These methods are independent of the ML algorithm used and easy to implement. In wrapper methods, a model is built on a subset of features and its performance evaluated. For optimal performance of the model, features are either added or removed from the subset. It is basically a search problem for identifying the best set of features for classification. Some examples of this approach include forward selection, backward selection, and recursive feature elimination methods. This approach is computationally more intensive compared to filter-based approach. Embedded methods combine features of both filter and wrapper methods and are generally included in ML algorithms with built-in methods such as LASSO, RIDGE regression, etc., to penalize overfitting.

In biological data analysis, the feature selection method helps in identifying features that would help in determining the disease class or differentiate between disease and normal cells. Typically, only a few genes are directly linked to the disease, while the majority only exhibit a weak or indirect association. The goal of the selection algorithm is to be able to distinguish between relevant and noisy/redundant ones. Most importantly, the result of the algorithm should be interpretable and feasible for clinical use. However, in most cases, the number of features returned by ML algorithms is too large, making it impractical to be used in a clinical setting and/or give non-interpretable results. Some of the algorithms claim to achieve both small and interpretable set of features, but may not be always accurate as desired. Major steps in feature selection in any ML approach are discussed below.

5.2.1 MAIN STEPS IN FEATURE SELECTION

The objective of any feature selection process is to identify a relevant set of features that are strongly correlated to the traits of interest and few features that are weakly correlated but still important for the classification of samples and for avoiding noisy features.

5.2.1.1   Preprocessing Step

Genome-wide analysis results in thousands of genes (features), which poses a major hurdle in the learning phase of ML algorithms when the number of samples is few. This is generally handled by subjecting raw datasets to some initial level of filtering based on statistical relevance of the features and/or removal of noisy signals—for example, filtering genes based on signal-to-noise ratio (Golub et al., 1999), differential expression of genes with respect to control (Xiao et al., 2018), correlation of genes to the trait of interest (Tabl et al., 2018), etc. The resultant dataset with a reduced number of features may include many correlated and redundant features. Selection of an optimal set of features from this resultant set involves some of the steps discussed below.

5.2.1.2   Determining the Direction of Selection

The selection algorithm may start with an empty set, a complete set, or a random selection of genes. That is, genes are either added one by one to a set of candidate genes or removed one by one from the initial set of genes, or a hybrid approach of adding and removing genes simultaneously is applied based on some criteria that improve the classification capability of candidate genes.

5.2.1.3   Determining the Stopping Criteria

The above process of adding/removing genes needs to be terminated to obtain an optimal set of relevant genes and reduce redundancy. This is done by defining a stopping criterion that requires the candidate genes to have some attributes that differentiate them from others. This step can be done either separately or combined with the next step of feature selection, for example, setting a threshold for the error rate in the performance of the model. Naively, this can be achieved by prefer deciding the number of features/iterations the algorithm must run.

5.2.1.4   Evaluating the Selection

Feature selection algorithms are categorized as filter-based, wrapper, or embedded methods. Filter-based methods evaluate the performance of candidate genes after the selection process with evaluation methods such as LOOCV, k-fold CV, etc. The wrapper method does the performance evaluation during the selection process and the stopping criterion in such cases is to continue adding or removing of genes till the performance improves. But with a change in the classification algorithm, the gene selection process may also change in this case. Embedded methods integrate classification and gene selection algorithms such that the performance of classification accuracy decides the selection of features.

5.2.1.5   Validation Methods

Cross-validation, use of confusion matrix, or various methods evaluating the similarity of selected genes, error rates, etc., are some of the validation methods commonly used.

5.2.2 CHALLENGES IN FEATURE SELECTION

The set of features selected can affect the performance of classification algorithms, and hence care should be taken when choosing feature selection methods that are robust and provide stable results. That is, change in the dataset or methods for feature selection should not affect the selected set of features. However, several factors are observed to affect the stability of the result. "Curse of dimensionality" is one major factor when the sample size is significantly small compared to the size of a feature set. This may result in problems such as missing important features or undue emphasis given to irrelevant features, leading to reduction in the performance of classifiers. Class imbalance is another important problem that causes prediction of classifier to be biased when some classes dominate others, i.e., when the number of samples in one or more classes outnumber the samples in other classes in a dataset. For example, in breast cancer datasets, Luminal A subtype is the most common subtype of breast cancer, while Normal-like subtype is observed with least frequency, resulting in class imbalance. Different standards followed by different microarray platforms, such as Agilent, Affymetrix, etc., and sequencing platforms in gene expression profiling incur difficulties in the analysis of cross-platform data, making it difficult to merge datasets across different platforms for increasing the sample size.

5.3 OVERVIEW OF CLASSIFICATION METHODS

Machine Learning is slowly replacing traditional classification approaches for the analysis of cancer samples due to high volumes of data resulting from next-generation sequencing technologies and the complexities involved in data interpretation. The classification algorithms are broadly categorized into three categories: supervised, semisupervised, and unsupervised algorithms. Supervised methods use labeled data for classification purposes, e.g., linear regression (Seber and Lee, 2012), random forest (Breiman, 2001), and support vector machine (Cortes and Vapnik, 1995). Unsupervised algorithms do not require labeled data, e.g., clustering algorithms ("Unsupervised Learning: Clustering," n.d.), self-organizing feature maps (Marsland, 2011), etc. Semisupervised algorithms are a mixture of both the techniques wherein prediction is improved with labeled data and using some discriminant methods to classify/predict. These methods generally depend on the techniques, such as eigenvector expressions of the datasets, probabilistic modeling, distance metrics, hierarchical/ agglomerative techniques, etc. Supervised learning methods are the most common learning methods used in the classification of disease/control or subtyping of microarray datasets. Unsupervised and semisupervised methods are less studied but appear to be promising and more suitable for gene expression profiles where labeling of data is very costly and availability of a large number of samples is not common.

5.3.1 OVERVIEW OF POPULAR ML ALGORITHMS

In this section, some of the most widely used ML methods are discussed followed by those combining ML with other non-ML methods in this domain. The well-accepted

ML methods in the domain of gene expression data analysis are SVM and its variants, regression-based methods, random forest, clustering approaches, and neural networks. Commonly used non-ML methods for gene selection are statistical models. Many studies consider a combined strategy to improve the results. Other methods, among many, proposed for classification include genetic algorithm for preselection of genes for multiclass classification using a maximum likelihood (MLHD) classifier (Ooi and Tan, 2003), t-statistic for gene pair scoring and feature selection for a binary class problem (Bø and Jonassen, 2002), and maximum relevance minimum redundancy (mRMR) approach using an entropy-based method for assessing relevance (Liu et al., 2005).

Support Vector Machine: SVM and its variants are supervised ML algorithms widely used because of their robustness and performance (Cortes and Vapnik, 1995). The first application of SVM in cancer classification dates back to 2000. Linear and non-linear SVMs are the most primitive categories of SVMs. Other variants include soft margin SVMs and hard margin SVMs (based on regularization penalty), support vector regression (SVR) (based on objective function), and binary and multiclass SVMs (based on number of classes). Depending on the loss function and kernels used, SVMs are of many types. Limitations of SVM are difficulty in parameter selection and extensive memory and time requirements. Non-interpretability of the features used for classification is another major drawback of SVMs in medical applications.

Support vector machine finds a maximum margin hyperplane (linear or non-linear) to split the data points into separate classes. A hyperplane is defined as set of points, X, satisfying the following equation:

$$\vec{W} \cdot \vec{X} - b = 0 \tag{1}$$

where $\vec{W}$ is a vector normal to the hyperplane. For linearly separable data, the two hyperplanes that would segregate the data into two different groups with a maximum margin between them are defined by the following equations:

$$\vec{W} \cdot \vec{X} - b \geq 1 \quad \text{and} \quad \vec{W} \cdot \vec{X} - b \leq -1 \tag{2}$$

where all points on or above the first inequality are labeled "1," and those on or below the second inequality are labeled "−1." Thus, the classifier is determined by parameters $\vec{W}$ and b, and $\vec{X}$ that lie near the hyperplanes form the support vectors. When an additional parameter λ is introduced, the hyperplanes have soft margins to separate non-linear data points, with loss function given by

$$\max\left(0, 1 - Y_i\left(\vec{W} \cdot \vec{X} - b\right)\right) + \lambda \left\|\vec{W}\right\|^2 \tag{3}$$

where Y_i is the ith target and $\vec{W} \cdot \vec{X} - b$ is the current output. For smaller values of λ, the hyperplane behaves as a hard margin. Further, if instead of simple dot product, non-linear kernel functions are used, the SVM becomes a non-linear classifier. In the study by Huang et al. (Huang et al., 2017), SVM ensembles with linear kernels and bagging method are shown to perform well on a preprocessed set of genes (a small-scale dataset) for predicting breast cancer, whereas an SVM ensemble with radial basis function (RBF) kernels with boosting method shows better performance on a large-scale dataset.

Regression: These models estimate conditional probability of a class label given the observations and are widely used for prediction tasks. Regression predicts continuous values of the dependent variable, whereas in classification a categorical value is predicted. For high-dimensional data, regression models can also be used to understand which among the independent variables are more related to the label and thereby help in dimensionality reduction. In linear regression, the dependent variable is defined as follows:

$$\hat{y}_i = \beta_1 x_{i1} + \beta_2 x_{i2} + \cdots + \beta_p x_{ip} + \varepsilon_i \tag{4}$$

where x_{ij} is the ith observation of the pth independent variable β_i, the parameters, and ε_i is an error term. In non-linear regression, the function of independent variables is non-linear in nature, viz., power functions, Gaussian, etc. For fitting a model to data, the parameters are learned by minimizing sum of squared residuals (SSR):

$$SSR = \sum_{i=1}^{n} e_i^2 \tag{5}$$

where $e_i = y_i - \hat{y}_i$, y_i is the true value of the dependent variable, $\hat{y}_i$ is the predicted value, and n is the sample size, or by mean squared error (MSE):

$$MSE = \frac{SSR}{n-p} \tag{6}$$

After model construction, the goodness-of-fit measure of the model and statistical significance of the parameters are estimated using R-squared analysis, F-test, or t-test. Logistic regression is a classification algorithm where the dependent variable can take only discrete values. The categories are binomial or multinomial (based on the number of values the dependent variable takes), or ordinal if the values are ordered. Model fitting is done by maximum likelihood estimation. Other types of regressions based on penalty terms include LASSO, RIDGE, elastic net regression, etc. An elastic net penalized logistic regression was used for classifying breast cancer samples as normal versus tumor with aberrant RAS pathway activity (Tabl et al., 2018). Advantages of the regression model are that it identifies relative importance of variables which influence the decision and its ability to identify the outliers. These models are not suitable in case of incomplete data as then all the variables that contribute to the prediction may not be captured, or when the correlation is interpreted falsely as causation, as then the algorithm returns a higher number of features which would be misleading. To overcome these disadvantages, a structured penalized logistic regression method was recently proposed (Liu and Wong, 2019). Here, a modification to the regularization term in the penalized regression equation is proposed:

$$F(\beta) = \lambda\alpha \sum_{j=1}^{p} \theta_j |\beta_j| + \lambda(1-\alpha) \sum_{i=1}^{p} \sum_{j=1}^{p} w_{ij} \left(\mu_i\beta_i - \mu_j\beta_j \right)^2 \qquad (7)$$

where the weight w_{ij} measures similarity between the pair of variables X_i and X_j. It controls the second regularization term in the above equation by penalizing the coefficients based on the structure of the data. The parameter θ_{ij} in the first regularization term selects features that correlate strongly and β_j introduced into the pairwise structured regularization term reduces the number of relevant features.

Random Forest (RF): It is another supervised learning algorithm and is used for classification or regression tasks (Breiman, 2001). It constructs multiple decision trees during the training phase and reports the mean or majority prediction of the individual decision trees as the algorithm's output. As shown in Figure 5.1, decision tree has a directed graph structure wherein each internal node represents an evaluation of an attribute, each branch denotes the outcome of that evaluation, and the terminal or leaf node represents a class label. The ensemble of decision trees is built using bagging method and the samples are selected with replacement. The features are selected randomly, and the best feature is used for splitting the node in a tree. The algorithm is widely used because of its good accuracy and ease of measuring the importance of features used for prediction, which helps in identifying and ranking

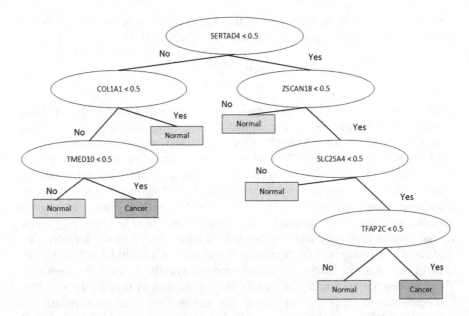

FIGURE 5.1   A representative decision tree.

the genes for classification purposes. In the study by Díaz-Uriarte and Alvarez de Andrés (2006), RF was used to select the minimum number of genes for classification. The disadvantage of decision tree is that it overfits, but random forests do not overfit the data if the number of trees in the forest is sufficiently large. Though with the increase in the number of decision trees the accuracy of the model improves, the algorithm becomes slower. The model is a predictive tool and not a descriptive one as it lacks interpretability. To improve its interpretability, various methods have been proposed. For example, the advantages of RFs have been combined with those of a generalized linear model to achieve interpretability of results by Song et al. (2013).

Neural Networks: These are non-linear, statistical, decision-making tools based on the working principle of biological neurons. It involves a set of processing elements connected to each other either densely or sparsely. The network may consist of a single layer or multiple layers of such connections, called hidden layers, apart from input and output layers. Neural networks can be used in supervised as well as unsupervised learning approaches. The learning here happens by updating the model parameters in iterations based on backpropagation of the error using techniques like stochastic gradient descent.

Neural networks propagate the input via hidden layers to the output layer such that the input to neuron j (successor) from neuron i (predecessor) is given by the propagation function:

$$p_j(t) = \sum_i o_i(t) \cdot w_{ij} + w_{0j} \tag{8}$$

where w_{ij} is the weight assigned to the connection between node i and node j and w_{0j} is the bias. Learning in neural network happens by minimizing a cost function, backpropagating the error, and updating the weights of the network. The cost function depends on the task to solve, for example, $C = E\left[\left(f(x) - y\right)^2\right]$ minimizes the cost over the sample data by minimizing $\hat{C} = \frac{1}{N} \sum_{i=1}^{N} f\left(x_{(i)} - y_i\right)^2$, thus solving the task in an optimal way by learning from the individual samples.

Neural networks were proposed in the early 1990s and its first application on gene expression microarray analysis was in a study conducted by Khan et al. in 2001 for classifying small round blue cell tumor (SRBCT) samples into four different tumor categories (Khan et al., 2001). Neural networks combined with various other gene selection strategies have been proposed in subsequent years, with the most recent being application of deep learning networks. As the number of layers increases, the neural network is called a deep neural network. With deeper layers, the network is able to capture better subtle features within the data and the deep learning concepts are widely used in genomics, proteomics, drug discovery, etc.

Deep learning networks are a category of artificial neural networks that make use of error backpropagation technique to automatically learn relevant patterns in the data. It is essentially a neural network with several layers of nodes (approximately hundreds) built according to the depths required by the problem. Automatic feature extraction is done within the layers of the network. Figure 5.2 shows a typical deep learning network's architecture extracting features of a handwritten digit and classifying it. It learns higher levels of features from the compositions of lower level features in a hierarchical fashion. Thus, it is a representation learning method with representations of data at multiple levels, obtained by non-linear transformations of the representations at one level to a higher level of abstraction in the next level. There are different types of deep learning networks based on the architecture of the network, e.g., convolutional neural networks (CNN) (Fukushima, 1980), deep belief networks (DBN) (Hinton et al., 2006), deep stacking networks (DSN) (Deng and Yu, 2011), and AutoEncoders (AE) (Bengio and Lecun, 2007).

Clustering: An unsupervised learning method, clustering has been widely used in gene expression analysis. In clustering approaches, set of objects are grouped such that objects within a group are more similar than those between groups, with similarity being defined in terms of distance between objects, distribution of the objects, density of objects, clique in the case of graph-based models, etc. These algorithms can be broadly classified as connectivity-based (hierarchical), density-based, centroid-based, and distance-based approaches. Connectivity-based clustering requires the user to specify the distance to consider two objects to be in a cluster and the linkage criterion between objects, while hierarchical clustering forms clusters at various distances which can be represented using a dendrogram. In centroid-based clustering, distance of objects is computed from the centroid of a cluster to place the objects in appropriate clusters. Distribution-based clustering models make use of distribution models so that the objects belonging to the same cluster are more likely from the same distribution. In density-based clustering, clusters are identified as regions with higher density of objects and have been applied for feature selection in the classification of various cancer types (Loscalzo et al., 2009). Figure 5.3 presents examples of the different clustering techniques.

Probabilistic graphical models: Probabilistic graphical models, as the name suggests, bring together graph theory and probability theory and provide a framework for modeling high-dimensional data and the interactions between them (Koller and Friedman, 2009; Hartemink et al., 2000). In such a model, uncertainties associated with the data are represented using the probability values and the interactions

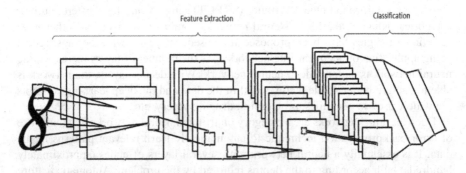

FIGURE 5.2 Representative deep learning network architecture.

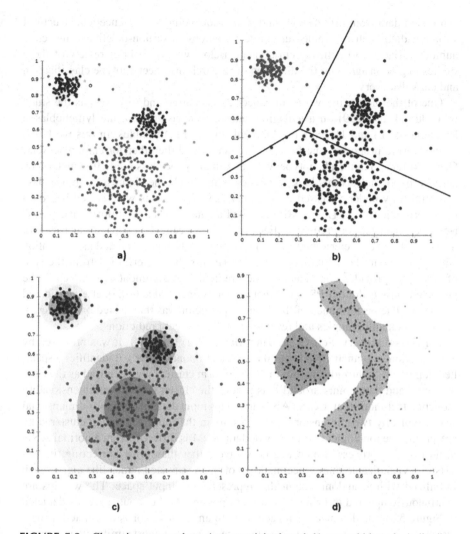

FIGURE 5.3 Clustering approaches: a) connectivity-based, b) centroid-based, c) distribution-based, d) density-based. (*Source:* https://en.wikipedia.org/wiki/Cluster_analysis.

among the variables are represented in a graph. The probabilities of the model are learned from the data and predictions made from the conditional probability calculations for the variable of interest given the observed variables. This is based on conditional independence assumption among variables.

5.4 RECENT APPLICATIONS OF ML IN CANCER DIAGNOSIS/CLASSIFICATION

Over the past two decades, various machine learning approaches have been proposed in the analysis of cancer samples. The methods vary from the analysis of gene expression data from microarrays and RNA sequencing to sequence and structural variation data such as single-nucleotide variations, insertion-deletions, and copy number variations to pathway enrichment. Below we give a brief review of these studies to give insight into the direction of research in cancer subtype classification and class discovery.

One of the pioneering works in cancer classification and discovery is the study by Golub et al. (1999) on a leukemia dataset comprising 27 acute lymphoblastic leukemia (ALL) and 11 acute myeloid leukemia (AML) samples. In this work two methods were proposed, one for class prediction and the other for class discovery. Genes correlated to the phenotype were identified by the class prediction method by neighborhood analysis that looks for genes exhibiting higher expression in one class and uniformly underexpressed in the other class. The genes were sorted based on their correlation to ALL or AML class and a small subset of "informative genes" (~50) were selected for prediction. Each informative gene then votes for a class with the strength of vote determined by the magnitude of its expression and its correlation with a particular class. Prediction strength (PS) is then determined from the sum of votes and provides confidence to the prediction. Assignment of samples to the predicted class is done if PS is above a predetermined value (~0.3), else considered uncertain. The performance of the 50-gene predictor was then tested on a different set of 34 leukemia samples and resulted in 29/34 correct predictions.

For class discovery, Self-Organizing Map (SOM) was used. It was proposed by Teuvo Kohonen as an artificial neural network (Kohonen, 1990). It identifies a specified number of "centroids" within the data to form clusters with centroid as the cluster center and data points around it as part of the cluster. SOM is a dimensionality reduction technique that uses an ANN and maps input data on to a lower dimensional space, typically two-dimensional. This results in the input data being clustered by preserving the topological properties of data. SOM is different from a normal ANN in its learning process, which is competitive rather than error correcting. It consists of a visualizable map space made up of interconnected nodes like a grid, each initialized with a random weight that represents the input space. The weights are continuously updated to bring it as close as possible to the input space, as depicted in Figure 5.4. The distance from each node to an input vector is calculated using a distance function, usually Euclidean distance, to identify most similar node to input

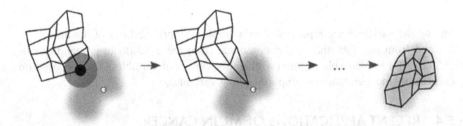

FIGURE 5.4 Illustration of training of self-organizing map. (*Source:* https://en.wikipedia. org/wiki/Self-organizing_map

vector, called a best matching unit (BMU). The neighboring nodes are identified with a neighborhood function based on the distance between BMU and a node. The process is repeated for each input for a number of iterations. As training proceeds, the magnitude of change in weights decreases and finally the output nodes unwind the pattern in the input data. SOM was applied to the same leukemia dataset of 38 samples and resulted in correctly grouping 24/25 samples of ALL and 10/13 samples of AML. The class discovery method was also applied to discover novel classes and evaluated using class prediction technique. The cross-validation of both the techniques, the neighborhood analysis and SOM, reported high accuracies.

In the study by Liu et al. (2004), various methods, namely, feature selection by Wilcoxon rank-sum test, clustering, and principal component analysis, followed by t-test and classification using three neural network models were carried out. In PCA, orthogonal linear transformation of the data matrix to a new coordinate system is done such that maximum variance is observed on the first coordinate, next higher variance on the second coordinate, and so on. By using multiple feature selection methods, the authors attempted to obtain a hypothesis that is closer to the true hypothesis by averaging over multiple hypotheses. Wilcoxon rank-sum test helped in identifying the top correlated genes, while PCA captured most of the variations in the samples and provided clustering information. This was followed by t-test for identifying lower ranked genes that may be associated with important biological pathways. An ensemble neural network was then chosen to classify the samples with the selected features and provided improved accuracy over a unitary network. The individual networks built using bagging method of resampling exhibited better performance over boosting approach in microarray data which are typically noisy. The results from multiple networks were combined using majority voting approach with confidence of each network output as voting value, instead of zero-one voting scheme. In this analysis, performance of the approach was evaluated on three categories of datasets: binary class with and without testing samples and multiclass. Seven cancer datasets were used for the analysis, viz., leukemia (binary class), lung, prostate, ovarian, DLBCL, colon, and leukemia (multiclass). The proposed method exhibited better or similar performance with other methods such as SVM, decision trees, etc., using LOOCV and 10-fold cross-validation methods.

In the study by Gevaert et al. (2006), a probabilistic model with a dependency structure was used to integrate microarray expression data and clinical data to extract relevant genes and other clinical characteristics contributing to the prognosis of breast cancer. The dependency structure captures the interdependency between the variables and is represented by directed edges, with no closed loops allowed. The probability distribution of how the variables depend on their parent variables is captured by using conditional probability tables (CPT). Probability of the variables is given by

$$p(x_1,\ldots,x_n) = \prod_{i=1}^{n} p\big(x_i|Pa(x_i)\big) \tag{9}$$

where $Pa(x_i)$ are the parents of x_i. The model building in this case involves learning the dependency structure and the parameters for CPTs as described below.

Structure Learning: In this case, the variables of interest are first arranged in a random order and model building is done by iterating the process with different permutations of ordering. The structure learning is through a greedy-based search strategy with the search space restricted by the order of variables, i.e., a variable is considered a parent only if it precedes the current variable in the ordered set. The searching algorithm starts with an empty set, iterates over the variables for finding the structure of the network by adding parents to a variable if the score of the structure, computed using Bayesian Dirichlet (BD) scoring metric (given by Equation (10)), improves on adding the parent variable to the structure. If not, the algorithm continues to the next variable in the ordered set. Once the entire list is exhausted, the algorithm terminates and the network with maximum score is selected.

$$p(S \mid D) \propto p(S) \prod_{i=1}^{n} \prod_{j=1}^{q_i} \left[\frac{\left(\Gamma(N'_{ij})\right)}{\Gamma\left(N'_{ij} + N_{ij}\right)} \prod_{k=1}^{n} \frac{\Gamma\left(N'_{ijk} + N_{ijk}\right)}{\Gamma\left(N'_{ijk}\right)} \right] \qquad (10)$$

where N_{ijk} denotes number of samples that have variable i in state k with parent having jth instantiation in structure S. N_{ij} corresponds to samples with variable i summed over all states, N'_{ij}, similar to N_{ij}, requires prior knowledge for assertion of parameters. In the absence of prior knowledge, it is given by $N/r_i q_i$, where N is the sample size, r_i is the number of states the variable can assume, q_i is the number of instantiations of its parents, and $p(S)$ gives prior probability of structure S.

Parameter Learning: The next step in the model building process involves parameter estimation in CPTs corresponding to the structure learned in the previous step. Considering the outcome variable as "Prognosis" that takes two values: "poor" (recurrence of disease within 5 years after treatment) and "good" (5-year disease-free period), parent variables could be a gene expression (overexpressed [on]/under-expressed [off]) or a clinical characteristic (age ≥ 50 or < 50). The Dirichlet score of the parameters which is initialized with a uniform prior value is updated during the parameter learning process. This is done by taking the maximum a posteriori (MAP) parameterization of Dirichlet distribution given by

$$p(\theta \mid D, S) = Dir\left(\theta_{ij} \mid N'_{ij1} + N_{ij1}, \ldots, N'_{ijk} + N_{ijk}, \ldots, N'_{ijr_i} + N_{ijr_i}\right) \qquad (11)$$

Integration of microarray and clinical data involves full, partial, or decision-based integration. Of these, decision and partial integration methods are identified to be equally good. After integration from different orderings of training data, 100 models were trained and one with maximum area under the curve was chosen. Given the Markov blanket, defined as the parents of a variable, children, and their other parents in a Bayesian network, a variable becomes conditionally independent of other variables. So, the Markov blanket of the outcome variable, prognosis in this case, is only required for classification purposes. Based on their analysis, age, grade, and angioinvasion, 13 genes were identified to fall under the Markov blanket.

There are very few unsupervised or semisupervised approaches applied to the analysis of gene expression data. One such study by Liu et al. (2006) is based on

SVD and seeded region growing clustering approach, a semisupervised algorithm. Singular value decomposition is an important concept in ML wherein a matrix is factorized into its components such that the resultant components are easy to handle. A real/complex matrix A can be decomposed as $U \sum V^T$, where the columns of matrices U and V are called left and right singular vectors of A, respectively, and $\sum$ is a diagonal matrix with non-negative real numbers representing the singular values of A. Orthonormal eigenvectors of AA^T and A^TA are the left and right singular vectors, respectively, and the non-negative singular values are the square roots of non-negative eigenvalues of AA^T and A^TA. By doing the conversion into factors, principal components of the matrix A are identified which can be further used for reducing the dimensions in the original matrix.

Spectral biclustering involves data normalization, bi-stochastization, and seeded region growing clustering. In data normalization step, logarithm of gene expression matrix A is obtained. Few cycles (5–10) of subtracting mean (or median) of rows and columns (i.e., genes and conditions) is performed followed by few cycles of row-column normalization. For bi-stochastization, first a matrix of interactions, K_{ij}, is defined by taking mean of rows (A_i), mean of columns (A_j), and mean of the matrix $(A_\cdot)$ as

$$K_{ij} = A_{ij} - A_i - A_j + A_{\cdot\cdot}. \tag{12}$$

Then SVD of the matrix is performed and eigenvalues determined. The eigenvectors corresponding to the largest s eigenvalues are also determined. The similarity measure between eigenvector and the genes is found using cosine similarity and for each eigenvector a set of genes which exhibit high similarity is chosen. The combination of genes chosen for each selected eigenvector is considered for evaluating their performance in classification using SVM and the set giving highest accuracy is chosen. Two datasets, lymphoma and liver cancer, were used to demonstrate the performance of the algorithm. Two pairs of genes from two eigenvectors were able to divide the samples into three types of lymphoid malignancies: chronic lymphocytic leukemia (CLL), follicular lymphoma (FL), and diffuse large B-cell lymphoma (DLBCL). One gene from two eigenvectors gave highest accuracy in classifying the samples into non-tumor and hepatocellular carcinoma (HCC).

A novel approach proposed by Zhang and Deng (2007) is based on Bayes error results in very few genes for classification. In this work, Based Bayes error Filter (BBF) method is implemented, which uses Bhattacharyya distance to identify genes that exhibit highest joined significance to the cancer class and simultaneously minimizes redundancy in the selected genes. The redundant genes thus identified by Bhattacharyya distance minimizes the Bayes error, known to be the lowest error probability achievable using a classifier according to Bayesian decision theory. It depends only on the features (genes) selected and not on the model used, which is the motivation behind this method. The classification error in this case is indirectly controlled by the Bhattacharyya distance as it gives an approximation to Bayes error. A preselected gene set with their individual relevance to cancer classes is used as input to the BBF method.

The algorithm comprises two steps. In the gene preselection step, relevant candidate genes are selected based on Wilcoxon rank-sum test with family-wise error rate (FWER ≤ 0.05) to evaluate the discriminative power of each gene in classifying a sample into one of the target classes. The second step applies redundancy filter using Bayes error to the preselected genes for removing redundancy. Starting with a single gene, the algorithm computes Bhattacharyya distance of every other gene from this gene. If the error exceeds a predefined cutoff, the gene is selected along with the first gene to the final list. The process is iteratively applied to the remaining genes till the required number of genes is selected, or the threshold on Bayes error is not met. The algorithm is evaluated using two classifiers, KNN and SVM with LOOCV, with error rate as the metric. In comparison to other methods such as minimum redundancy maximum relevance, simulated annealing, normalized mutual information, signal to noise ratio, information gain, etc., the proposed method chooses very small number of genes for attaining lowest error rates. The cancer datasets used in the study were colon, DLBCL, leukemia, prostate, and lymphoma. The number of genes identified with lowest error rate using KNN was 12, 6, 3, 11, and 8, respectively, and using SVM it was 20, 5, 2, 13, and 3, respectively, for the five cancer datasets.

Loscalzo et al. (2009) use dense group feature selection algorithm to identify group of features from a user-specified number of subsamples of the dataset. It finds core groups in the gene set with Kernel density estimation and iterative mean shift process. When the mean shift procedure converges, the nearby features of the mean will be grouped and returned by the algorithm. For every pair of genes, the algorithm computes a weight based on how often they were grouped together per subsample. With these weights, a hierarchical clustering of features is performed to form consensus groups. For every consensus group, a representative feature is selected and its relevance computed. On ordering the features based on relevance measure, k features are selected. A pairwise similarity comparison is done for calculating the similarity between features from different subsamples. Performance is evaluated using the genes selected for classification with SVM and KNN. Consensus group stable (CGS) feature selection is shown to have higher stability and accuracy than features selected by the algorithm DRAGS (dense relevant attribute group selector) and SVM-RFE.

Several methods proposed for cancer classification involves integration of more than one method for improving the performance. One such approach proposed by Song et al. (2013) has attempted to incorporate the advantages of RF algorithm and a generalized linear model (GLM). Random forest, even though highly accurate, is not interpretable, whereas a GLM can be used as a multipurpose model for binary/multiclass outcome prediction. The interpretability is better compared to RF because of forward variable selection of the features in the proposed approach. The method initially generates a number of equal-sized datasets, "nbags," from the original data using a bootstrap method by sampling with replacement. A random set of features chosen from each bag are sorted based on their correlation to outcome variable, considering absolute value of correlation coefficient to the output variable. The high ranked features were selected based on an input parameter "nCandidateCovariates" (default value 50) for each bag on which the forward variable selection method was applied to build a multivariable generalized linear model for each bag. The predictions from each model were then aggregated to give the final ensemble prediction. Results carried out on 20 disease-related and synthetic expression datasets and other UCI ML benchmark datasets showed better prediction accuracies with their method compared to SVM, KNN, and LDA.

Apart from expression data, mutation profiles of patients have also been used for cancer classification. In the study by Hofree et al. (2013), gene interaction networks for stratifying somatic mutation profiles of patients into biologically and clinically relevant subtypes have been proposed. The somatic mutation profiles are digital signals representing whether a gene is mutated or not while all other data types like gene expression provide continuous values for a measurement. Hence, the somatic mutation profiles give more precise results and are robust to noise. These profiles were projected onto gene interaction network and the mutations propagated to its network neighborhood using network propagation technique. The clustering of network-smoothed matrix of patient profiles was performed using non-negative matrix factorization method. Clustering result was further improved using consensus clustering technique. STRING, HumanNet, and PathwayCommons were the network data resources used for the analysis. Performance analysis of network-based stratification (NBS) to assign correct subtypes was carried out on ovarian tumor mutation data from TCGA, full exome sequence data of uterine, and ovarian and lung cancers from TCGA with standard consensus clustering without any network knowledge. The testing was also carried out on other data types, including copy number variations, mRNA expressions, methylation data, and protein profiles. The NBS subtypes were shown to give better performance and overlapped with results from other types of datasets.

Another clustering approach, a bottom-up hierarchical multiclass tree model, proposed by Tabl et al. (2018) uses Ward's linkage to discriminate different classes of samples by minimizing the within-cluster variance. In each branch of the tree, classifiers such as Naive Bayes and random forests were used to determine biomarker genes with most discriminative power for separating the classes and SVM was used to optimize the classifier's parameters. In this study, 347 out of 2433 breast cancer samples were categorized into six classes based on the available information about treatment given (hormone therapy, radiotherapy, or surgery) and the patient's status (alive or dead). Initial feature selection was done using chi-square, Info-Gain, and mRMR (minimum redundancy maximum relevance) methods. The class imbalance problem was addressed with methods such as SMOTE and resampling. The small set of genes selected by the algorithm for predicting the therapy was confirmed by enrichment analysis as the most responsive ones.

It is expected that different types of tumors may share some common features and this concept can be used to address the problem of limited data. The work of Liu et al. (2018) is one such study which integrates data from multiple domains to infer common functional modules, e.g., gene expression data across multiple types of tumors. It proposes considering association among domains by spectral clustering method to identify different clustering structures across multiple domains. It then computes consistency of the clustering structure to determine how associated domains may influence the clustering results. The approach makes use of domain relevance to build better clusters in each individual domain with the help of block Laplacian matrices B. The optimization problem in this case is to minimize the trace $(U^T BU)$ subject to $U^T U = I_k$, where matrix U gives the assignment of objects to clusters. The eigenvector associated with smallest eigenvalue of Block signed Laplacian matrix is used to identify the initial candidate cluster. If the intracluster variance of the initial cluster is larger than a given threshold, it is split into more candidate clusters. When all intracluster variances are within a predefined cutoff, the algorithm proceeds to find intracluster variances based on the next eigenvector. In each iteration, adjacency matrix between domains is updated based on the clustering structure of the respective domain. Performance of the algorithm was evaluated on datasets of neural activity, gene expression data from colon, two types of kidney tumors, and another cohort of data from two types of lung, ovarian, and uterine cancers. The algorithm was able to find strongly and weakly correlated domains and overlapping genes from these domains along with better clustering in each domain. Gene ontology enrichment analysis and pathway enrichment analysis were carried out to confirm the correctness of results.

Another approach in classification studies is to apply ML algorithms at multiple levels such that input of the classifier at one level is fed as input to the second level and so on to improve the accuracy of classification. Xiao et al. (2018) proposed an ensemble of Machine Learning models in which prediction from models in the first stage form input to the models in the second stage. Five different classifiers were used in the first level: KNN, SVM, RFs, decision trees, and gradient-boosting decision trees. An ANN was used in the second stage to capture non-linear patterns for improving the prediction accuracy. In this study, DESeq (Anders and Huber, 2010) was used to identify differentially expressed genes (DEGs) and fed as input to the first-level model for classification. The second-level model was then trained on the predictions from the previous level for final classification.

In the first level, the dataset was divided into five subgroups D_1 to D_5 containing labeled points drawn independently and identically from the same distribution. In the first iteration, four subgroups D_1 to D_4 were combined to form training set and the remaining fifth group formed test set, where $D_i = \{x_i y_i\}$, x_i represents gene expression and y_i the corresponding label. For a given input x_1, five different models perform the classification and propose the corresponding hypotheses, $h_1(x_1), h_2(x_2), \ldots, h_5(x_5)$, where $h_i(x_1)$ is a binary variable. Predictions of each model were assembled into $H_1 = [h_1(x_1), h_2(x_2), \ldots, h_5(x_5)]$ along with corresponding label y_1, which forms the input dataset D_{10} for the second level. The fivefold cross-validation was performed by repeating the procedure five times to generate five new datasets, $D_{i0} = \{H_i, y_i\}$, $i = 1, 2, \ldots, 5$.

In the second level, a five-layer ANN is used to classify the samples into normal/tumor. Five models obtained in the first stage are given as input to this model. Each hidden layer consists of different number of nodes and the output layer consists of a single node that predicts 0/1 for normal/tumor samples, respectively. A fivefold cross-validation is employed at this level also and the mean value is taken as the outcome. This ensemble approach of multiple models with a deep neural network reduces generalization error by considering the predictions from the first level as features in the second level compared to independently training the model using the data. The relationships among the first-level classifier's outcomes are learned automatically, resulting in improved prediction. Experiments were conducted on breast, stomach, and lung cancer RNASeq data from TCGA. Raw read counts were used for identifying differentially expressed genes and FPKM values for classification. The proposed deep learning method exhibited higher accuracies compared to the first-stage models and majority voting algorithm.

Under the assumption that there exist common features among different tumor types, Sevakula et al. proposed a transfer learning approach to train an autoencoder to learn its initial parameters and later fine-tune the parameters to specific problems (Sevakula et al., 2018). These methods make use of (general) solutions of similar problems in improving solutions for new (specific) problems. Autoencoders are multilayered neural networks that reconstruct the input data by generating an intermediate representation of the input features with fewer nodes in hidden layers. Since input is required to be reconstructed at output with minimal loss, the autoencoders learn the best possible latent space with a fewer number of features in the intermediate layers.

Initial feature selection in this case was done to rank features using the individual training error reduction (ITER) ranking method. A linear classifier was trained independently for each feature in the input data resulting in as many trained classifiers. The features were sorted based on training error and those with least training errors selected. Selected feature values were then normalized using zero-one normalization method or mean-variance normalization method. The weights in each layer of the neural network were initialized using autoencoders. For each layer, the autoencoder has a structure matching the corresponding layer. After the weights were learned, the weighted input was propagated to the next layer. This data serves as input to another autoencoder, having the same architecture for the next layer, to learn the weights for the next layer. This process of initialization of weights was continued till the last hidden layer. After initialization, weights of the deep neural network (DNN) were fine-tuned (median-based method) based on the target problem. The data when sent through the DNN was transformed to a more appropriate representation for classification. The newly constructed features were then fed to three classifiers: Softmax classifier, RF, and kernel SVM. In this study, unlabeled data from seven different types of tumor were considered for learning the abstract similarities of gene expression pattern, and two other types of tumor data for binary classification problem. The DNN used in the study had three hidden layers with respective dimensions of 900, 800, and 750. The dimension of the input layer was 1024, equal to the features selected based on ITER ranking. Using this DNN, the proposed algorithm statistically outperformed several classification approaches such as SVM, RF, PCA, and sequential forward selection.

5.5 WEB-BASED TOOLS

Various web-based tools based on Machine Learning approaches are available for analysis of gene expression and variation profiles and pathway enrichment (Lim and Wong, 2014). Few popular and recent tools are briefly discussed in this section.

A web-based tool, gene-set activity toolbox (GAT), to integrate gene expression data with gene networks to identify biomarkers of various cancers and classification of samples has been developed (Engchuan et al., 2016). It provides gene expression analysis and performance assessment of selected features with k-fold cross-validation. Functional analysis of the selected features and network visualization can also be performed. The classification of samples can be done using SVM, RF, or logistic regression.

The role of sequence and structural variants is well known in tumorigenesis. A decision support tool for variant reporting that makes use of RF and logistic regression models has been developed by Zomnir et al. (2018) to address the problem of understanding the output of complex bioinformatics pipeline for next-generation sequencing data. It provides a score in the range of 0–1 that represents the variant calling from no to yes, which can be verified by a pathologist and help to understand the reason behind the model's decision. That is, the model selection also takes into consideration the interpretability factor of the results.

The ML approach to predict *Ras* activity in solid tumors has been proposed by Way et al. (2018) and the code is available at https://github.com/greenelab/pancancer. It helps in categorizing abnormal pathway activities in tumors and the analysis of transcriptomes of patients who fail to respond to treatments. It has integrated RNASeq data, copy number variations, and small-sequence variations in 9075 tumors from 33 forms of cancers from PanCanAtlas project from TCGA. A supervised classifier, logistic regression with stochastic gradient descent, was trained on this data to predict whether the gene is activated or wild type. Only non-silent genic mutations and mutations at splice sites are considered. Additionally, data from oncogenes (*KRAS*, *NRAS*, and *HRAS*) for functional gain (by mutation or copy gain) and tumor suppressor *NF1* (copy loss) are integrated.

Numerous methods have been proposed for cancer subtype classification. A representative list of different categories of approaches is given in Table 5.1.

5.6 CONCLUSION

There is considerable research going on in applying Machine Learning and deep learning approaches for classification and feature selection of cancer samples. Major studies covered in this chapter discuss the analysis of microarray gene expression data and also few recent studies on RNA sequencing data and variation data. Most studies use some feature selection algorithm before applying a classification algorithm, of which filter-based approaches are most common. Few studies that consider wrapper, embedded, or hybrid methods are also discussed along with their advantages and limitations. The application and development of embedded methods in gene expression data analysis would provide a direction for future research.

It is observed that SVMs are most popular compared to other classification methods in gene expression analysis. This is probably because compared to other methods such as KNN, hierarchical clustering, etc., SVMs use distance functions that can operate in high-dimensional feature space. Because of this property, SVMs can accommodate the high correlations among genes and still find a hyperplane to

TABLE 5.1

A Representative List of Feature Selection and Classification Methods

Feature Selection Methods	Classifier	Validation Method	Datasets	Performance Metrics	Reference
SNR	Weighted voting SOM	CV	Leukemia	Accuracy	Golub et al., 1999
Wilcoxon rank-sum test, PCA, clustering followed by t-test	NN	LOOCV, 10-fold CV	Leukemia, lung, prostate, ovarian, DLBCL, colon	Accuracy	Liu et al., 2004
Bayesian network with K2 algorithm	Bayesian network with K2 algorithm	–	Breast	AUC, Standard deviation	Gevaert et al., 2006
SVD	SVM	10-fold CV	Lymphoma, liver	Accuracy	Bing Liu et al., 2006
Wilcoxon rank-sum test	KNN, SVM	LOOCV	Leukemia, prostate, lymphoma, DLBCL, colon	Error rate	Zhang and Deng, 2007
CGS	SVM, KNN	10-fold CV	Leukemia, colon, lung, lymphoma, prostate, SRBCT	Accuracy, stability	Loscalzo et al., 2009
–	RGLM predictor	3-fold CV	Adenocarcinoma, brain, breast, lung, leukemia, colon, lymphoma, NCI60, prostate, DLBCL, SRBCT, multiple, sclerosis, psoriasis	Accuracy	Song et al., 2013
–	Negative matrix factorization, clustering	–	Ovarian, uterine, lung	–	Hofree et al. 2013
Chi-square, information gain, mRMR	Hierarchical bottom-up agglomerative clustering, Naive Bayes, RF	–	Breast	Accuracy, sensitivity, specificity, F-measure	Tabl et al., 2018

(Continued)

TABLE 5.1 (CONTINUED)

A Representative List of Feature Selection and Classification Methods

Feature Selection Methods	Classifier	Validation Method	Datasets	Performance Metrics	Reference
Graph clustering	K-means	–	Lung, kidney, ovarian, uterine, colon	Number of overlapped genes, enrichment analysis	Liu et al., 2018
–	KNN, SVM, DT, GBDT, RF, NN	Fivefold CV	Lung, stomach, breast	Precision, recall, accuracy	Xiao et al., 2018
Individual training error reduction ranking	SVM-linear, SVM-RBF, NN, RF	10-fold CV	Breast, lung, ovary, prostate, omentum, kidney, colon, endometrium, uterus	AUC, Friedman test, Bonferroni-Dunn test	Sevakula et al., 2018
Two sample t-statistic	DLD, FLDA, KNN	LOOCV, LKOCV	Colon, leukemia	Accuracy	Bø and Jonassen, 2002
Based on genetic algorithm	Maximum likelihood estimator	LOOCV	NCI60, GCM	Accuracy	Ooi and Tan, 2003
mRMR	K-means	LOOCV	SRBCT, breast, colon	Error rate	Liu et al., 2005
Structured penalized logistic regression	Structured penalized logistic regression	–	Leukemia, Lung, Colon, DLBCL, prostate	Youden Index, F1-score	Liu and Wong, 2019
RF	RF	OOB	Adenocarcinoma, brain, breast, leukemia, colon, lymphoma, NCI60, prostate, SRBCT	Accuracy, error rate	Díaz-Uriarte and Alvarez de Andrés, 2006
PCA, Relief-F, gain ratio, information gain	SVM, RF, logistic regression, multilayer perceptron	k-fold cross-validation	Breast, lung, colorectal	AUC, recall	Engchuan et al., 2016

SNR: signal-to-noise ratio, SOM: self-organizing map, CV: cross-validation, PCA: principal component analysis, NN: neural network, LOOCV: leave-one-out cross-validation, DLBCL: diffuse large B-cell lymphoma, AUC: area under ROC curve, SVD: singular value decomposition, SVM: support vector machine, KNN: K-nearest neighbor, CGS: consensus group stable, RF: random forest, RGLM: random generalized linear model, SRBCT: small-round-blue-cell tumor, mRMR: minimum redundancy maximum relevancy, DT: decision tree, GBDT: gradient boosting decision tree, SVM-RBF: SVM-radial basis function, DLD: diagonal linear discriminant, FLDA: Fisher's linear discriminant analysis, LKOCV: leave-K-out cross-validation.

distinguish between classes in the dataset. Further, its ability to rank features based on their distance from the hyperplane helps in selecting best features for discrimination. However, the results of SVM are not interpretable; it behaves like a black box and does not reveal much on why the decision was made for a particular non-linear kernel function chosen. Due to the properties like interpretability and ability to measure importance of variable, RFs are equally widely used in gene expression analysis. The random sampling and ensemble strategies applied in RFs are observed to result in better accuracies and generalizations. KNN is another classification method that has been used for over two decades in this field due to its simplicity. It is the simplest Machine Learning algorithm to use if the number of classes in a dataset is known a priori. Clustering approaches are popular in gene expression data analysis due to the ease of understandability. Neural networks and deep learning networks are finding a fresh and unmatchable application in many domains, including gene expression analysis. The power of deep learning networks to capture the relationships among genes and high accuracies in decision-making are the reasons behind their acceptance. These networks are capable of handling high-dimensional data and give intermediate feature representations with much lesser dimensions. There definitely is lot of scope in exploring these models for interpretability of results which would make them more suitable for use in cancer detection and subtype classification in clinical settings.

Majority of the classification methods reviewed here fall under the supervised category and require a huge number of labeled samples for training the model. The limited availability of cancer datasets makes the application of these methods difficult because of the problem of overfitting. Data merging is a possible solution to this problem, but integrating data from multiple platforms and from different technologies is a tedious task. Research can be directed toward the area of data integration which can be a breakthrough in gene expression data analysis and related fields. Unsupervised and semisupervised algorithms may be further explored as most available gene expression data are unlabeled.

REFERENCES

Anders, S., & Huber, W. (2010). Differential expression analysis for sequence count data. *Genome Biology, 11*(10), R106. doi: 10.1186/gb-2010-11-10-r106

Ang, J. C., Mirzal, A., Haron, H., & Hamed, H. N. A. (2016). Supervised, unsupervised, and semi-supervised feature selection: A review on gene selection. *IEEE/ACM Transactions on Computational Biology and Bioinformatics, 13*(5), 971–989. doi: 10.1109/TCBB.2015.2478454.

Bengio, Y., & Lecun, Y. (2007). Scaling learning algorithms towards AI. *Large-Scale Kernel Machines*. Retrieved from https://nyuscholars.nyu.edu/en/publications/scaling-lea rning-algorithms-towards-ai.

Bing Liu, Wan, C., & Lipo Wang. (2006). An efficient semi-unsupervised gene selection method via spectral biclustering. *IEEE Transactions on NanoBioscience, 5*(2), 110–114. doi: 10.1109/TNB.2006.875040.

Bø, T., & Jonassen, I. (2002). New feature subset selection procedures for classification of expression profiles. *Genome Biology, 3*(4), RESEARCH0017.

Breiman, L. (2001). Random forests. *Machine Learning, 45*(1), 5–32. doi: 10.1023/A:10 10933404324.

Cortes, C., & Vapnik, V. (1995). Support-vector networks. *Machine Learning, 20*(3), 273–297. doi: 10.1007/BF00994018.

Deng, L., & Yu, D. (2011). *Deep Convex Network: A Scalable Architecture for Speech Pattern Classification*. Retrieved from https://www.microsoft.com/en-us/research/publication/deep-convex-network-a-scalable-architecture-for-speech-pattern-classification/.

Díaz-Uriarte, R., & Alvarez de Andrés, S. (2006). Gene selection and classification of microarray data using random forest. *BMC Bioinformatics, 7*, 3. doi: 10.1186/1471-2105-7-3.

Engchuan, W., Meechai, A., Tongsima, S., Doungpan, N., & Chan, J. H. (2016). Gene-set activity toolbox (GAT): A platform for microarray-based cancer diagnosis using an integrative gene-set analysis approach. *Journal of Bioinformatics and Computational Biology, 14*(4), 1650015. doi: 10.1142/S0219720016500153.

Fukushima, K. (1980). Neocognitron: A self-organizing neural network model for a mechanism of pattern recognition unaffected by shift in position. *Biological Cybernetics, 36*(4), 193–202. doi: 10.1007/BF00344251.

Gevaert, O., De Smet, F., Timmerman, D., Moreau, Y., & De Moor, B. (2006). Predicting the prognosis of breast cancer by integrating clinical and microarray data with Bayesian networks. *Bioinformatics (Oxford, England), 22*(14), e184–e190. doi: 10.1093/bioinformatics/btl230.

Golub, T. R., Slonim, D. K., Tamayo, P., Huard, C., Gaasenbeek, M., Mesirov, J. P., … Lander, E. S. (1999). Molecular classification of cancer: Class discovery and class prediction by gene expression monitoring. *Science (New York, N.Y.), 286*(5439), 531–537.

Hartemink, A. J., Gifford, D. K., Jaakkola, T. S., & Young, R. A. (2000). Using graphical models and genomic expression data to statistically validate models of genetic regulatory networks. *Biocomputing, 2001*, 422–433. doi: 10.1142/9789814447362_0042.

Hinton, G. E., Osindero, S., & Teh, Y.-W. (2006). A fast learning algorithm for deep belief nets. *Neural Computation, 18*(7), 1527–1554. doi: 10.1162/neco.2006.18.7.1527.

Hofree, M., Shen, J. P., Carter, H., Gross, A., & Ideker, T. (2013). Network-based stratification of tumor mutations. *Nature Methods, 10*(11), 1108–1115. doi: 10.1038/nmeth.2651.

Huang, M.-W., Chen, C.-W., Lin, W.-C., Ke, S.-W., & Tsai, C.-F. (2017). SVM and SVM ensembles in breast cancer prediction. *PLOS ONE, 12*(1), e0161501. doi: 10.1371/journal.pone.0161501.

Khan, J., Wei, J. S., Ringnér, M., Saal, L. H., Ladanyi, M., Westermann, F., … Meltzer, P. S. (2001). Classification and diagnostic prediction of cancers using gene expression profiling and artificial neural networks. *Nature Medicine, 7*(6), 673–679. doi: 10.1038/89044.

Kohonen, T. (1990). The self-organizing map. *Proceedings of the IEEE, 78*(9), 1464–1480. doi: 10.1109/5.58325.

Koller, D., & Friedman, N. (2009). *Probabilistic Graphical Models: Principles and Techniques*. MIT Press.

Lim, K., & Wong, L. (2014). Finding consistent disease subnetworks using PFSNet. *Bioinformatics (Oxford, England), 30*(2), 189–196. doi: 10.1093/bioinformatics/btt625.

Liu, B., Cui, Q., Jiang, T., & Ma, S. (2004). A combinational feature selection and ensemble neural network method for classification of gene expression data. *BMC Bioinformatics, 5*, 136. doi: 10.1186/1471-2105-5-136.

Liu, C., & Wong, H. S. (2019). Structured penalized logistic regression for gene selection in gene expression data analysis. *IEEE/ACM Transactions on Computational Biology and Bioinformatics, 16*(1), 312–321. doi: 10.1109/TCBB.2017.2767589.

Liu, X., Krishnan, A., & Mondry, A. (2005). An entropy-based gene selection method for cancer classification using microarray data. *BMC Bioinformatics, 6*, 76. doi: 10.1186/1471-2105-6-76.

Liu, Y., Ng, M. K., & Wu, S. (2018). Multi-domain networks association for biological data using block signed graph clustering. *IEEE/ACM Transactions on Computational Biology and Bioinformatics, 17*(2), 1–1. doi: 10.1109/TCBB.2018.2848904.

Loscalzo, S., Yu, L., & Ding, C. (2009). Consensus group stable feature selection. In *Proceedings of the 15th ACM SIGKDD International Conference on Knowledge Discovery and Data Mining,* 567–576. doi: 10.1145/1557019.1557084.

Marsland, S. (2011). *Machine Learning: An Algorithmic Perspective* (1st ed.), Chapman and Hall/CRC. doi: 10.1201/9781420067194.

Network-based stratification of tumor mutations | Nature Methods. (n.d.). Retrieved March 22, 2019, from https://www.nature.com/articles/nmeth.2651.

Ooi, C. H., & Tan, P. (2003). Genetic algorithms applied to multi-class prediction for the analysis of gene expression data. *Bioinformatics (Oxford, England), 19*(1), 37–44.

Seber, G. A. F., & Lee, A. J. (2012). *Linear Regression Analysis.* John Wiley & Sons.

Sevakula, R. K., Singh, V., Verma, N. K., Kumar, C., & Cui, Y. (2018). Transfer learning for molecular cancer classification using deep neural networks. *IEEE/ACM Transactions on Computational Biology and Bioinformatics, 16*(6), 1–1. doi: 10.1109/TCBB.2018.2822803.

Song, L., Langfelder, P., & Horvath, S. (2013). Random generalized linear model: A highly accurate and interpretable ensemble predictor. *BMC Bioinformatics, 14,* 5. doi: 10.1186/1471-2105-14-5

Tabl, A. A., Alkhateeb, A., Pham, H. Q., Rueda, L., ElMaraghy, W., & Ngom, A. (2018). A novel approach for identifying relevant genes for breast cancer survivability on specific therapies. *Evolutionary Bioinformatics Online, 14,* 1176934318790266. doi: 10.1177/1176934318790266

Unsupervised Learning: Clustering. (n.d.). 54.

Way, G. P., Sanchez-Vega, F., La, K., Armenia, J., Chatila, W. K., Luna, A., … Greene, C. S. (2018). Machine learning detects Pan-cancer Ras pathway activation in the cancer genome atlas. *Cell Reports, 23*(1), 172–180.e3. doi: 10.1016/j.celrep.2018.03.046

Xiao, Y., Wu, J., Lin, Z., & Zhao, X. (2018). A deep learning-based multi-model ensemble method for cancer prediction. *Computer Methods and Programs in Biomedicine, 153,* 1–9. doi: 10.1016/j.cmpb.2017.09.005.

Zhang, J.-G., & Deng, H.-W. (2007). Gene selection for classification of microarray data based on the Bayes error. *BMC Bioinformatics, 8*(1), 370. doi: 10.1186/1471-2105-8-370.

Zomnir, M. G., Lipkin, L., Pacula, M., Dominguez Meneses, E., MacLeay, A., Duraisamy, S., … Lennerz, J. K. (2018). Artificial intelligence approach for variant reporting. *JCO Clinical Cancer Informatics,* (2) 1–13. doi: 10.1200/CCI.16.00079.

6 Pancreatic Cancer Detection by an Integrated Level Set-Based Deep Learning Model

Arti Taneja, Priya Ranjan, Amit Ujlayan,
and Rajiv Janardhanan

CONTENTS

6.1 INTRODUCTION

On the basis of the patient history and clinically apparent symptoms, the diagnosis of the pancreatic pseudocysts has become difficult in recent medical scenarios. The basic diagnostics requires computed tomography (CT) images of the round, fluid-filled structures of cysts [1]. The pseudocysts and the pancreatic mucinous cysts are hard to discriminate in some images. Pancreas segmentation is an essential step in the early computer-aided diagnosis for quantitative analysis. But an accurate segmentation of pancreatic images is a challenging task due to its shape, size, and location in the abdominal region [2]. Pancreas is an anatomical variable organ within which the abdominal cavity varies from patient to patient [3]. The boundary contrast may vary due to the quantity of visceral fat in the proximity of the pancreas. This makes segmentation of the pancreas a challenging task. Hence, the pancreas segmentation becomes more difficult than other segmentation tasks with the statistical models [4]. The application of Convnets shows good promising results with the progressive pruning.

The factors which have a great impact on classification are features, edges, and appearance consistency and inconsistency. Hence, the important visual cues for the segmentation process are in obtaining hierarchical features corresponding to the boundary and interior [5]. Achieving accuracy and pixel-level labeling consistency requires these important visual cues. Image segmentation, object detection, and localization are generalized with the neural network formulation due to their flexibility and limited modifications. Recently, various research studies have shown that computed tomography [6, 7] is an efficient method to estimate pancreatic atrophy in patients. The review of image features such as mass size, location, shape, wall thickness, cyst configuration, and signal intensity of the lesions with heterogeneity is performed. The cystic fibrosis–related diabetes (CFRD) [8] is a different form of diabetes mellitus (DM) and hence improvement in care and treatment is required. CFRD hypothesizes that there are differences in the size and morphology of the pancreas of patients with cystic fibrosis (CF). It projects two objectives such as the comparison of the volume and features of patients with and without CFRD, and The correlation between the pancreas volume with age-matched non-CF patients as well as long-standing type 1 diabetes mellitus (T1DM) with healthy controls. The cystic pancreatic lesions are majorly non-malignant lesions consisting of pseudocysts, mucinous cystic neoplasms, intraductal papillary mucinous neoplasms (IPMN), solid pseudo-papillary tumor (SPT), and lymph epithelial cysts. Among these, the IPMN, mucinous cyst adenomas, and SPT have malignant potential but less frequent. Also, the malignant lesions of the pancreas are comprised of cystic variants like endocrine tumors, metastases, and ductal adenocarcinomas. Conversely, cystic variations in large pancreatic lesions generally exist in adenocarcinomas and endocrine tumors [9]. The pancreatic cancer patients have poor diagnosis in which most of the patients affected with pancreatic cancers are diagnosed at advanced stages. This poor diagnosis causes difficulty in diagnosing pancreatic cancer early. Most of these pancreatic cancers arise from the branches of the pancreatic duct. Generally, the diameter of the pancreatic duct is 2–3 mm. If small duct cell pancreatic carcinoma is presented in the branch, the lesion can be detected due to the obstruction [10]. The ultimate objective of the proposed work is to efficiently segment the pancreas from the abdominal images irrespective of the probable map variations and to improve the accuracy and Dice coefficients effectively. An integrated framework of Gaussian formulation with the double-well level set function predicts the region of interest (ROI) effectively. The multi-angular n-ternary pattern extraction predicts the features that describe the edge information clearly. Diverse patterns based on multi-directions efficiently support the clear image analysis. The integration of level set formulation with the convolution neural network (CNN)-based classification increases the classification performance, which highly contributes towards the early detection applications. The rest of the chapter is organized as follows: Section 6.2 describes the related work available for the pancreas segmentation. Section 6.3

discusses the implementation process of the proposed integrated framework of level set function with the convolution Neural network (IF-CNN) to segment the pancreas in the input images. Section 6.4 describes the performance analysis of the proposed work. This chapter concludes with Section 6.9.

6.2 RELATED WORK

Roth et al. [11] presented the fully automated bottom approach to segment the pancreas in CT abdominal images. Based on the coarse to fine classification of local image regions, the extraction of superpixels was carried out by a method called simple linear iterative clustering (SLIC) [12]. The assignment of distinct probabilities was the prior stage in SLIC to state whether the region was pancreas or not. Roth et al. [13] extended their approach by applying the dense labeling of local image patches by integration of SLIC with the nearest neighbor fusion. The application of these integrated methods improved the Dice similarity coefficient in both training and testing stages. Besides, Roth et al. [14] utilized holistic learning through the integration of semantic midlevel cues with the interior and boundary maps. The generation of boundary preserving pixel-wise labels was the necessary stage for pancreas segmentation. An analysis of statistical differences of the CT features was performed with two different tests: Student's test and Fisher's test. Age, size, and the total number of locules in tumors in two groups were compared in Student's test. The shape, location, wall thickness, and cyst configuration were analyzed using Fisher's test. Farag et al. [15] presented the fully automated bottom-up approach to segment the pancreas into four stages: (i) decomposition of image slices into the disjoint boundary-preserving superpixels, (ii) probability estimation through the dense patch labeling, (iii) pooling of intensity and probability features for cascaded random forest, and (iv) connectivity-based postprocessing. The segmentation through the deep patch labeling confidences was the stable approach against the small deviations in parameter variations. Moeskops et al. [16] investigated the issues of single CNN training to segment the MRI brain images, pectoral images, and the coronary arteries in the heart through the learning of image modalities and their visual anatomical structures. The single system utilization to perform the diverse segmentation tasks without any training was achieved. Cai et al. [17] formulated the pancreas segmentation as the graph-based decision fusion, which was integrated with the deep CNN models in the MRI scans. Two models—tissue detection and boundary detection—were employed with the spatial intensity context and semantic boundaries allocation, respectively. The final segmented output was generated through the initialization of conditional random field (CRF) [18] framework with the fusion of results obtained from the above processes. Wang et al. [19] presented the novel-patch-based label propagation approach, which uses the relative geodesic distances to define the patient-specific systems as spatial context to overcome the issues in the existing methods. Wolz et al. [20] applied the automatic intensity learning model with the incorporation of high-level spatial knowledge to handle the inter-subject variation. They evaluated the segmentation performance on 150 manually segmented images against the various existing methods. The generation of target-specific priors was a major issue in an automatic segmentation method. Tong et al. [21] applied the postprocessing step based on graph-cut (GC) methods. Besides, the voxel-wise local atlas selection strategy was proposed to handle the intersubject variations effectively. Lucchi et al. [22] proposed the automated graph-partitioning methods that incorporate the shape and distinctive shape learning for better recognition. They demonstrated better computational efficiency and segmentation quality. Lucchi et al. [22] concluded that a suitable weight estimation and a multilevel set formulation are required to provide the optimal trade-off between the accuracy improvement and clear image analysis. The automated assisted reading (AAR) technique used in the cervical screening process has less error rates and maximum productivity, depending on the accurate segmentation of abnormal cells. Zhang et al. [23] proposed the global/local scheme with the graph-cut approaches that utilized the combination of normal and abnormal cells. The tumor histopathology characterization defined the nuclear regions from the hematoxylin and eosin stained tissue sections. Chang et al. [24] performed the automated analysis by using the nuclear segmentation formulation within the graph framework. They presented the multi-reference graph cut (MRGC) with the prior knowledge regarding the reference and local image features. Zhang et al. [25] introduced the autofocusing method that rejected the coverslip and the actual focal plan was extracted. The hybrid global and local schemes segmented the normal and abnormal cells by CNN-based approach with three-dimensional filters. The existing CNN approaches on medical image segmentation allowed full access to three-dimensional structures. But they had some challenges such as high-class imbalance in the ground truth, high memory requirement, and shortage of labeled data. To overcome the above-mentioned issues, two modifications in CNN were incorporated and discussed in this work. Here a network architecture related to the U-net architecture was used. The two modifications in this architecture were that the multiple segmentation maps created at various scales were combined and the feature maps were forwarded from one stage to the other stage of the network by using element-wise summation. Litjens et al. [27] reviewed the major deep learning concepts related to medical imaging analysis. Various methods such as CNN, fCNN, RNN, and auto-encoders and stacked auto-encoders such as U-net and V-net were discussed in this survey. Their performance analyses were evaluated and compared. Milletari et al. [28] proposed an approach to 3D image segmentation based on the volumetric, fully conventional neural network. Here a novel objective function was introduced to optimize the system based on the Dice coefficient. The histogram matching and random non-linear transformations were applied to manage with the limited number of annotated volumes in training. The major drawback was the segmentation of volumes with multiple regions and higher resolutions. Sudre et al. [29] investigated the behavior of loss functions and sensitivity of rate tuning due to the presence of various label imbalance rates in the 2D and 3D segmentation processes. Also, a known metric for assessing the segmentation was proposed by using class rebalancing properties of generalized Dice overlap.

6.3   INTEGRATED LEVEL SET-BASED DEEP LEARNING

The proposed work comprises four new methods to segment the pancreas from the abdominal images. First, the Laplacian-based filtering is used to remove the noise present in the image and enhance the quality level. Then, the Gaussian operator is integrated with the level set formulation to segment the pancreas among other organs from the abdominal images due to high anatomical variability across patients from diverse genetic makeup. Second, the weight update with the level set estimates the region of interest (ROI-pancreas). Here, the N-ternary pattern extracts the texture pattern features of the pancreas in the form of angle variations. Finally, the CNN model predicts the classes of normal and abnormal effectively. The periodical weight update by level set, N-ternary patterns, and CNN improved the performance effectively.

6.4   LAPLACIAN-BASED PREPROCESSING

Noise removal is the initial stage in a proposed algorithm which includes the Laplacian of Gaussian (LoG) function for noise filtering in images. The Laplacian operator is considered as the 2D isotropic model, which measures the second spatial derivative of the input image $I(x,y)$. The rapid changes in the pixel intensity values are highlighted with this operator. Traditionally, the Gaussian filter is used to remove the noise present in the images. But its sensitivity to the noise variations is high and hence an approximation is required. The Laplacian operator is applied to provide such a smoothening effect on the images. The Laplacian $L(x,y)$ of the input image $I(x,y)$ is expressed as follows:

$$L(x,y) = \frac{\partial^2 I}{\partial x^2} + \frac{\partial^2 I}{\partial y^2} \tag{1}$$

Due to the image representation in a discrete set of pixels, an approximation of second-order derivatives was obtained by computing the discrete set of kernels, as shown in Figure 6.1. With these kernels, the LoG function is estimated by the standard convolution methods. Prior to the differentiation step, the reduction of high-frequency noise components was performed using the Laplacian operator. The convolving of Gaussian with the Laplacian operator followed by convolving of this hybrid filter with the image provides the required noise-free image effectively.

The two-dimensional LoG function with the zero mean and standard deviation σ is expressed as follows:

$$\log(x,y) = \frac{-1}{\pi\sigma^4}\left[1 - \frac{x^2 + y^2}{2\sigma^2}\right]e^{\frac{-x^2+y^2}{2\sigma^2}} \tag{2}$$

The calculation of the second spatial derivative of the image means that the LoG response is zero for the regions having constant intensity. If there are any changes in pixel intensities, then the Laplacian response is positive for the darker side and it

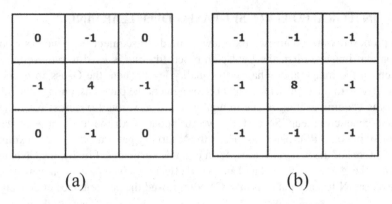

FIGURE 6.1   Kernels matrix for Laplacian of Gaussian preprocessing of the image.

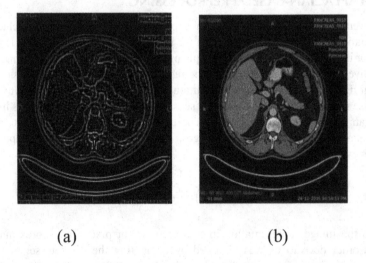

FIGURE 6.2   CT images before and after preprocessing step to make segmentation step more accurate.

is negative for the brighter side. The edge extracted from the Laplacian operator is sharp across the different pixel intensities. Figure 6.2 (a) and (b) show the Gaussian-filtered and Laplacian-smoothened images, respectively.

After obtaining the preprocessed images, the ROI (the pancreatic region) in the abdominal image is necessitated. In order to accomplish such a refined delineation of the original abdominal image, the integrated level set segmentation procedure is employed.

6.5   INTEGRATED LEVEL SET-BASED SEGMENTATION

The proposed workflow comprises four new methods to segment the pancreas from the abdominal images. First and foremost, the Laplacian-based filtering has been used to remove the noise present in the image and enhance its quality (Figure 6.3).

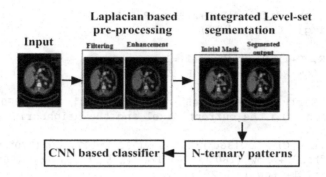

FIGURE 6.3 Operational steps of the designed system: (i) original image, (ii) filtered and enhanced image, (iii) initial mask as an input to the level set algorithm and ROI segmentation using level sets, (iv) feature extraction, and (v) convolutional neural networks for classification into categories benign and malignant.

6.6 N-TERNARY PATTERNS

The traditional N-ternary pattern described in Reference [30] is considered as the base for the proposed pattern extraction. The modeling of lower and upper ternary patterns corresponding to the 5 × 5 pixel to represent the image highly contributes to the clear information extraction by using the comparison among the center and neighborhood pixels. Initially, the enhanced image set is processed through our proposed LNTP algorithm and the major difference that lies between the existing N-ternary patterns and our algorithm is the pixel value selection for comparison. In the traditional approach, the center pixel value is selected for comparison. Alternatively, the median value is selected in proposed LNTP (median value 2). Then, the row (R) and column (C) values corresponding to the pixel values of (3, 4), (2, 4), (2, 3), (2, 2), (3, 2), (4, 2), (4, 3), and (4, 4) are updated by subtracting the median value (*med*). The algorithm to extract the patterns for the enhanced image set is listed as follows.

Local N-ternary pattern
Input: Segmented image (*seg$_i$*)
Output: Output patterns for categorized images

Procedure:
```
Initialize I (m,n)=size(seg_i) // Consider image size (m,n)=
(256x256)
Let D= [0°,45°, 90°,135°,180°,225°,270°,315°,360°]
For R= 3,C=3 to m-2,n-2
Select the 5x5 pixel window from I, img=I(R-2:R+2, C-2:C+2)
Med= Min C(Min R(img)) //median value
Let k=2;
//For 0° angle :

If(abs _dif(img(R,C+2)-img(R,C+1) ) > abs_dif(img(R,C+1)-med))
Set Low (R, C+1)=1; Up(R, C+1)=0;
```

```
Else if ( abs_dif(img(R,C+2)-img(R,C+1) ) <
abs_dif(img(R,C+1)-med+k))

Set Low(R, C+1)=0; Up(R, C+1)=1;
Else Set Low(R, C+1)=0; Up(R, C+1)=0;
End if;
// simil Early compute in 45°, 90°, 135°,180°, 225°, 270°,315°,
360° considering the current pixel and the neighboring pixel.

LowPattern(R,C)= Low(360°)*2^8+Low(315°)*2^7+ Low(270°)*2^6+
Low (225°)*2^5+ Low (180°)*2^4+ Low (135°)*2^3+ Low (90°)*2^2+
Low (45°)*2^1+ Low (0°)*2^0;
UpPattern(R,C)= Up (360°)*2^8+Up (315°)*2^7+ Up (270°)*2^6+ Up
(225°)*2^5+ Up (180°)*2^4+ Up (135°)*2^3+ Up (95°)*2^2+ Up
(45°)*2^1+ Up (0°)*2^0;
End for R,C;
```

6.7 CNN-BASED DEEP LEARNING

The output patterns from N-ternary are passed to the CNN, as shown in Figure 6.4. The CNN in machine learning is a deep, feedforward artificial neural network which can be used for analyzing the visual imagery. Generally, it uses a variety of multi-layer perceptron, which is designed for the requirement of minimal preprocessing. It comprises an input layer, an output layer, and three hidden layers. These hidden layers mainly contain convolution layers, pooling layers, normalized layers, and fully connected layers. In the convolution layer, a sliding window is running through the image. The subimages are convolved with the size and number of kernel/filters used in each layer at each step of the convolution layer, which produces a new layer while increasing the depth. The volume down-sampling is done by the pooling layer by using some aspects along with the spatial dimensions. This makes the model more efficient by reducing the size of the representations and the number of parameters. It also helps to avoid overfitting. The max-pooling layer is the most used pooling layer

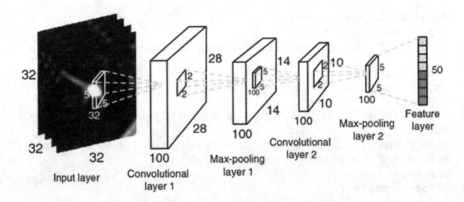

FIGURE 6.4 CNN classification.

which uses the maximum value of the cluster of neurons from the previous layer of each down-sampled block.

A non-linearity which mapped the score at each neuron can be applied after each layer in CNN. It helps to improve the speed, accuracy, and training time of the system. Generally, the sigmoid function is used in this non-linearity function, but here the *tanh* function is used which maps the real numbers in the interval of $[-1, -1]$ and this can be represented as

$$\tanh(x) = \frac{\left(e^x - e^{-x}\right)}{e^x + e^{-x}} \tag{15}$$

In this work, the *tanh* function is integrated with the most popular non-linearity function, which is termed as rectified linear unit (ReLU). In this, *tanh* is computed after the convolution and therefore a non-linear activation functions like a sigmoid. Due to its simple and linear form, this ReLU function has become more popular in activation function, which also helps to improve the speed of stochastic gradient descent (SGD). Moreover, it does not involve any experimental validations, so it is easy to evaluate. Even though these ReLUs are fragile, they can die permanently while training. In order to overcome the above-mentioned problem, leaky ReLU is used which contains a small negative slope for negative inputs. But the ReLU helps to enhance the accuracy and training time. The definition of ReLU function is described as

$$f(x) = \max(0, x) \tag{16}$$

Initially, the labels are initialized as n and $L = 1$. The patterns corresponding to the edge are assigned as P. The maximum and the mean of patterns are computed, and they can be regarded as M and N, respectively. The limit of subdivided intervals for the classification process lies in the range $(1 < \frac{1}{n} < N)$. Then, the rules necessary to perform the classification process are extracted as follows:

$$R = SF(M - N)* \tag{17}$$

where SF is the selected feature of a matrix.

The neighbor link parameter (ρ_t) and the kernel function (K) are necessary for accurate classification:

$$\rho_t = SF^{-1} TS(t) \tag{18}$$

$$K = R^{-1}\varnothing(t) \tag{19}$$

where SF^{-1} is the selected feature of the inverse matrix.

TS is the tested feature set.

The training feature set with the neighbor link and the kernel parameter for the mapping process is constructed by

$$P_i = K_i + \rho_i = R^{-1}\varnothing(i) + \rho_i \tag{20}$$

The probability distribution on feature set for neighboring features to update the kernel function is computed as follows:

$$\varnothing(t) = \frac{1}{(2\pi)^{\frac{n}{2}}} \frac{1}{N_i} \sum_{i=1}^{N_i} e^{\left[\frac{-(T_{l_i}-p_t)^{-1}(T_{l_i}-R_j)}{2\sigma^2}\right]} \tag{21}$$

Finally, the kernel function checks whether the value of patterns is compared with the probability distribution for each column (t) ($p_t > \varnothing(t)$) defined in Equation (25). The kernel function formulation for the class labels are listed as follows:

$$V_t(TP) = \sum_{n=1}^{N}\sum_{m=1}^{M}\left(\frac{\partial P_{p,m}}{\partial t_i} TP_{p,m}\right) \tag{22}$$

where *TP* is the testing pattern.

If the probability distribution function is greater than the count of patterns *P*, then the corresponding label is ($C=L(\varnothing(t))$).

6.8 PERFORMANCE ANALYSIS

The authors collected the images to validate the effectiveness of proposed IF-CNN. The input dataset contains 256 training points and Table 6.1 presents the comparative analysis of proposed IF-CNN with the SVM [16] on the basic performance parameters for pancreas images.

Figure 6.5 shows the comparative analysis between Machine Learning methods IF-CNN and SVM in terms of sensitivity, specificity measures, precision recall, and various other performance metrics for both normal and abnormal cases of pancreatic cancer. The optimal weight update by the integrated level set formulation and the N-ternary patterns improves specificity values. The numerical values of sensitivity and specificity for SVM are 100% and 52.0833%, respectively. But the proposed IF-CNN provides 97.2222% and 98.0392%, respectively. Compared to SVM, the IF-CNN offers 46.87% improvement specificity values.

Figure 6.6 shows the comparative analysis of accuracy, precision, and recall values for IF-CNN and SVM formulation. The SVM offers 85.2564%, 82.4427%, and 100%, respectively. The proposed IF-CNN offers 96.7949%, 96.3303%, and 97.2222%, respectively. The IF-CNN formulation and novel pattern extraction methods improve accuracy and precision by 11.92% and 14.42%, respectively.

Figure 6.7 shows the comparative analysis of Jaccard, Dice, and kappa coefficient for IF-CNN and SVM formulation. The SVM offers 85.2564%, 92.0415%, and

TABLE 6.1

Comparative Performance Analysis of IF-CNN with SVM for Images of Pancreas

Parameters	IF-CNN	SVM
True Positive (TP)	108	105
True Negative (TN)	42	23
False Positive (FP)	3	23
False Negative (FN)	3	5
Sensitivity (%)	97.2222	100
Specificity (%)	98.0392	52.0833
Precision (%)	96.3303	82.4427
Recall (%)	97.2222	100
Jaccard coefficient (%)	97.7564	85.2564
Dice overlap (%)	98.8655	92.0415
Kappa coefficient	99.04	60.08
Accuracy (%)	96.7949	85.2564

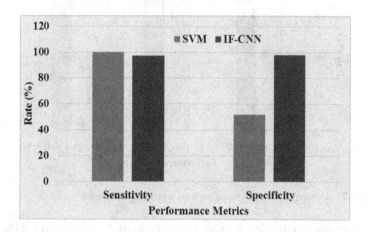

FIGURE 6.5 Sensitivity/specificity analysis.

60.08% and the IF-CNN offers 97.7564%, 98.8655%, and 99.04%, respectively. The integrated level set formulation with the IF-CNN improves the accuracy, precision, and recall by 12.79%, 6.92%, and 39.34%, respectively.

Figure 6.8 shows the loss over time of the proposed work; this represents the validation loss and training loss. By considering the time, the validation loss and training loss reduce with respect to the increasing time.

Table 6.2 shows the performance of the proposed system using various algorithms. Here various algorithms such as U-Net, Deformed U-Net, V-Net, Holistically Nested Network (HNN), Holistically Nested Network-Random forest (HNN-RF) are used to evaluate the performance of the proposed system. The V-net algorithm is analyzed

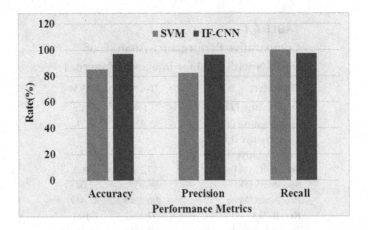

FIGURE 6.6   Analysis of accuracy, precision, and recall.

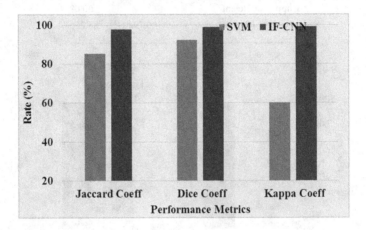

FIGURE 6.7   Comparative analysis of various similarity measures.

with this proposed system by the evaluation of parameters such as average Dice coefficients and average Hausdorff distances of the predicted delineation to the ground truth annotation. The performance of the U-Net model is evaluated by using the measures such as inducing loss, false positive rate, and false negative rate. Also, the error rates 1 and 2 are estimated.

6.9   CONCLUSION

A high-anatomical variation in the pancreas region resulted in the reduced performance of traditional segmentation approaches to demarcate/differentiate the pancreas region from the other organs in the CT abdominal imagery. The state-of-the-art image processing and computer vision techniques like segmentation and filtering classification already witnessed (e.g., **K-means clustering, level set Segmentation,**

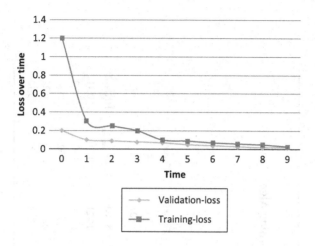

FIGURE 6.8 Loss over time.

region growing, Otsu segmentation, Fuzzy C-means clustering, Bilateral filtering, Angular Texture pattern etc.) have successfully eradicated some of the above-mentioned issues. However, image segmentation algorithms rarely adapt well to the changes in the imaging system or to a different image analysis problem, so there is a demand for solutions that can be easily modified to analyze different image modalities, which are more accurate than the existing ones. To overcome these demerits faced by the above-mentioned customized segmentation approaches and to enhance segmentation precision, we need to design a model that gives us more finer segmentations and that clearly demarcates the location of the pancreas. Initially, the proposed work employed the Laplacian formula to filter the noisy regions from the images and the second-order formulation to sharpen the edges of images. The multi directional angle-based feature extraction methodology extracts the different patterns in the images. We propose a novel integrated segmentation approach that joins both level sets and deep neural networks to significantly improve the more accuracy of the segmentation and correctly distinguish between pancreatic and non-pancreatic imagery via assigning exact labels. The main idea behind this dual approach is to improve the segmentation accuracy by first utilizing level sets which comprise the following steps to gauge the initial boundary of the pancreas region. The initial level contour grows and shrinks based on the principle of energy minimization to finally surround the pancreatic region. Subsequently, the post-segmentation results can be further fine-tuned by providing the correct hyperparameters for the training of our proposed level-set-based CNN model (IFCNN) and by giving abundance of examples to our learning algorithm to depict the exact labels for classification. Hence, customized image processing solutions for pancreas segmentation can be replaced by a trainable method which can be applicable to a large variety of image data instead of solving only one specific problem. The comparative analysis between the proposed CNN-based learning models and the various methods like SVM, V-Net, and U-NET are then performed and extracted performance parameters such as Jaccard, Dice, and

TABLE 6.2
Performance Analysis of the Proposed System Using Various Machine Learning Algorithms

Algorithm	Average Dice	Average Hausdorff
V-Net	$0.872^{+0.034}_{-}$	$0.547^{+1.20}_{-}$

Algorithm	Loss	FN	FP	Error1	Error2
U-Net	0.1456	5	10	70	43
Deformed U-Net	0.1001	2	4	60	9

	$HNN_{meanmax}$	HNN-RF	$HNN_{meanmax}$	HNN-RF	$HNN_{meanmax}$	HNN-RF	$HNN_{meanmax}$	HNN-RF
Mean	80.15	81.54	65.21	69.21	25.25	16.21	0.54	0.41
Standard	7.5	6.21	9.5	8.21	12.62	10.5	0.35	0.32
Median	83.54	82.57	70.54	70.57	17.8	15.2	0.32	0.31
Min	45.26	50.65	28.95	33.54	5.84	5.30	0.20	0.21
Max	90.98	89.25	78.53	80.24	78.51	70.54	1.2	2.12

Average Hausdorff ensure the effectiveness of the early diagnosis by the proposed model. Furthermore, we can improve our segmentation by introducing end-to-end training architecture CNN, e.g., semantic segmentation, for dense pixel classification and generate segmentation maps independent of any size of the image. This could be extrapolated to other organs of high anatomical variability along with improved performance of the segmentation task.

REFERENCES

1. Clores, M. J., Thosani, A., & Buscaglia, J. M. (2014). Multidisciplinary diagnostic and therapeutic approaches to pancreatic cystic lesions. *Journal of Multidisciplinary Healthcare*, 7, 81.
2. Fritz, S., Bergmann, F., Grenacher, L., Sgroi, M., Hinz, U., Hackert, T., ... & Werner, J. (2014). Diagnosis and treatment of autoimmune pancreatitis types 1 and 2. *British Journal of Surgery*, 101(10), 1257–1265.
3. Rosenberger, I., Strauss, A., Dobiasch, S., Weis, C., Szanyi, S., Gil-Iceta, L., ... & Plaza-García, S. (2015). Targeted diagnostic magnetic nanoparticles for medical imaging of pancreatic cancer. *Journal of Controlled Release*, 214, 76–84.
4. Trikudanathan, G., Walker, S. P., Munigala, S., Spilseth, B., Malli, A., Han, Y., ... & Beilman, G. J. (2015). Diagnostic performance of contrast-enhanced MRI with secretin-stimulated MRCP for non-calcific chronic pancreatitis: A comparison with histopathology. American Journal of Gastroenterology, 110(11), 1598–1606.
5. Brugge, W. R. (2015), Diagnosis and management of cystic lesions of the pancreas. *Journal of Gastrointestinal Oncology*, 6, 375.
6. Lee, J. H., Kim, J. K., Kim, T. H., Park, M. S., Yu, J. S., Choi, J. Y., ... & Kim, K. W. (2012). MRI features of serous oligocystic adenoma of the pancreas: differentiation from mucinous cystic neoplasm of the pancreas. *The British Journal of Radiology*, 85(1013), 571–576.
7. Legrand, L., Duchatelle, V., Molinié, V., Boulay-Coletta, I., Sibileau, E., & Zins, M. (2015). Pancreatic adenocarcinoma: MRI conspicuity and pathologic correlations. *Abdominal Imaging*, 40(1), 85–94.
8. Sequeiros, I. M., Hester, K., Callaway, M., Williams, A., Garland, Z., Powell, T., ... & Bristol Cystic Fibrosis Diabetes Group. (2010). MRI appearance of the pancreas in patients with cystic fibrosis: a comparison of pancreas volume in diabetic and non-diabetic patients. *The British Journal of Radiology*, 83(995), 921–926.
9. Barral, M., Soyer, P., Dohan, A., Laurent, V., Hoeffel, C., Fishman, E. K., & Boudiaf, M. (2014). Magnetic resonance imaging of cystic pancreatic lesions in adults: An update in current diagnostic features and management. *Abdominal Imaging*, 39(1), 48–65.
10. Hanada, K., Okazaki, A., Hirano, N., Izumi, Y., Teraoka, Y., Ikemoto, J., ... & Yonehara, S. (2015). Diagnostic strategies for early pancreatic cancer. *Journal of Gastroenterology*, 50(2), 147–154.
11. Roth, H. R., Lu, L., Farag, A., Shin, H. C., Liu, J., Turkbey, E. B., & Summers, R. M. (2015, October). Deeporgan: Multi-level deep convolutional networks for automated pancreas segmentation. In International conference on medical image computing and computer-assisted intervention (pp. 556–564). Cham: Springer.
12. Achanta, R., Shaji, A., Smith, K., Lucchi, A., Fua, P., & Süsstrunk, S. (2012). SLIC superpixels compared to state-of-the-art superpixel methods. *IEEE Transactions on Pattern Analysis and Machine Intelligence*, 34(11), 2274–2282.

13. Roth, H. R., Farag, A., Lu, L., Turkbey, E. B., & Summers, R. M. (2015, March). Deep convolutional networks for pancreas segmentation in CT imaging. In *Medical Imaging 2015: Image Processing* (Vol. 9413, p. 94131G). International Society for Optics and Photonics.

14. Roth, H. R., Lu, L., Farag, A., Sohn, A., & Summers, R. M. (2016, October). Spatial aggregation of holistically-nested networks for automated pancreas segmentation. In International Conference on Medical Image Computing and Computer-Assisted Intervention (pp. 451–459). Cham: Springer.

15. Farag, A., Lu, L., Roth, H. R., Liu, J., Turkbey, E., & Summers, R. M. (2016). A bottom-up approach for pancreas segmentation using cascaded superpixels and (deep) image patch labeling. *IEEE Transactions on Image Processing*, 26(1), 386–399.

16. Moeskops, P., Wolterink, J. M., van der Velden, B. H., Gilhuijs, K. G., Leiner, T., Viergever, M. A., & Išgum, I. (2016, October). Deep learning for multi-task medical image segmentation in multiple modalities. In International Conference on Medical Image Computing and Computer-Assisted Intervention (pp. 478–486). Cham: Springer.

17. Cai, J., Lu, L., Zhang, Z., Xing, F., Yang, L., & Yin, Q. (2016, October). Pancreas segmentation in MRI using graph-based decision fusion on convolutional neural networks. In International Conference on Medical Image Computing and Computer-Assisted Intervention (pp. 442–450). Cham: Springer.

18. Zheng, S., Jayasumana, S., Romera-Paredes, B., Vineet, V., Su, Z., Du, D., ... & Torr, P. H. (2015). Conditional random fields as recurrent neural networks. In *Proceedings of the IEEE International Conference on Computer Vision* (pp. 1529–1537).

19. Wang, Z., Bhatia, K. K., Glocker, B., Marvao, A., Dawes, T., Misawa, K., ... & Rueckert, D. (2014, September). Geodesic patch-based segmentation. In International Conference on Medical Image Computing and Computer-Assisted Intervention (pp. 666–673). Cham: Springer.

20. Wolz, R., Chu, C., Misawa, K., Fujiwara, M., Mori, K., & Rueckert, D. (2013). Automated abdominal multi-organ segmentation with subject-specific atlas generation. *IEEE Transactions on Medical Imaging*, 32(9), 1723–1730.

21. Tong, T., Wolz, R., Wang, Z., Gao, Q., Misawa, K., Fujiwara, M., ... & Rueckert, D. (2015). Discriminative dictionary learning for abdominal multi-organ segmentation. *Medical Image Analysis*, 23(1), 92–104.

22. Lucchi, A., Smith, K., Achanta, R., Knott, G., & Fua, P. (2011). Supervoxel-based segmentation of mitochondria in em image stacks with learned shape features. *IEEE Transactions on Medical Imaging*, 31(2), 474–486.

23. Zhang, L., Kong, H., Chin, C. T., Liu, S., Chen, Z., Wang, T., & Chen, S. (2014). Segmentation of cytoplasm and nuclei of abnormal cells in cervical cytology using global and local graph cuts. *Computerized Medical Imaging and Graphics*, 38(5), 369–380.

24. Chang, H., Han, J., Borowsky, A., Loss, L., Gray, J. W., Spellman, P. T., & Parvin, B. (2012). Invariant delineation of nuclear architecture in glioblastoma multiforme for clinical and molecular association. *IEEE Transactions on Medical Imaging*, 32(4), 670–682.

25. Zhang, L., Kong, H., Ting Chin, C., Liu, S., Fan, X., Wang, T., & Chen, S. (2014). Automation-assisted cervical cancer screening in manual liquid-based cytology with hematoxylin and eosin staining. *Cytometry Part A*, 85(3), 214–230.

26. Kayalibay, B., Jensen, G., & van der Smagt, P. (2017). CNN-based segmentation of medical imaging data. arXiv preprint arXiv:1701.03056.

27. G. Litjens, T. Kooi, B. E. Bejnordi, A. A. A. Setio, F. Ciompi, M. Ghafoorian, et al. (2017). A survey on deep learning in medical image analysis. *Medical Image Analysis* 42, 60–88.

28. F. Milletari, N. Navab, and S.-A. Ahmadi. (2016). V-net: Fully convolutional neural networks for volumetric medical image segmentation. In *3D Vision (3DV), 2016* Fourth International Conference on, pp. 565–571

29. Sudre, C. H., Li, W., Vercauteren, T., Ourselin, S., & Cardoso, M. J. (2017). Generalised Dice overlap as a deep learning loss function for highly unbalanced segmentations. In *Deep Learning in Medical Image Analysis and Multimodal Learning for Clinical Decision Support* (pp. 240–248). Cham: Springer.

30. Wang, S., Wu, Q., He, X., Yang, J., & Wang, Y. (2015). Local N-Ary pattern and its extension for texture classification. *IEEE Transactions on Circuits and Systems for Video Technology*, 25(9), 1495–1506.

7 Early and Precision-Oriented Detection of Cervical Cancer
A Deep-Learning-Based Framework

Vandana Bhatia, Priya Ranjan, Neha Taneja,
Harpreet Singh, and Rajiv Janardhanan

CONTENTS

7.1 INTRODUCTION

The abnormal growth of cells of any organ in the human body can be the effect of cancer. The abnormal growth of cells of different body organs can affect both males and females. Some types of cancers are very frequent in women such as breast cancer and cervical cancer. A significant proportion of these cancers are burdened with poor clinical outcomes due to delay in detection as well as misdiagnosis. For example, breast cancer impacts 2.1 million women worldwide every year and is the major cause of mortality among women. In 2018, it was estimated that breast cancer took the lives of around 627,000 women—approximately 15% of all cancer-associated deaths taken together (Wang, Khosla, Gargeya, Irshad, & Beck, 2016).

Similarly, cervical cancer is the fourth most common cancer among women, with an estimation of around 570,000 new cases in 2018, i.e., 6.6% of all female cancers. Roughly 90% of deaths take place due to cervical cancer in low- and middle-income countries (Kessler, 2017; Kumar & Tanya, 2014; Srivastava, Misra, Srivastava, Das, & Gupta, 2018). It is the second most prominent cause of female cancer among women in the age group 15–44 years in India. Annually, around 96,922 new cervical cancer cases are detected in India (Bobdey, Sathwara, Jain, & Balasubramaniam, 2016; Bray et al., 2018). While cervical cancer cases are declining in the developed countries, they pose a heavy burden on developing countries, where the risk of developing cervical cancer is 35% greater compared to developed countries (Bray et al., 2018). India accounts for approximately 25% of the mortality globally because of cervical cancer (Kumar & Tanya, 2014).

Early detection of solid tumors is critical for improving the clinical outcomes in patients afflicted with reproductive cancers such as breast cancer and cervical cancer. For example, early detection has been shown to correlate with more than 80% five-year survival rate; however, this rate decreases quickly in patients with advanced stages, reaching 15–20% population at stage IV (Meiquan et al., 2018).

Fortunately, cervical and breast cancers have an adequate premalignant time, which provides an opportunity for treating and screening before it turns to be aggressive cervical cancer. Pap smear or cytology-based population screening is a crucial secondary preventive measure that precedes a high-cure rate among patients suffering from cervical cancer. Early detection and treatment via screening can prevent nearly 80% of the cases of cervical cancers in developed countries, where efficient screening programs are in place (Srivastava et al., 2018). In developing countries, however, there is limited access to wide-scale and effective screening, leading to increased deaths due to cervical and breast cancers (Srivastava et al., 2018).

For providing context, the first step of any cancer diagnosis is the visual examination, in which a specialized doctor examines a lesion of interest with the assistance of devices. If the doctor considers the lesion to be cancerous in nature, or the initial opinion is unpersuasive, the primary healthcare physician will recommend a follow-up with a biopsy, which is indeed invasive and uncomfortable for the patients. The Institute of Medicine at the National Academies of Science, Engineering and Medicine has discoursed that "diagnostic errors account for approximately 10 percent of patient deaths," and also reports for 6–17% of complications at hospitals (Kessler, 2017). It is worthwhile to mention here that a general physician's performance cannot be calculated by false prediction of cancer. Researchers worldwide have attributed a variety of factors to a wrong diagnosis:

- Ineffective collaboration and integration of technology for efficient diagnostics.

- Disparities in communication among clinicians, patients, and their caretakers.
- Inadequate support provided to the diagnostic process by the healthcare work system.

The amalgamation of digital colposcopy for cervical cancer screening in the place of manual diagnosis can significantly strengthen the precision. Applications of Artificial Intelligence (AI) in medical diagnostics in both low- and middle-income countries (LMICs) are in the early adoption phase across healthcare settings (Kessler, 2017). These applications have the potential to revolutionize the provisioning of not only healthcare but also the clinical outcomes of patients affected with reproductive cancers such as breast cancer and cervical cancer in a real-time frame.

Artificial Intelligence along with Machine Learning has proved to be very efficient as classifier for the early detection of both cervical cancer (Menezes, Vazquez, Mohan, & Somboonwit, 2019) and breast cancer. AI-based approaches have been used widely in literature for the diagnosis of many deadly cancers (Anagnostou, Remzi, Lykourinas, & Djavan, 2003; Lisboa & Taktak, 2006). The accuracy and efficiency depend predominantly on the experience and in this case for training an AI-based model: the more the data, the better the experience. It might be pertinent to mention here that AI-based deep learning models, in vogue since the beginning of the 21st century, have been extensively used for image-analytics-based detection of anomalous tumors (Hu et al., 2018; Razzak, Naz, & Zaib, 2018).

Deep learning is a neural-network-based model which exploits multiple layers for efficient processing (Zhang & Chen, 2014) and has been extensively used for the detection of breast cancer (Hu et al., 2018; Togaçar & Ergen, 2018) and cervigram image analysis-based diagnosis of cervical cancer (Alyafeai & Ghouti, 2020; Hu et al., 2018; Togaçar & Ergen, 2018). It has proved to be very efficient when the data are very large. In literature, deep learning models such as convolutional neural networks (CNNs) were broadly used for cervical cancer classification (Alyafeai & Ghouti, 2020). In this chapter, the efficiency of CNN for the classification of cervical cancer has been discussed at length. It will be interesting to observe the capability of an AI-based approach for early detection of cervical cancer.

This chapter is organized as follows: deep learning models will be discussed in Section 7.2. In Section 7.3, related work done for detection of cancer with the help of deep learning has been discussed. Section 7.4 provides a deep-learning-based framework for cervical cancer classification. Section 7.5 provides results and observations of classification. Section 7.6 discusses the limitation of deep learning models for cancer prediction. Section 7.7 concludes the chapter and focuses on the way forward.

7.2 DEEP LEARNING NETWORKS AND CERVICAL CANCER

Intelligent diagnosis of cervical cancer is the need of the current time. Generally, five types of cervical precancerous data (i.e., cytology, fluorescence in situ hybridization [FISH], electromagnetic spectra, cervicography, and colposcopy) can be utilized for an intelligent screening of cervical cancer. However, the computer system based on cytology data and electromagnetic spectra data attained improved accuracy than the other data (Taneja, Ranjan, & Ujlayan, 2018). For example, by using the pap smear in neural networking system (PAPNET), equipped with neural network, cancer cells can be identified in repeatedly misdiagnosed pap smears (Lisboa & Taktak, 2006). The last two decades have witnessed an increasing use of computer-based intelligent techniques for solving complicated problems in the medical science domain such as perinatology, cardiology, urology, liver pathology, oncology, gynecology, and thyroid disorders (Anagnostou et al., 2003; Fein, Wong, Rosa-Cunha, Slomovitz, & Potter, 2018; Meiquan et al., 2018; Palefsky, 2009). The main aim of using Artificial Intelligence tools in medical science is to enable the development of intelligent decision support systems that can act as adjunct clinical aids in improving the diagnosis of cervical cancer.

In literature, AI-based approaches have been observed to be very popular among researchers for helping healthcare professionals toward the timely diagnosis of cancer. Wen et al. (2016) predicted prostate cancer patient survivability using four different Machine Learning techniques—decision tree, support vector machine, k-nearest neighbor and Naive Bayes—and achieved a satisfactory 85.67% accuracy (Wen et al., 2016). AI-based approaches have been extensively used for the diagnosis and classification of cancer. Wu and Zhou (Wu & Zhou, 2017) used support vector machine for the diagnosis of cervical cancer. They considered 32 risk factors that help in categorization into four target diagnosis methods.

Deep-learning-based approaches have also been proposed in literature for the classification of cervical cancer. A fully automated approach was proposed by Alyafeai and Ghouti (2020) for cervical cancer classification using deep learning. Mesut et al. (Togaçar & Ergen, 2018) have used a deep learning approach for breast cancer detection (Togaçar & Ergen, 2018). However, most of the proposed approaches have been tested on a relatively small dataset consisting of less than 100 images. Deep learning models provide better results in the presence of larger sample data. In this chapter, more than 1000 images are considered for training deep learning models.

7.3 DEEP LEARNING MODELS

Deep learning is a special kind of Machine Learning technique that utilizes the "learning by example" approach for training of the computer model. It has been used in many domains such as network clustering (Bhatia & Rani, 2019), image classification (Arel, Rose, & Coop, 1988), and recommendation systems (Fu, Qu, & Yi, 2019), to name but a few examples. This kind of technique is similar to how humans learn. Deep learning models are trained to directly perform classification tasks on images, text, sound, and so on and so forth. Some of the deep learning models are known to achieve very high accuracy levels, even exceeding that of humans. The key features of deep-learning-based models are that they are trained over very large datasets of labeled data and are designed using neural networks with several layers.

Deep learning models use artificial neural networks to train, which is why they are often called deep neural networks also. Deep learning is called "deep" because

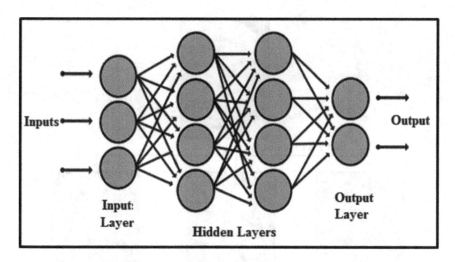

FIGURE 7.1 Neural network with two hidden layers and binary output.

of the various hidden layers that are present in the neural network. While most neural networks consist of around two to three hidden layers, deep neural networks can contain much more, about 150 hidden layers, as shown in Figure 7.1.

It will be interesting to observe the performance of deep learning for the identification of cervical cancer lesions. There are various challenges like image segmentation, efficient feature extraction from cervigrams that can be solved using Artificial Intelligence approaches such as deep learning and EMD if used together.

7.4 DEEP-LEARNING-BASED CLASSIFICATION OF CERVICAL CANCER

A deep-learning-based CNN model is used for the classification task. First, data augmentation is performed. Then the region of interest (ROI) is extracted so that features can be extracted efficiently. Further classification is performed using CNN. The main steps that are performed are as follows.

7.4.1 IMAGE PREPROCESSING AND DATA AUGMENTATION

Images are rarely gathered without any noise in them. Often, the dataset contains images with noise and corrupted data. Thus, image preprocessing is required so that any neural network can have increased effectiveness in classifying the images. In the case of the cervical cancer dataset, the noise which can be seen pertains to human error, similarities between various classes as well as specular reflection. First, image normalization was performed. An image is nothing but a matrix of numbers, and

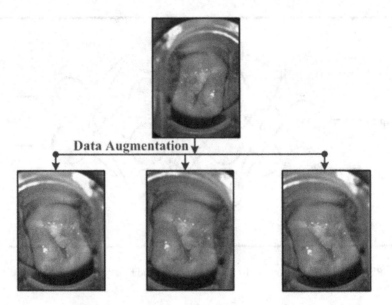

FIGURE 7.2   Augmentation of cervigrams using scaling, cropping and flipping.

these numbers are generally in the range of 0–255, which can be disruptive to the learning of the neural network, and thus the values of every pixel are normalized to fall between 0 and 1. Further, to avoid any outliers in the dataset, blurred images were manually removed.

After preprocessing, data augmentation was performed, as shown in Figure 7.2. Deep learning requires a lot of data to perform well and thus a larger dataset is required than that available in the Intel and MobileODT repository. Image augmentation is therefore used to create new images from the existing dataset to feed the network with adequate images; we augmented the images based on random rotations of the datasets based on the rotation angles.

7.4.2   REGION OF INTEREST EXTRACTION

Instead of handling images, the first step involved the extraction of the region of interest. ROI was the designated region from which the subsequent images would be analyzed for performing classification. The images in themselves are very large in size and thus make training a very long and time-consuming process along with a lot of noise in them, causing the accuracy of the neural network to drop, thereby significantly compromising the quality of the images.

We used UNET to resolve the issue. UNET is essentially a convolutional neural network developed (Wen et al., 2016) for the application in biomedical image segmentation.

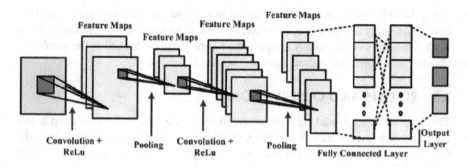

FIGURE 7.3 Architecture of convolutional neural network for classification of cervical cancer.

7.4.3 FEATURE EXTRACTION AND MAPPING

Convolutional neural networks are among popular deep learning models used for many tasks like image classification, object recognition, etc. CNN can be used on any device and are proven to be computationally efficient by many researchers. CNN performs parameter sharing by using special convolution and pooling operations for feature extraction and mapping. In this work, the CNN model was used by performing multiple convolutional and pooling operations that were followed by a number of fully connected layers. The building block of CNN is the convolutional layer.

In it, mathematical operations were performed to merge two sets of information such as an image matrix and a filter or kernel. Rectified linear unit (ReLU) activation function was used for a non-linear operation. The output of ReLU was calculated as follows:

$$f(x) = \max(0, x) \tag{1}$$

The purpose of ReLU's activation function was to add the non-linearity in the proposed approach. As the real-world data had many non-negative linear values, the deep-learning-based model should be able to learn from them.

In the proposed model, the activation function in the output layer was SoftMax, as multiclass classification needed to be performed. The detailed model is shown in Figure 7.3. The deep learning model will consist of several convolutional layers combined with non-linear and pooling layers. When the images are passed through one convolution layer, the output of the first layer is passed as the input for the next layer. The same process was continued for further convolutional layers as well.

7.4.4 CERVICAL CANCER CLASSIFICATION

After the completion of series of convolutional, pooling, and non-linear layers, using a fully connected layer was necessary. The fully connected layer took the output information from convolutional networks and provided the final classification. Connecting a fully connected layer in the end of the convolutional neural network results in a vector with N dimensions, where N can be defined as the number of classes from which the desired class was selected.

7.5 RESULTS AND OBSERVATIONS

The deep learning model was implemented using the Python-3-based deep learning package named Keras along with Google TensorFlow. For implementation, the Google Collaboratory platform was used by exploiting various features available such as GPU processing.

7.5.1 CERVICAL CANCER DATASET

Intel and MobileODT jointly have provided the cervical cancer screening dataset. The dataset of screening is available publicly on Kaggle portal ("Kaggle, Intel& Mobile ODT cervical cancer screening dataset," 2020). The Intel & MobileODT dataset was used mainly for training the machine and deep learning models so that they can perform classification for the cervix types correctly. All the images of cervigram that were used for training are gathered from women who have no history of cervical cancer. Such images were used for extracting the region of interest. These images are not expected to train for the object detection using deep-learning-based models; thus, the cervical region of interest must be annotated manually first. A subset of physically annotated data by a human expert is considered ("Kaggle, Manual annotation of intel&mobileodt cervical cancer screening dataset," 2020).

The type of the cervix is closely related to the transformation zone location ("Kaggle, Intel&MobileODT cervical cancer screening dataset," 2020). Table 7.1 provides a summary on cervix type classification across the Intel & MobileODT dataset. It should be observed that 1500 images were accurately annotated only in the aforementioned dataset ("Kaggle, Manual annotation of intel&MobileODT cervical cancer screening dataset," 2020).

7.5.2 MODEL VALIDATION

The UNET was used to segment the images and acquire the region of interest from the images. This is done by applying a CNN over the images. Train error and test error metrics are considered for the model validation. Train loss is the value of

TABLE 7.1
Dataset Characteristics

Cervigram Type	Type 1	Type 2	Type 3
Number of images	1241	4348	2426
Train data	992	3478	1940
Test data	243	870	486

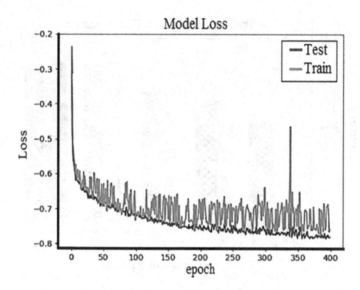

FIGURE 7.4 Image segmentation and classification using UNET: Lower test loss indicates good performance.

objective function which is being optimized by the model. Test loss is calculated over the unseen data. When the training loss is smaller than the testing loss, there are chances that the model is suffering from overfitting; and when the training loss is much higher than the testing loss, the model may have the problem of underfitting.

The goal of any good model is to minimize the loss. Loss can be considered as a penalty for wrong prediction. Lower loss values are an indication of a better model. For perfect prediction, loss should be equal to zero. The results acquired from the CNN model are shown in Figure 7.4. As it can be observed, the testing loss decreases when the number of epochs increases. There is a noticeable reduction in testing errors.

This is essential as the risk cannot be taken when the model is making predictions for a very sensitive problem such as cervical cancer prediction. In such problems, patients may have different characteristics. However, the train error is fluctuating between −0.6 and −0.7. It indicates that the model is neither overfitted nor underfitted (Figure 7.5).

7.5.3 CLASSIFICATION RESULTS

A fully connected layer in a convolutional neural network will perform the final classification. The results are analyzed based on accuracy. In classification, accuracy can be given as follows:

$$\text{Accurancy} = \frac{\text{Number of correctly classified target}}{\text{Total number of classification}} \qquad (2)$$

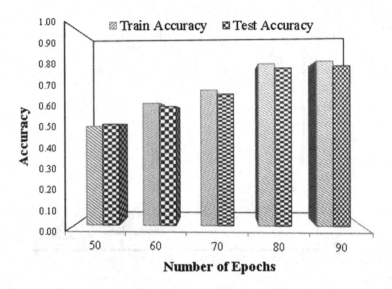

FIGURE 7.5 Train and test accuracy trade of the proposed solution indicating better performance in terms of train and test accuracy.

The test accuracy and training accuracy are illustrated in Figure 7.5. Training accuracy is computed based on the data; the model was trained on. Test accuracy is computed over the data that is unseen to the model. For a perfect blend, training accuracy should not be much higher than the test accuracy as the larger difference signifies that the model is suffering from the problem of overfitting. As shown in figure, we have tested the model on a different number of epochs of CNN. As the number of epochs increases, the complexity of the model will also increase. As observed, there is not much difference in accuracy received when we run the model for 80 epochs and when we run the model for 90 epochs. As healthcare professionals expect a prompt and timely reply from an AI-based prediction model, we have considered 80 epochs because it will save a significant amount of time. It can be observed from the figure that the proposed model is not suffering from overfitting as the training accuracy and test accuracy are almost the same in the case of all the epochs.

7.6 LIMITATIONS OF DEEP LEARNING FOR CANCER PREDICTION AND FUTURE POSSIBILITIES

Despite all the work done in literature involving deep learning for cervical cancer diagnosis, it is frequently treated as a black box approach. For critical applications like cancer detection, the algorithmic relevance is as important as algorithmic performance. And, the model interpretability is vital for convincing medical professionals to use deep-learning-based models for recommendations, which does not even provide the basis of the prediction (Razzak et al., 2018).

Another challenge in using a deep-learning-based model for cancer detection lies in its complexity. The power required by a system machinery for training the deep learning model can be the major reason for not using it in handy devices. If health-care professionals rely on deep learning for cancer prediction or classification, they expect to get the result in a shorter span of time. However, due to the complexity of deep learning models, it is also a big challenge.

The data storage is also an issue as deep learning models require large amounts of data for maintaining precision. Although this problem can be resolved by training deep learning models on the top of cloud and edge processing so that they can learn using all the available data centrally. But healthcare professionals will not prefer to pass their data on the cloud due to security concerns. It also requires affirmation from patients, which in most cases is denied (Razzak et al., 2018).

However, the recent burst in the growth of the medical device sector has witnessed companies making several attempts to diagnose solid tumors in an accurate and reliable manner, as development of niche-specific and reliable diagnostic tools might capture a percentage of this profitable market. Better infrastructure in healthcare will play a vital role in implementation of deep learning approaches for assisting the specialized professional in diagnosis and making critical decisions.

7.7 CONCLUSION

In this chapter, the cervical classification model was performed using deep learning. Convolutional neural network, a popular deep-learning-based model, was used for image classification. The use of CNN for cervical cancer classification was done by providing cervigrams as input. Data augmentation was performed on the images to provide input to the CNN model. The images were then processed to get the region of interest. Further feature mapping was performed to extract desired features from images. Further, images are classified as normal and abnormal. Deep learning is observed to provide 0.79 training accuracy and 0.72 test accuracy. In the end, the limitations and challenges of using CNN for cervical cancer prediction have been discussed.

The results of this research have shown a strong capability of foreseeing data. More specific usage of the variants of deep-learning-based models will be very much helpful to people with high risk by providing timely screening and positive precaution measures.

ACKNOWLEDGMENTS

We acknowledge the Indian Council of Medical Research, New Delhi, for support as grant-in-aid to Dr Rajiv Janardhanan and Dr Priya Ranjan (Grant Id No. 2029-0416-No. ISRM/12(23)/2019).

REFERENCES

Alyafeai, Z., & Ghouti, L. (2020). A fully-automated deep learning pipeline for cervical cancer classification. *Expert Systems with Applications*, *141*, 112951. doi: 10.1016/j. eswa.2019.112951.

Anagnostou, T., Remzi, M., Lykourinas, M., & Djavan, B. (2003). Artificial neural networks for decision-making in urologic oncology. *European Urology, 43*(6), 596–603.

Arel, I., Rose, D., & Coop, R. (1988). DeSTIN : A scalable deep learning architecture with application to high-dimensional robust pattern recognition. *Biologically Inspired Cognitive Architectures*, 11–15.

Bhatia, V., & Rani, R. (2019). A distributed overlapping community detection model for large graphs using autoencoder. *Future Generation Computer Systems, 94*, 16–26. doi: 10.1016/j.future.2018.10.045.

Bobdey, S., Sathwara, J., Jain, A., & Balasubramaniam, G. (2016). Burden of cervical cancer and role of screening in India. *Indian Journal of Medical and Paediatric Oncology: Official Journal of Indian Society of Medical \& Paediatric Oncology, 37*(4), 278.

Bray, F., Ferlay, J., Soerjomataram, I., Siegel, R. L., Torre, L. A., & Jemal, A. (2018). Global cancer statistics 2018: GLOBOCAN estimates of incidence and mortality worldwide for 36 cancers in 185 countries. *CA: A Cancer Journal for Clinicians, 68*(6), 394–424.

Fein, L. A., Wong, A., Rosa-Cunha, I., Slomovitz, B., & Potter, J. (2018). Anal cancer risk factors and utilization of anal pap smear screening among transgender persons. *Papillomavirus Research, 5*, S4.

Fu, M., Qu, H., & Yi, Z. (2019). A novel deep learning-based collaborative filtering model for recommendation system. *IEEE Transactions On Cybernetics, 49*(3), 1084–1096.

Hu, Z., Tang, J., Wang, Z., Zhang, K., Zhang, L., & Sun, Q. (2018). Deep learning for image-based cancer detection and diagnosis- A survey. *Pattern Recognition, 83*, 134–149.

Kaggle, Intel & mobileodt cervical cancer screening dataset. (2020, May).

Kaggle, Manual annotation of intel&mobileodt cervical cancer screening dataset. (2020, May).

Kessler, T. A. (2017). Cervical cancer: Prevention and early detection. In *Seminars in Oncology Nursing* (Vol. 33, pp. 172–183). WB Saunders, 2017.

Kumar, H. H. N., & Tanya, S. (2014). A study on knowledge and screening for cervical cancer among women in Mangalore city. *Annals of Medical and Health Sciences Research, 4*(5), 751–756.

Lisboa, P. J., & Taktak, A. F. G. (2006). The use of artificial neural networks in decision support in cancer: A systematic review. *Neural Networks, 19*(4), 408–415.

Meiquan, X., Weixiu, Z., Yanhua, S., Junhui, W., Tingting, W., Yajie, Y., … Longsen, C. (2018). Cervical cytology intelligent diagnosis based on object detection technology.

Menezes LJ, Vazquez L, Mohan CK, Somboonwit C. (2019). Eliminating cervical cancer: A role for artificial intelligence. In *Global Virology III: Virology in the 21st Century*, 405–422. doi: 10.1007/978-3-030-29022-1_13.

Palefsky, J. (2009). Human papillomavirus-related disease in people with HIV. *Current Opinion in HIV and AIDS, 4*(1), 52.

Razzak, M. I., Naz, S., & Zaib, A. (2018). Deep learning for medical image processing: Overview, challenges and the future. In *Classification in BioApps* (pp. 323–350). Springer.

Srivastava, A. N., Misra, J. S., Srivastava, S., Das, B. C., & Gupta, S. (2018). Cervical cancer screening in rural India: Status & current concepts. *The Indian Journal of Medical Research, 148*(6), 687.

Taneja, A., Ranjan, P., & Ujlayan, A. (2018). Multi-cell nuclei segmentation in cervical cancer images by integrated feature vectors. *Multimedia Tools and Applications, 77*(8), 9271–9290.

Togaçar, M., & Ergen, B. (2018). Deep learning approach for classification of breast cancer. In *2018* International Conference on Artificial Intelligence and Data Processing (IDAP) (pp. 1–5).

Wang D, Khosla A, Gargeya R, Irshad H, Beck AH. (2016). Deep learning for identifying metastatic breast cancer. *ArXiv Preprint ArXiv:1606.05718*. Retrieved from https://arxiv.org/abs/1606.05718 Last accessed on 14-01-2020

Wen, H., Li, S., Li, W., Li, J., and Yin, C. (2016). Comparison of Four Machine Learning Techniques for the Prediction of Prostate Cancer Survivability. In *2018* 15th International Computer Conference on Wavelet Active Media Technology and Information Processing (ICCWAMTIP) (pp. 112–116).

Wu, W., & Zhou, H. (2017). Data-driven diagnosis of cervical cancer with support vector machine-based approaches. *IEEE Access*, *5*, 25189–25195.

Zhang, K., & Chen, X. W. (2014). Large-scale deep belief nets with mapreduce. *IEEE Access*, *2*, 395–403. doi: 10.1109/ACCESS.2014.2319813.

8 Transformation of mHealth in Society

Ankur Saxena, Mohit Saxena, Anveshita Deo,
and Alejandra Rodríguez Llerena

CONTENTS

8.1 WHAT IS mHEALTH?

mHealth refers to mobile health. mHealth can share data continuously, not for a limited time but for longer duration in order to see the difference between statistics and the behavioral patterns of an individual [1]. It is a constituent of eHealth, which is concerned with the electronic processes and communication in the field of healthcare. It deals not only with Internet medicine but also with virtual examination, diagnosis, and telemedicine. Mobile health thus greatly emphasizes the usage of different mobile devices such as smartphones, smart clothing, smart chips, wireless devices, personal digital assistants (PDAs) and other patient monitoring devices, as shown in Figure 8.1, which are easily accessible for users, professional medical practitioners, and healthcare advisors [2]. This new digital healthcare system makes healthcare more attainable for the rising population and more manageable for the healthcare providers, by having a steady data storage system and tracking of the significant changes in the user for better diagnosis and treatment. mHealth can be a great asset to track physical health as well as mental health [3].

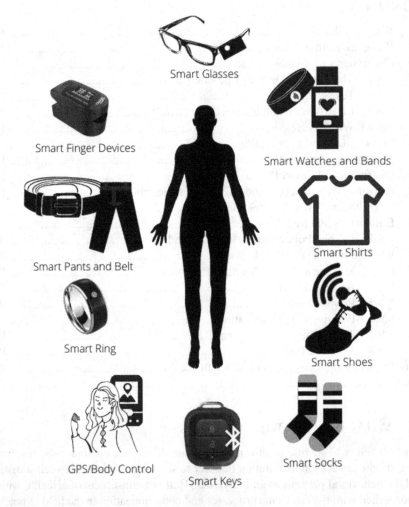

FIGURE 8.1 Patient monitoring with smart devices.

There are numerous sensory devices available on the market today—smart watches, smartphones, smart jewelry (e.g., band, ring, etc.), and other smart wearable devices (e.g., shirts, pants, belt, shoes, socks, etc.)—that aim to keep a check on physical health. Recent advancements and adaptability in technology have proven that this technology could also keep a check on mental and emotional well-being[4].

mHealth technology, being user-friendly, has integrated deep into our daily lives, enabling us to easily store data in real time. The monitoring of daily activities constantly gives a lot of meaningful data related to heart rate, pulse, oxygen saturation, perspiration, geo-location, physical exercise, etc. These data help both the users and their healthcare professionals to better diagnose if there are some serious fluctuations in the vital physiological cycle of an individual. Such healthcare databases when compiled together can give a pictorial or graphical representation of the medical history as well as the present health state of a person along with special cases like chronic diseases and the body's reaction to a certain kind of medications. It can thus help physicians in better monitoring the medical situation in real time, leading to early diagnosis and prediction of disease and a better understanding of disease progression and effect of medication [5].

On the contrary, mental health is the state of mind where a person can cope with day-to-day normal stresses and find solutions to the problems faced by any individual. This is also considered as the "mental sanity" of an individual, where a person recognizes their potential to encounter a situation or circumstance before them. There are several factors that might hamper the mental health of an individual. This may include emotional trauma, corporate load, problems in personal lives, accidents, and senescence, which impact the mental health in a massive manner leading to conditions like psychosis, dementia, attention-deficit hyperactivity disorder (ADHD), posttraumatic stress disorder (PTSD), schizophrenia, and depression, the last of which is one of the most neglected mental disorders [6].

mHealth uses and works on the basic utility of mobile phones, which involves short messaging service (SMS) and voice clips from the voice calls, nexus of functions and applications like Bluetooth technology, general packet radio service (GPRS), global positioning systems (GPS), and third- and fourth-generation mobile telecommunications (3G and 4G systems). These applications when working in a collaborative manner produce a personalized health data of the user which can be easily stored and accessed with the users' consent. These data can be relayed or shared to the medical practitioners and healthcare professionals for the detailed analysis of one's medical condition [7].

Smartphones are one of the most common mobile devices used by the general population all around the globe. These smartphones are equipped with a number of sensors, as shown in Figure 8.2, which help in the collection of essential data constituting the healthcare database. A few sensors that are ubiquitously available in smartphones and wearable sensory devices are microphones, GPS sensors, gyroscopes, and accelerometers. With the assistance of such sensors, the calculation

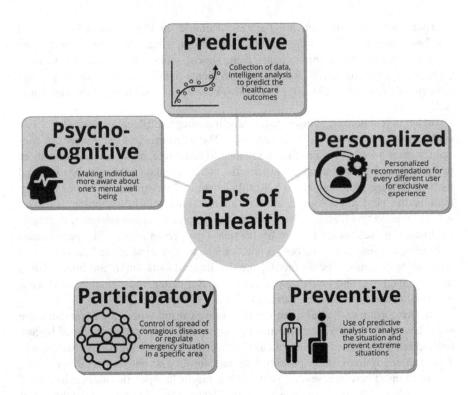

FIGURE 8.2 Five P's of mHealth.

and monitoring of sleeping pattern, pulse, heart rate, blood pressure, oxygen and hydration level, etc., can be enabled. They cumulatively give rise to the real-time data regarding the health information of the user. Any sudden shift from the normal pattern and medical condition will immediately send the "alert notification" to the user and the emergency contact information provided by the user, before the unnoticed symptoms transform into a serious cause of illness physically or mentally [7, 8].

Such advances in the applications of the healthcare system have given us some well-renowned health platforms in mHealth: Apple HealthKit, Google Fit, WHOOP, Shealth, and many more. These applications can be used by both iOS and android users. mHealth also has an advantage when it comes to data processing and storage. The smartphones and smart devices have cloud computing platforms such as Google cloud and Amazon Web Services; however, when big data processing is involved, Hadoop is more conveyable. These progressions are possible due to the advancement in Artificial Intelligence (AI), Machine Learning (ML), and natural language processing (NLP). These revolutionary changes make mHealth more compatible with the population [5, 8–11].

8.2   P'S OF mHEALTH

With the global rise in population, advancement in technology, and improvement in living standard, the demand for better healthcare facilities has increased drastically, which means that healthcare professionals are now overwhelmed with work in order to meet the public healthcare demand. In this scenario, mHealth offers exactly what is the need of the hour. By incorporating information technology (IT) along with medicines and healthcare, the channel between the medical professionals and the mHealth users has become more accessible, making the availability of medical care for the user as well as the healthcare professionals at convenience.

With the real-time analysis of this acquired data retrieved from smartphones, smart devices, and other sensory devices, mHealth can be regarded as a tool to narrow the gap between the mHealth user and healthcare system. The mHealth sensory system works on the principle of 5 potential P's (Predictive, Personalized, Preventive, Participatory, and Psychocognitive), by which it assesses the real-time data of an individual [1, 2, 12]

a. *Predictive mHealth*

The predictive nature of mHealth collects the user's data from their day-to-day life and analyzes the pattern in their everyday routine. Different sensors of smart devices fetch mHealth a large amount of information about the user, their habits, and day-to-day activities, which results in the accumulation of data in a healthcare database that includes a predictive nature of the user for a better understanding of their normal routine. For instance, if the user is a swimmer and he trains himself daily in the evening, the predictive nature of mHealth automatically gets used to his active vitals for a specific duration during the day by taking into account the geo-location, which means that the increased heart rate and the pulse recorded by the sensors is a normal routine for that individual during active hour; however, if a person leading a sedentary lifestyle happens to have a shooting heart rate and pulse at a specific time period, mHealth will regard it as an anomaly until it happens in a repetitive cycle.

b. *Personalized mHealth*

The personalized factor of mHealth focuses on treating every individual in a specific manner, which is totally customized according to the individual's own needs. Every person has a different demand for their body and mHealth provides that personalized monitoring by recommending the mHealth apps that suits the requirement of the individual according to the bio-psycho-social characteristics to provide non-redundant data. For instance, a user belonging to an athletic background will need mHealth apps with advanced accelerometer to record his efficiency to perform better; however, a person engaged with indoor work can achieve desired monitoring with the basic mHealth apps to track their daily heart rate, pulse, and caloric intake.

c. *Preventive mHealth*

The preventive factor aims at excluding the possibility of a serious ailment by monitoring every single detail of an individual's vitals and comparing it with the database formed so far to notice any significant difference or fluctuation which may indicate the proper consultation with the medical professionals for a thorough diagnosis. For instance, if the data achieved from the athlete shows the oxygen saturation of the individual in the range of 96–99, but a sudden drop in the oxygen saturation is recorded for consecutive days, the individual will be alerted to consult a doctor to get himself checked for any underlying reasons behind the situation. Thus, by closely monitoring one's physical activity in real time, many serious diseases or medically important conditions can be detected before it transforms into a chronic disease or a life-threatening situation.

d. *Participatory mHealth*

The participatory mHealth factor recognizes the individuals who are active participants toward their physical and mental health. Users who make active decisions for health will be given feedback and suggestions according to their demands and, on the contrary, the inactive users will be notified to push themselves to achieve their targeted goal. For instance, an individual who has routine checkups scheduled all by himself in his calendar, that person might not be sent multiple alert notifications for the doctor consultations. However, an individual who has not got himself under medical inspection for a significant period might be asked to visit the doctor to update their medical database, especially when a certain anomaly is detected in their routine according to the statistics achieved from the daily vitals database.

e. *Psychocognitive Strategy of mHealth*

The psychocognitive strategy of mHealth focuses on making an individual self-sufficient and more liable toward their health and well-being. This involves the individual actively with their self-statistics and vitals, propelling them toward making an active choice for choosing healthier and better lifestyle for their well-being. For instance, when an individual with a fondness for sugar discovers his increased blood sugar levels and heart rate at regular intervals, he will start cutting down his sugar intake in an active manner. This shift may or may not be drastic, but it will definitely be the initiation toward a healthier life choice.

8.3 CONSTITUENTS OF mHEALTH

mHealth functionality depends on the basic four pillars that enable it to perform, providing the users and the medical professionals the easiest and hassle-free experience without hindering their routine activities. The four essentials that constitute mHealth are mobile health sensory devices, telehealth (teleconsultation

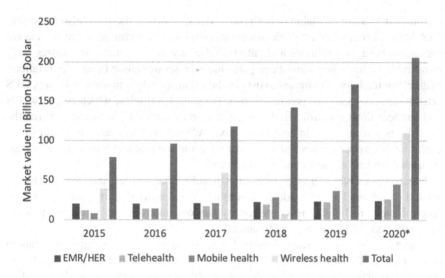

FIGURE 8.3 Constituents of mHealth.

or robo-consultation), electronic health record (EHR)/electronic medical record (EMR), and wireless health. The data processing of these constituents combined gives a better user-specific data that makes it more personalized toward physical and mental healthcare. Figure 8.3 shows the progressive growth of mHealth during recent years and suggests it as a promising tool for improved healthcare outcomes in the coming future.

8.3.1 THE SENSORY DEVICE OR MOBILE HEALTH

Sensory devices perform detection based on external stimuli from the user. They are readily available on the market in recent times. They are cost-effective as well as user-friendly. Every stratum of the population needs some kind of monitoring toward their health—it can be physical health or the mental health. The only thing that can monitor this in real time without intervening with the routine of the modern and busy user are the sensors which are available in smartphone and other mobile devices. These sensors may not be restricted just to smartphones or smart watches; even fitness trackers, implants, smart jewelry, head accessories, patches, clips, etc., can also be used to track minute to minute activities of an individual. When the smart sensor technology of smartphones is combined with the biosensor technology in smart wearable sensors, the accuracy of data is greater than that of data obtained from a professional, single sensory device.

Smartphones and smart watches are some of the most common sensory devices that are majorly preferred across the globe. They are equipped with multiple sensors that monitor multiple health statistics, as mentioned in the previous sections.

Certain sensors are available in both the devices; however, there are also some sensors that are exclusively available in a certain device. A few common sensors that are present in both smartphones and smartwatches are accelerometer (measures body movements to track steps and sleep patterns), gyroscope sensor (measures rotation), magnetometer sensor (compass assists in the accuracy while motion tracking), GPS sensor (detects location), pressure sensor (measures altitudes, which helps cyclists and runners during uphill climbing), hydration or humidity sensor (measures the intensity of a workout, skin health, and toxin release), and temperature sensor (measures the difference between skin temperature and the ambient temperature for better understanding of the intensity of exercise).

Smartphones have an edge over smartwatches due to their use, size, complexity and presence of various additionl sensors. The sensors that are present solely in smartphones are light sensors, proximity sensors, microphones, fingerprint scanners, cameras, and CMOS image scanners.

There are more serviceable sensors that are incorporated in a smartphone than in a smartwatch. There are certain sensors which are available and are more utilitarian for smart watches such as oximetric sensor, skin temperature sensor, skin conductance sensor, and heart rate monitor. Since a smartwatch is closer to the wrist and in direct contact with the skin and the pulse, the statistics obtained by these sensors are relatively more accurate.

8.3.2 TELEHEALTH

Telehealth refers to receiving healthcare services remotely via telecommunication or digital communication. It has become one of the most accepted health consultation techniques in recent years. Due to its 24/7 availability to the user and the emergency services it provides, it is possible for the user to record and consult on the telephone and avoid the hassles of traveling, except in case of emergency. Teleconsultation/robo-consultation help people with long term medical conditions as well as healthy individuals, especially those in remote and rural areas, in self-managing their health. The user needs to record their vitals and the teleconsultation techniques tell the self-care measures that should be implicated by the individual, except for such medical conditions when self-care precautions are not enough and the user has to reach out for expert medical help. It not only makes the user self-aware of their own conditions, but also makes them self-dependent for minor health ailments which can be treated by adaptation of certain healthy habits. Even in emergency situations when there is no expert doctor available, primary healthcare providers and nurses can seek necessary advice of the senior doctor through telephone or other digital devices and thus can help the patient stabilize and get relief from immediate stress until the patient reaches the hospital. The advancement in telehealth skyrocketed when the first shoulder surgery was performed in Avicenne Hospital (AP-HP) on December 5, 2017, with the virtual assistance. The surgery took place on the HoloPortal platform from TeraRecon and Microsoft developed HoloLens holographic computer. During the surgery, 3D patient's internal anatomical images could be modeled and visualized in real time by the expert doctor panel. The relevant data about the surgery could also be shared and stored. The HoloLens enabled the proper accurate imagery, assisting the doctor in placement of the prosthesis. This ground-breaking experience of the mixed reality connected the external world to the live medical surgery.

8.3.3 ELECTRONIC HEALTH RECORDS

EHR and EMR both go hand in hand to deal with the patients' data, which medical professionals can share for a better understanding of any ailment faced by an individual. The data that are stored in these databases are comparatively more secure than any other means of data storage software systems.

The difference between EHR and EMR is that EMR is the patient's chart that is retrieved from one consultation session only. It is generally present in the doctor's office and is not followed up if the patient changes the doctor. So, it is more likely for the doctor's reference. EHR on the other hand comprises a chart with details of several consultation sessions, test reports, and follow-up records, giving a more vivid picture about the patient's medical condition, especially of chronic diseases. If a patient has to refer to a different doctor for further treatment, this record can be further shared for a better understanding of the patient's medical history and medication that the patient undertook.

8.3.4 WIRELESS HEALTH

Wireless health is the integration of sensors or wireless technology into the trivial medicinal practice. In other words, any health record or data that is shared wirelessly, by means of Internet, comes under wireless health. The mobile devices and the sensory devices are supposed to monitor, store, and share the data with proper access to Internet connectivity. This will not only help ensure the proper storage of data but also eliminate any possibility of the redundancy of the data. Since all the data are collected and stored by cloud syncing, the real-time data become more accurate for the doctors to follow up.

8.4 SERVICES OFFERED BY mHEALTH

The acceptance of mHealth in society has been possible due to services it provides and advancement that is made in the existing technologies over the years. It has its ramifications in almost all the fields and has been developing personalized services for individual's personal requirements. The data collection and data analysis of distinct fields require a different and specific approach, which is managed by mHealth in a very simplified manner for the general population. Apart from this, the data collected from the users are stored according to the necessity of the target demand of the user. Some of the major services offered by mHealth that will be discussed in further sections are shown in Figure 8.4; these services include health, productivity, sports, geo-tracking, meditation, quantified self, sleep, brain training, period tracking, and nutrition.

FIGURE 8.4 Services offered by mHealth applications.

One of the most highlighted and prominent services provided by mHealth is healthcare. There are numerous mHealth apps, as shown in Figure 8.5, which are developed solely for tracking the health of an individual. A few popular mHealth apps for healthcare are Fitbit, Apple Heart Study, Google Fit, Samsung Health, BlueStar, and AliveCor's KardiaMobile. These apps aim towards monitoring the general health of an individual. Apart from this, the patients who have undergone major surgery or are suffering from any chronic disease are recorded in the database of these apps, which enables monitoring of medications and treatment. Patient rehabilitation costs are reduced dramatically as the mHealth app guides the patients or the user on self-care and self-maintenance unless professional medical help is the need of the hour. In addition, the patients can also be sent medication reminders and instructions for speedy recovery postsurgery. In this way, the patient stays under constant supervision because the statistics and the instructions are provided to the patient by the medical professionals through this mobile channel (Figure 8.12).

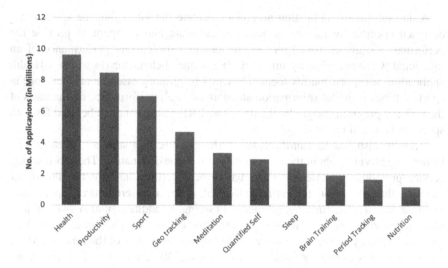

FIGURE 8.5   Graph showing people's interest in mHealth services.

In today's busy lifestyle and hectic schedule, mHealth applications also provide platforms that enhance the productivity of an individual. Due to industrialization, workforce has increased. The growing network also has its impact on a person's life. It has been seen that Internet and social media has a huge traffic, with the majority of the population being youth, who keep themselves busy on social media and the web. There are certain mHealth applications that keep a check on the hourly indulgence of an individual on the internet. The user can customize their needs accordingly. For instance, if the user feels that being active on social media is consuming a lot of time, the mHealth application responsible for productivity can help in customizing the daily hours of social media usage. In this manner, the user is obligated to get back to the immediate and pressing concerns for which he/she has customized the mHealth application settings. In a way, this also helps the user in self-restraining from excessive screen time and ultimately gets better at time management. Artificial Intelligence used in these applications enables them to be active in the background monitoring the activity of other applications used by the user and it sends an alert if the daily usage limit which is set by the user is crossed.

Sports has been one of the largest industries as people have started becoming more aware and cautious about their health. Not only the athletes but also all those who aspire to maintain good health and are inclined toward fitness need to keep a check on their vitals to track their performance and progress. mHealth applications provide them with a platform that is sports specific, which means these applications are specifically designed to monitor vigorous training and intense workouts.

A normal health application may just calculate the vitals, but the applications designed specifically for sports activities calculate and compare to provide the performance statistics based on the previous and the current performance of an individual. Cardiorespiratory fitness (CRF) is one such factor on which mHealth applications for sports mainly focus. The cardiorespiratory assessment when done in sports settings provides information about an athlete's performance on the basis of the training program chosen by the user. The CRF assessment can be used for both sports and clinical purposes [13].

mHealth also has its ramifications in the geo-tracking services. Geo-trackers inform an individual about their location as well as the destination. The geo-tracking service provided by mHealth is the base where certain data are calculated, for instance, the number of steps of an individual, distance covered during sports, and vigorous activity like running, hiking, and cycling. In addition, it also gives an idea about the distance to be covered if the user has set up a destination location. Taxi and food delivery services are some of the popular examples of the services where geo-tracking is extensively used in our daily lives. We are able to track the driver and the estimated time of arrival. Similarly, by use of such services, similar kinds of data could be provided by mHealth applications. The geo-tracking services are not just confined to taxis, food, and calculation of physical steps. It can also be helpful in the state of emergencies. Multiple user-friendly applications aim to provide safety services in the state of emergencies. These apps work on the principle of sharing location. If a user is in danger, they can send location-specific details to the police authorities as well as their emergency contacts for immediate help. This revolutionary advancement has made help readily available by immediate reinforcement from concerned authorities for appropriate action.

People with vivid interests are inclined toward different forms of health and fitness programs. One such program is meditation. It not only builds physical strength but also has a strong effect on mental strength, which is why people all around the world prefer meditation. Since it hardly requires any heavy weights and equipment, it is user-friendly with respect to time and space.

mHealth services not only focuses on being instrumental to the user in every possible means; it also extends its help to enable users to build self-care programs. These applications form meditation plans according to the person's need. Some people adopt meditation as a daily practice in their routine; however, others require it as a break from their daily stressful lives. These applications help in building programs according to the state of an individual's mind. It also guides people in the progressive format which assists them in understanding how to follow instructions.

In 2017, the mobile application "Calm" was awarded "2017 app of the year" by Apple. This was followed by apps "Aura" and "Headspace." These apps help people suffering from conditions like insomnia and daily stress to attain mental peace. For instance, playing of nature sounds in a relaxing tone helps the user sleep [14].

It has become difficult to have a regular sleep cycle in today's life, especially in metropolitan regions. The growing stress levels and work anxiety are the major reasons for such issues. Recent studies show that almost 30% of the population from all age groups are suffering from insomnia. Since their brain is loaded with multiple thoughts and stress, it is nearly impossible to get mental peace, which results in over-working of the brain [15].

Mental stress can not only lead to insomnia; it might also cause extra hours of sleep. It is clinically proven that a person suffering from mental stress may sleep for unusual extra hours to avoid the feeling of depression. To help prevent people falling into such vicious cycles, mHealth has brought applications that help people attain mental peace and have adequate amount of sleep in order to keep their brains healthy. A few examples of such applications are Calm, Headspace, Noisli, Sleep Cycle, etc. These applications are not necessarily used to encounter mentally stress-ful problems; they can also be used by people facing temporary issues like jet lag after intercontinental travel. In order to set up a proper circadian rhythm, people tend to require some extra help which can lead them toward a proper sleep cycle. These are some of the concerns addressed by the mHealth app with respect to the sleep cycle of an individual.

Extensive studies about the brain have led to the conclusion that with today's lifestyle and old age, people are more prone to suffering from memory disorders like dementia and Alzheimer's disease. These disorders are escalating at an alarm-ing rate each year and are affecting a large number of population. People who are entering old age are comparatively at a higher risk of suffering with these disorders than it was a few decades earlier. This happens due to weak cognitive function-ing of the brain. Increased stress levels in society have led people toward poor development of the cognitive functioning of their brains. The symptoms are often small when compared to the humongous effects of the poorly developed cognitive functioning of the brain.

mHealth introduces Assistive Technology (AT) which involves therapeutic train-ing of the brain, making it more efficient to conduct tasks and memorize the details in their daily lives. The application designed to assist in the cognitive training of the brain mainly focuses on (a) activities of daily living (ADL) based cognitive training, (b) monitoring, (c) dementia screening, (d) reminiscence and socialization, (e) track-ing, and (f) caregiver support.

With these measures, the application assists the individual with the daily monitor-ing of the cognitive fitness of the individual's brain. Constant training of the brain helps individuals to understand their brain health and to take actions accordingly with respect to their mental fitness [16].

Menstrual cycle trackers have been introduced in society in a recent couple of years, making the hormonal cycle tracking easier for millions of women all around the world. This might not be the most accurate way to track menstruation, but it has certainly proven to calculate the approximate time that different events take place in the menstruation cycle, including the ovulation period, bleeding phase, and the hormonal mood fluctuations experienced by women.

Since the menstrual cycle is considered an indication of women's health, it is important to ensure that reproductive health is also monitored like the overall health of an individual. Monitoring the menstrual health also tells a lot about a woman's mental health and the stress levels influencing the cycle. It helps women to be aware of their own fertility and also assists the couples who are planning to conceive. For such activities, it is important to track the ovulation period for the better understanding of their own body [17].

Furthermore, it helps in practicing contraception and maintaining an overall healthy reproductive system. This application enables the women toward self-care and symptom management. The behavioral change patterns, irregular menstruation cycle, and other symptoms can be some of the primary symptoms of chronic hormonal disorders like PCOD (polycystic ovarian disease) and PCOS (polycystic ovarian syndrome). These disorders not only affect the reproductive health of a woman but also affects physical health, which is marked by sudden weight gain or weight loss, mood swings, and discomfort [18].

Food nutrition can be tricky when it comes to consuming a balanced diet with all the macronutrients, micronutrients, vitamins, and minerals. We all know proteins, carbohydrates, fats, and essential elements are required by our body, but keeping track of them can be a tedious job. Since everybody is different with different body compositions, it is crucial to keep in mind that the nutrient requirements will also vary from individual to individual.

The mHealth services enable people to calculate the amount of nutrients required by the body against the nutrients actually consumed. The mHealth application related to monitoring the nutrition makes sure that the food consumed and the nutrients acquired by it by the body is according to the BMI (Body Mass Index) of an individual, which varies in males and females. When such calculations are put on the algorithms, it becomes easier for the user to keep track of everything consumed by the body. These applications can be set up in order to achieve the fitness goals that are desired by the user. The applications can be manually set to the desired plans like weight loss, muscle gain, and even maintaining a toned muscle. In this way, the mHealth applications provide services as a weight tracker, calculator, weight loss assistant, nutritionist, and food tracker [19]. Different subcategories of mHealth are shown in Figure 8.5.

8.5 PENETRATION OF mHEALTH INTO SOCIETY

Technology has become an integral part of our life. It is practically impossible to imagine our day-to-day life without a smartphone and smart devices. Integration of Artificial Intelligence and Machine Learning into smart sensing technology has led to the vivid range and increased potential of smart technology in our daily lives.

By the time you will be reading this book, there will be over 3.5 billion smartphone users (most of them coming from urban and suburban areas) in the world, which constitutes approximately 44.9% of the total world population; however, there are over 5.2 billion smart feature phones in the world, which constitutes over 66.8% of the world population who owns a mobile phone with over 10 billion active mobile connections, which accounts to approximately 128.9% of total world population, among which 5.23 billion are the unique mobile subscribers according to GSMA real-time intelligence survey and UN digital analyst estimate.

FIGURE 8.6 Distribution of mHealth in society.

These figures clearly state that the number of smartphone users has increased drastically, with over a 40% increase between 2016 and 2020. This increase could be the result of globalization and digitalization policies adopted by most of the countries across the world, reduced smartphone costs due to advancement in technology, and improved living standards. More and more people are connecting to the smart technology and a bigger proportion of youth and elderly population are getting inclined toward a healthy lifestyle.

Penetration of smartphone, smart devices, and other mobile devices is not same in every corner of the globe. For instance, China has the maximum number of smartphone users (due to its population). However, China's smart device penetration rate is approximately 60% when, on the contrary, Switzerland has the lowest number of smartphone devices in a country but the penetration of devices is as high as 73%. This is due to high living standards, awareness about the features, and better affordability.

The United Kingdom has the highest smartphone penetration with about 83% of population, i.e., 55.5 million people, having at least one smart device, whereas Nigeria has the lowest penetration rate of about 14.9% or 30 million users, as shown in Figure 8.6, reflecting promising growth of mHealth in upcoming years.

8.6 DISTRIBUTION OF SMART DEVICES

The sale of smart devices has been increasing with the addition of new technologies into smart devices. People do not restrict themselves to the usage of smartphones and smart watches. Smart homes have also become one of the trendsetters in using smart devices and making our daily work to our convenience, where all the commands can be accessed with just the voice activation of an individual. The smart STB is one of the applications which allows user to access "anything on anything." This means that this application can be installed on any device like smart TV, smartphones, or computers where it allows the user to open their own portal to the world of IPTV. This also takes care of the wireless and remote-less access to these services, provided that there is a stable Internet connection.

Virtual reality (VR) is another smart device that is often used for recreational activities. It is a simulated experience that gives a life-like experience that may or may not be related to the actual world. It can serve various purposes like educational purposes. The entertainment platform has been the most popular one which enables an individual to play videogames along with having an experience of being in the game. Virtual reality also has its contribution to the educational platform where it provides certain beneficial training like military training and medical training. The virtual reality enables the user to place themselves in a scenario which allows them to picture themselves in the training situations, giving them a vivid knowledge comparative to just theoretical knowledge. Furthermore, with mixed technology and augmented reality, they can also be referred to as XR, which is the abbreviation of extended reality. The virtual reality ramifications into text-based network VR is often termed as cyberspace and the immersive VR. The only difference between these two is that in immersive VR, when an individual moves or tilts their head, the view of the individual also changes. However, cyberspace is more concerned with calibrating the distance.

The other most popular smart device that is available on the market is the omni-directional (360 degrees) camera. It is supposed to capture approximately a sphere from its front view on a horizontal plane. The concept of omnidirectional cameras arose from the pictures that needed wide visual coverage like panoramic photography. These cameras are also used in scientific labs in the field of robotics, due to its wide-angle visual coverage.

Smart TV, on the other hand, has been another advancement in smart devices. It is often known as connected TV (CTV). It works on the principle of integration of the normal set-top box with the Internet connectivity along with the interactive Web 2.0 features. This makes the TV accessible to the users through the Internet so that they can access and stream videos and music even on their television. The smart TV, besides performing the traditional tasks of broadcasting media, can also provide the connectivity needed to stream Internet content and home networking access.

The number of wearable sensor devices all over the world has been increasing with time, as seen in Figure 8.7. Smartphones and smart watches are some of the common wearable smart devices that are available with the maximum population. Between 2015 and 2020, an upward trend in the usage of wearable smart devices has been observed. These devices have also been cost-effective and easily accessible, which means that people are more prone to buying them. Wearable devices have been trending in different regions of the world in the past five years. A combination

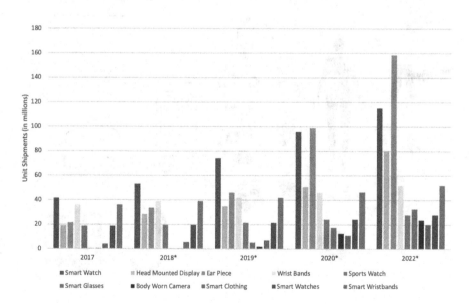

FIGURE 8.7 Global interest of people towards mHealth smart devices.

of different sensors from different mHealth devices could lead to reliable data and productive outcomes when shared using technology, could result into a mHealth network where user's information could be captured via different sensors, could be stored in real time in the portable smart device (smartphones usually), and could also be permanently stored in a medical database. This database could be accessed by physicians, healthcare providers, emergency services, and users themselves when necessary, as shown in Figure 8.8.

The North American region has been the highest consumer of wearable smart devices. In 2015, the number of connected wearable devices was approximately 36.65 million, which escalated to 217 million in 2017. It was followed by the Asia-Pacific region, which estimated around 30.4 million wearable devices in 2015, and 99.8 million and 155 million devices in 2016 and 2017, respectively, as shown in Figure 8.6b.

This rising pattern was also observed in the regions like Western Europe, Central and Eastern Europe, Middle East, and Africa and Latin America. In 2015 and 2016, the Asia-Pacific region accepted the wearable smart devices with open arms, which resulted in a high number of sales in such devices—30.4 million devices in 2015 and

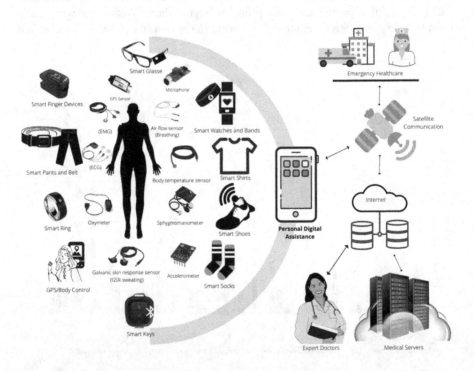

FIGURE 8.8 mHealth network architecture.

99.8 million devices in 2016. This statistical growth was followed in the regions like Western Europe, Middle East, and Africa and Latin America.

8.7   REASONS BEHIND SUCCESS AND FAILURES OF mHEALTH

mHealth has been a fast growing industry, providing services all across the globe with its new invention each day. It strives toward making the lives of the people more reliable toward themselves and stimulates the discipline and self-care required to keep oneself in a healthy state of mind and body. With the rising empire of mHealth, it has had numerous milestones in the journey with both success and failures. Where the industry of mHealth aims for higher goals after every successful invention and technological growth, it has also been careful about the failures and the reasons behind those failures. The setbacks help the mHealth industry to know their scope of growth. In this section, we will look into various reasons behind the success and failures of mHealth as an industry.

For an industry like mHealth to be successful, there are three factors that are highly essential: access, quality, and cost-containment. The acceptance of mHealth by society has mainly taken place due to these pillars of mHealth, which define the innovation's success in the society.

The accessibility of the mHealth devices makes it user-friendly. The user is able to easily understand the working of the device: how to operate and read the statistics and the steps to be taken with respect to the instructions provided by the device. The accessibility of the device is followed by the quality of the device. A technical device like mHealth device has to be built with good quality products as it has to monitor the day-to-day life activity in real time, which indicates that the device will be in constant use. The probability of wear and tear should be as low as possible, which will add to its usage life. Lastly, cost-containment plays a vital role in the triumph of the industry. Since these devices are so technologically advanced and user-friendly, they should also be cost-effective for the population to actually afford it and use it in their daily lives. It should not be merely a luxury device, rather an assistance to everyone.

The increasing demographic population and the increased number of elderly people put the industry in the position to produce more and more new innovative mHealth devices to assist people all around the world. However, in recent years, vast amounts of mHealth and eHealth interventions have failed in clinical implementations. All the industries around the globe have been developing, all incorporating mHealth in almost all the sectors. Due to this, with increasing industrialization, the demand for new innovation and technologies has been more than ever. This results in more and more failed prototypes of the inventions and the breach in mHealth promise toward providing good quality and services. There is still a huge stratum of population that finds the cost of mHealth devices expensive to be incorporated into their daily lives. Considering these setbacks, the mHealth industry has been working to overcome these odds [20]. The graph in Figure 8.9 shows a rough sketch about the reasons behind lagging of mHealth despite being a promising technology.

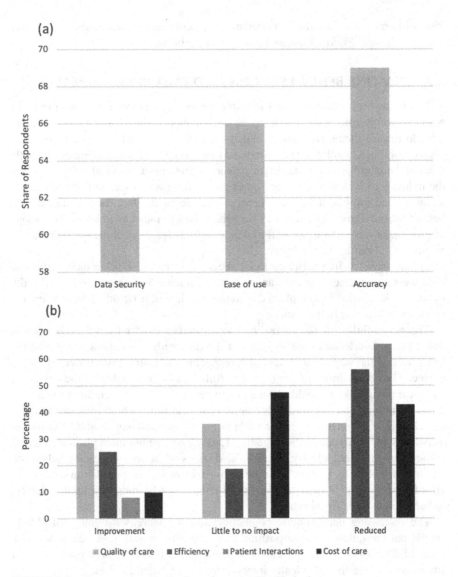

FIGURE 8.9 Acceptance and rejection of smart mHealth devices.

8.8 mHEALTH AND SISTER TECHNOLOGIES

The sister technology of mHealth includes not only the technologies that are available on our smartphones, smart watches, and wearables, but also the devices that are designed to monitor health statistics and data on a mobile platform. Certain devices may not be completely travel-friendly but they work on the principle of mHealth, which is monitoring health data for an individual. Unlike smart devices, these devices are specifically designed to monitor a specific variable of health. In this section, we will talk about the sister technologies of mHealth like sphygmomanometer, pulse oximeter, body temperature sensor, electromyography sensor (EMG), electrocardiogram sensor (ECG), airflow sensor, accelerometer, galvanic skin response sensor (GSR-sweating) [7].

Blood pressure monitor or sphygmomanometer is the device which is used to monitor blood pressure. It comprises an inflatable cuff which works on the artery by creating controlled pressure while collapsing and releasing pressure. The blood pressure in the artery is calculated by the mercury which indicates the systolic and the diastolic pressure. The manual sphygmomanometer is generally coupled with a stethoscope in order to calculate the blood pressure. There are also many automated sphygmomanometers available on the market, which show the readings in the digital format.

The pulse oximeter is a device used for clinical use and is user-friendly. The device is non-invasive in nature and calculates the blood oxygen saturation levels in the artery. The readings that are obtained from it are generally peripheral oxygen saturation. The sensor part of the device is placed on the earlobes or the fingertips, provided that the nails are not coated with any nail enamel paint for the sensor to provide an accurate reading. The device works by sending two wavelengths of light passing through the body part to the photodetector. The changing absorbance of the light is measured, which gives the absorbance due to pulsatile arterial blood.

As the name suggests, the body temperature sensor is used to measure the temperature of the body. It is also known as the thermometer. The thermometer has two parts. One is the temperature sensor, which is used to measure the temperature of the body, and the other is the device or a scale that can convert the reading into numeric form, which is easily accessible and understood by the user. The temperature sensor in the glass sensor is the bulb of the mercury; however, in the infrared sensor, it is the polymeric sensor. Similarly, in glass thermometers, the readings can be seen on the visible scale and in infrared thermometers, it is visible on the digital readouts.

Electromyography sensor (EMG) is another technology which can be used to calculate health statistics with the help of sensors. These sensors are used in the device electromyograph and the record is known as electromyogram. It is used to evaluate the electric potential that is produced by the skeletal cells. These cells are generally electrically or neurologically activated. With the help of this device, physical abnormalities or anomalies can be detected. In addition, EMG can also be used in the computer gestures to understand the human and computer interactions.

An ECG or the electrocardiograph is the device that works on the principle of electrical changes. The electrodes present in the device can detect even small significant electrical changes that are the result of the polarization and the repolarization of the cardiac muscles with each heartbeat. If there is a cardiac abnormality present in an individual, it will be recorded on the electrocardiogram, as the electric changes will differ from the normal pattern of the ECG.

An accelerometer is a sensor that senses the acceleration of a body. With the help of this device, an individual can calculate their acceleration rate with respect to their rest frame. Fitness enthusiasts can use this device to calculate their acceleration and velocity while training and keeping track of their daily fitness goals. Accelerometer sensors can be installed in multiple devices like smartphones, tablets, and smart watches.

Galvanic skin response (GSR) sensors work on the ectodermal activity and conductance. It can be used to measure the sweating and perspiration of an individual. Hence, this sensor can be used in the calculation of the physical health and the activity done by the user. It works on the electrical characteristics of the skin allowing the sensor to measure the reading consequential to the impulses.

Collectively, these microsensors inbuilt in smartphone and other smart devices monitor changes in the body's physiology and keep a track via mobile application or standard portable device. This data can be stored in the healthcare server and cloud storage and can be accessed anywhere using Internet. This could help in timely detection, better monitoring, and quick access to emergency healthcare as shown in Figure 8.10.

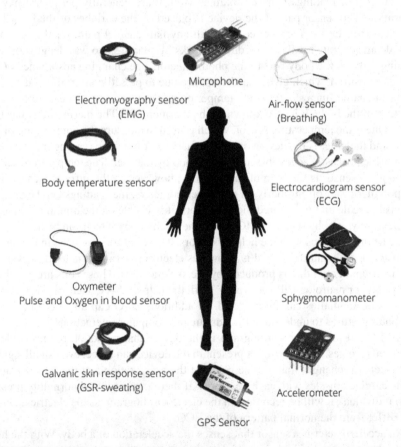

FIGURE 8.10   Sensors for mHealth smart devices.

8.9 LIMITATIONS AND REGULATIONS

The mHealth platform makes the electronic health medium available to people anywhere and everywhere. It mainly functions on the availability of Internet connectivity and database systems. To manage such intensive data, it is also important to keep in my mind that the data stored can always be misled and be compromised [21, 22]. In order to ensure that the confidentiality of the data is always safe and secured, several limitations, legislations, and regulations have been laid down, as shown in Figure 8.11.

8.9.1 PRIVACY POLICY AND TERMS AND CONDITIONS

The privacy policy and the terms and conditions should be easily accessible to the user. It should be documented in simple and plain language which can be understood by the user. The section of "terms and conditions" should contain a link or a logo so that it is easily visible to the user (Figure 8.12).

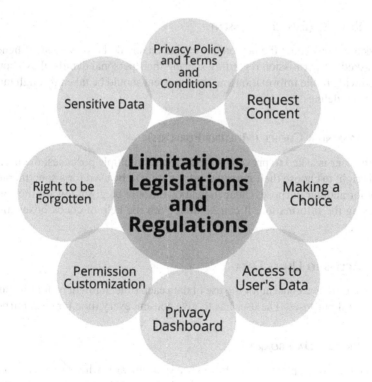

FIGURE 8.11 Legislations of mHealth.

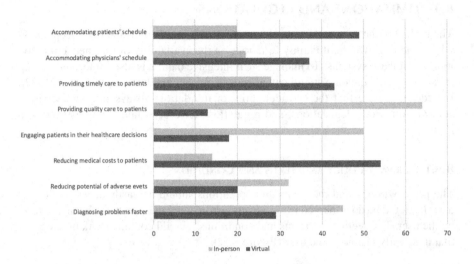

FIGURE 8.12   Face to face vs virtual acceptance of mHealth.

8.9.2   Request (Explicit) Consent

The specifications about the personal information should be very clear. Whenever a user is asked for permission regarding sharing their personal details, they should be provided with all the information and their consent should be taken through targeted and clear guidelines.

8.9.3   Making a Choice (Multiple Purposes)

When the user is asked to provide information for multiple purposes, the user must have the right to choose their personal information to be used for a specific purpose and not for another purpose. Clear indications should be given toward the specificity of using the information. It can be done with the help of check boxes and tick boxes.

8.9.4   Access to User's Data

The user has to give consent for the use of data each time. It might be for one purpose or for several purposes. The user has to give consent every time for each purpose.

8.9.5   Privacy Dashboard

The user should be provided with a privacy dashboard, where they can alter the usage of their privacy settings. Clear instructions should be provided stating the consequences of changing the settings and confirmation from the user should be asked before making any changes.

8.9.6 PERMISSION CUSTOMIZATION

All the permissions should be visible to the users. The users should also have the right to edit these permissions. The applications should be very descriptive with the permissions and the data access that will be granted.

8.9.7 THE RIGHT TO BE FORGOTTEN

The user should be able to edit the setting of their privacy and if needed to delete the data sharing options of certain data.

8.9.8 SENSITIVE DATA

The sensitive data, like biometric data, should be included in the special categories. The applications should be very particular about the user's consent if it requires data on such a personal category.

8.10 PROMISES AND CHALLENGES OF mHEALTH

mHealth is the provision for healthcare by which information is shared and stored through mobile technologies and personal digital assistants (PDAs). With the help of wearable sensors and smart devices, these services can reach people to influence them toward a better lifestyle and a better version of themselves. This has changed the society and the mindset of people toward healthcare in a drastic manner. It has revolutionized the conceptualization of the orthodox methods of healthcare, though it is still not replaced as in person consultation and treatment will always be an important parameter of healthcare. Despite this positive and promising nature of mHealth, there are also various challenges faced by mHealth. In this section, we will be focusing on the promises and the challenges faced by mHealth [23].

One of the major reasons behind mHealth's success is the promises it offers. Since mHealth works on the availability of the Internet, it makes sure that the data could be transferred to the clinicians and the practitioners in time, as seen in Figure 8.8. The in time monitoring and check of daily symptoms promise to track symptoms related to drug intake or even certain personalized allergies or medical conditions. Prediction of risk assessment is achievable with the combined data of the user with the help of Artificial Intelligence and other technologies. The passive data collection service provided by mHealth sets a benchmark for the positive development of technological growth [24].

Integration of Artificial Intelligence and Machine Learning in mHealth apps along with advancements in sensor technology has led to immense potential of mHealth technology. Several other factors contributed in this regard: acceptance of mHealth apps and generated data by medical practitioners and doctors, high level of digitalization in hospital and healthcare systems (such as telemedicine, teleconsultation, etc.), increased market size for smart devices, access to developers, political support and increase in available government funds to support the digital healthcare, increase in external collaborative support, and willingness of patients to pay for smart healthcare due to increased living standards, and awareness regarding healthcare, as shown in Figure 8.13a–c.

Analysis of voices, sleep-wake cycle, and active hours on social media helps in reading the behavioral pattern of the individual, which remarkably enables the assessment of the significant shift resulting in the precautionary alert to the user. With the advancement of technology and reduction in the cost of smart gadgets and biosensors, there is at our disposal a way to penetrate deep into the population beyond the socio-economic barriers. A careful analysis of real-time sensory data from both smartphones and sensory devices could prove to be just the tool needed to cope with these ever-increasing mental health issues.

During this ongoing pandemic, the world has shifted to digital platforms. The high rate of pathogenicity of virus has affected the medical system and led to shift of non-emergency cases to teleconsultation and remote consultation which created a boom in mHealth app downloads in different countries, as seen in Figure 8.13d. According to WHO, one out of four individuals is suffering from a mental or a physical ailment. mHealth provides us the opportunity to respect the rules regarding social distancing and making the individual self-aware by promoting patient empowerment. Apart from this, mHealth also makes the communication channel between the user and the clinician more transparent, which is both elaborative and

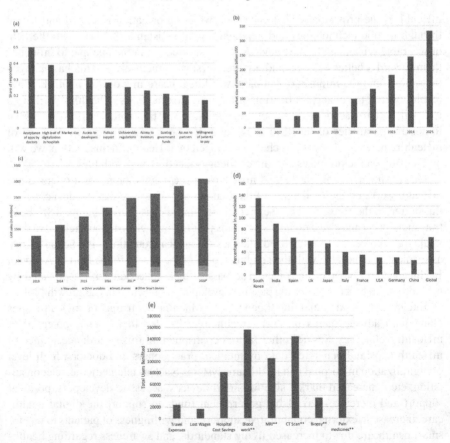

FIGURE 8.13 Factors behind acceptance of mHealth.

easily understood by the clinicians or medical practitioners and the users themselves. It provides user flexibility toward health with their schedule, while also being cost-effective (Figure 8.13e).

On the flip side, mHealth also faces multiple challenges. mHealth innovations require a massive amount of research to reduce the chances of incompetent validation and poor efficacy [25]. Since mHealth is still a new technology comparative to the one that already exists (evidence-based medicine), the medical practitioners and the general public are still coming to terms with accepting this and incorporating it as a part of their daily lives.

The mHealth industry is also concerned with ethical issues, security issues, as well as privacy issues for data sharing. It still has limited systematic integration and there is a huge gap between patient and the platform. Since it has not fully acquired as healthcare status, mHealth platforms are not covered under state or private insurances and are non-reimbursed. Moreover, these are a few controversial issues that have to be kept in mind while dealing with new technologies. The data consent is a sensitive topic and the handling of such data requires a lot of security and precautions. Since it is based on an individual's personal life and health statistics, any breach in the database can lead to severe repercussions. It is also important to take care of the flow of information between the user and the clinicians, so daily logging of information is mandatory (Figure 8.14).

FIGURE 8.14 Barriers to mHealth services.

REFERENCES

1. Saxena, M., A. Deo, and A. Saxena. *mHealth for Mental Health*. in International Conference on Innovative Computing and Communications. 2020. Springer.
2. Saxena, M. and A. Saxena. Evolution of mHealth Eco-System: A Step Towards Personalized Medicine. in International Conference on Innovative Computing and Communications. 2020. Springer.
3. Who, D.-G., *Report of the Review Committee on the Functioning of the International Health Regulations (2005) in Relation to Pandemic (H1N1) 2009*. Sixty-fourth World Health Assembly: World Health Organization, 2011, pp. 49–50.
4. Nilsen, W., et al., Advancing the science of mHealth. *Journal of Health Communication*, 2012, **17**(supl): 5–10.
5. Saxena, M., M. Arora, and A. Saxena, Advancements in systems medicine using big data analytics. *International Journal of Information Systems & Management Science*, 2018, **1**(2), pp. 3.
6. Iyawa, G.E., et al., mHealth as tools for development in mental health, in *Impacts of Information Technology on Patient Care and Empowerment*. 2020, IGI Global. Pp. 58–80.
7. Cao, Z. Mobile phone GPS and sensor technology in college students' extracurricular exercises, in International Conference on Machine Learning and Big Data Analytics for IoT Security and Privacy. 2020. Springer.
8. Hermes, S., et al., The digital transformation of the healthcare industry: Exploring the rise of emerging platform ecosystems and their influence on the role of patients. *Business Research*, 2020, 13, pp. 1–37, doi.org/10.1007/s40685-020-00125-x.
9. Saxena, M., O. Singh, and A. Saxena, *Big Data and Personalized Medicine for Oncology*, in *2019* 6th International Conference on Computing for Sustainable Global Development (INDIACom). 2019. IEEE, pid 1352.
10. Agarwal, A. and A. Saxena. Analysis of machine learning algorithms and obtaining highest accuracy for prediction of diabetes in Women, in *2019* 6th International Conference on Computing for Sustainable Global Development (INDIACom). 2019. IEEE.
11. Agarwal, A. and A. Saxena. Comparing Machine Learning Algorithms to Predict Diabetes in Women and Visualize Factors Affecting It the Most—A Step Toward Better Health Care for Women, in International Conference on Innovative Computing and Communications. 2020. Springer.
12. Saxena, M. and A. Saxena, Personalized medicine: a bio-medicine derived from big data analytics. *Space*. **22**: 23.
13. Muntaner-Mas, A., et al., A systematic review of fitness apps and their potential clinical and sports utility for objective and remote assessment of cardiorespiratory fitness. Sports Medicine, 2019, **49**(4): 587–600.
14. Huberty, J., et al., Efficacy of the mindfulness meditation mobile app "calm" to reduce stress among college students: Randomized controlled trial. *JMIR Mhealth Uhealth*, 2019, **7**(6): e14273.
15. Longyear, R.L. and K. Kushlev, Can Mental Health Apps Be Effective for Depression, Anxiety, and Stress During a Pandemic? 2020.
16. Yousaf, K., et al., A comprehensive study of mobile-health based assistive technology for the healthcare of dementia and Alzheimer's disease (AD). *Health Care Management Science*, 2020, 23: 287–309. https://doi.org/10.1007/s10729-019-09486-0.
17. Murthy, P. and M. Naji, Role of digital health, mHealth, and low-cost technologies in advancing universal health coverage in emerging economies, in *Technology and Global Public Health*. 2020, Springer. pp. 31–46.

18. Karasneh, R.A., et al., Smartphone applications for period tracking: Rating and behavioral change among women users. *Obstetrics and Gynecology International*, 2020, 2, 1–9.

19. Franco, R.Z., et al., Popular nutrition-related mobile apps: a feature assessment. *JMIR mHealth and uHealth*, 2016, **4**(3): e85.

20. Granja, C., W. Janssen, and M.A. Johansen, Factors determining the success and failure of eHealth interventions: systematic review of the literature. *Journal of Medical Internet Research*, 2018, **20**(5): e10235.

21. Muchagata, J. and A. Ferreira. Translating GDPR into the mHealth practice, in *2018 International Carnahan Conference on Security Technology (ICCST)*. 2018. IEEE.

22. da Silva, P.E.F., et al., Development of a software for mobile devices designed to help with the management of individuals with neglected tropical diseases. *Research on Biomedical Engineering*, 2020, 36: 1–11, doi.org/10.1007/s42600-020-00090-8.

23. Baldauf, M., P. Fröehlich, and R. Endl. Trust me, I'ma doctor–user perceptions of AI-Driven apps for mobile health diagnosis, in 19th International Conference on Mobile and Ubiquitous Multimedia. 2020.

24. Goodman, R., L. Tip, and K. Cavanagh, There's an app for that: Context, assumptions, possibilities and potential pitfalls in the use of digital technologies to address refugee mental health. *Journal of Refugee Studies*, 2020, doi.org/10.1093/jrs/feaa082.

25. Brault, N., Saxena, M. For a critical appraisal of artificial intelligence in healthcare: The problem of bias in mHealth. *J Eval Clin Pract*. 2020 Dec 23. doi: 10.1111/jep.13528. Epub ahead of print. PMID: 33369050.

26. Available at: www.statistica.com.

9 Artificial Intelligence and Deep Learning for Medical Diagnosis and Treatment

Jai Mehta

CONTENTS

9.1 INTRODUCTION

Machines have been surrounding our lives since past century. Since the development of light bulb and electricity in 1878 by Edison, the whole system has been controlled by machines. So, whether it is multiple power generators supplying to the grid to bulbs operated by motion sensors, the machines are getting smarter and smarter. However, all these activities required a level of human interference as most of the machine's decisions were purely based on logic fed into it and not on its ability to think independently. Therefore, the capabilities of these machines were restricted by the capacity of the developers. As times changed, the big idea of making machines intelligent just like humans capable of making decisions resulted in lots of sci-fi movies and less of real applications. But as times further changed, we faced tougher problems, which led to the quest for intelligent machines. This quest resulted in the discovery of Artificial Intelligence, and it was formally introduced as an academic discipline in 1955 (Crevier 1993).

A large number of algorithms come under the umbrella of Artificial Intelligence and boast of making smart decisions; however, in essence they are limited by the training data. While mathematicians and statisticians were developing powerful models to predict outcomes using mathematical modeling, experts in computer science got interested in how the human brain learns and in building machines that can simulate the same learning processes. This led to some of the breakthrough algorithms, and leading among them is deep learning.

9.2   DEEP LEARNING

Deep learning is inspired by how the human brain learns from examples and stores information in the series of interconnected neurons. Let us first try to understand the human brain. Our whole body is interconnected with neurons, which collect signals and transfer to the interconnecting neurons through synapses. The information is finally processed in the brain. For most time it is learning through the incoming signals and when needed, it makes its decision; for example, when we touch hot thing, we remove our hand. Figure 9.1a symbolizes how neurons collect instructions from the environment and transmit it to the next neuron. Figure 9.1b depicts the role of neurotransmitters in transferring information.

This idea was initially incorporated in a perceptron model, which is a single-layer neural network, followed by backpropagation, and recently adapted as deep learning. The fast adaptation to deep learning has been primarily driven by high computational resources and availability of open-source platforms such as TensorFlow, PyTorch, and CNTK.

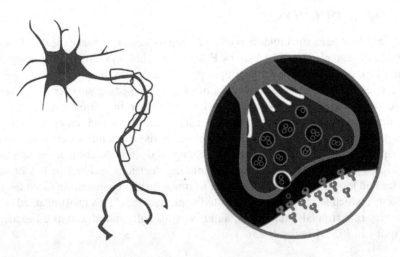

FIGURE 9.1   Communication of neurons in human brain.

9.3 DEEP LEARNING ARCHITECTURE

Deep learning architecture primarily consists of interconnected neurons. The number of input neurons and output neurons is decided on the type of problem we are trying to solve. In between the input and output neurons are the hidden neurons; the number of layers and the number of neurons in each layer vary based on the complexity of data. Each interconnection holds a weight, which at the start of training is assigned a random weight but the weight keep changing till the desired outcome is obtained.

9.4 TYPES OF DEEP LEARNING ALGORITHMS

Deep learning models are typical neurons connected in an architecture, by which predictions can be made. Different architecture and training methodologies have been developed to suit a wide range of applications. Here we discuss two of the common deep learning models:

1) **Feedforward Neural Networks (FNN):** One of the oldest training methodologies, FFN consists of fully interconnected neurons at each layer (Figure 9.2). The abstraction is captured in the interconnection between the hidden neurons. The model is trained with known outcomes and the error generated is backpropagated to modify the interconnecting weights using a stochastic gradient descent algorithm. The process of training is continued till the error sum of squares reaches the desired level. Multiple parameters need to be adjusted to achieve the desired learning and generalization levels.

2) **Convolutional Neural Networks (CNN):** Convolution neural networks are specialized type of deep learning networks and have a convolution layer along with other hidden layers (Figure 9.3). The convolution network is highly efficient in pattern recognition and therefore has been immensely

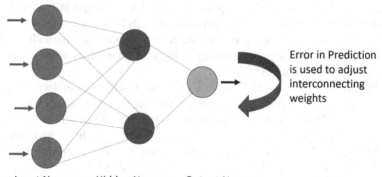

Input Neurons   Hidden Neurons   Output Neurons

FIGURE 9.2 This diagram represents the errors in prediction is used to adjust interconnecting weights.

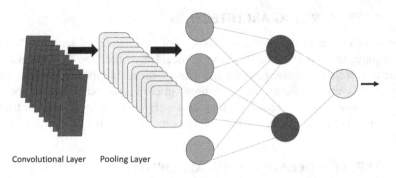

Convolutional Layer   Pooling Layer

FIGURE 9.3   Illustration of convolutional layer.

popular in making predictions from the image. This has led to huge popularity in medical diagnostics and has potential to be used for automated scanning of X-rays, CT scans, biopsy, mammograms, and other areas of clinical diagnostics.

9.5   DEEP LEARNING LIBRARIES

1) **TensorFlow:** TensorFlow developed by Google is the most widely used library for commercial application of deep learning algorithms. TensorFlow runs on Python environment and provides all the tools and techniques for fast development and deployment of deep learning models. There is a library for web and mobile development applications. For more details, visit https://www.tensorflow.org/. COLAB is a web-based environment for new learners and includes all the needed libraries for quick learning and development of deep learning models. For getting started, visit https://colab.research.google.com

2) **Microsoft Cognitive Toolkit (CNTK):** CNTK, developed by Microsoft, incorporates most of the deep learning models. It is specially suited for developers working on .NET environment. CNTK libraries are available in C#, C++, and Python and therefore provide opportunity for wider range of software developers. For more details, visit https://docs.microsoft.com/en-us/cognitive-toolkit/

3) **PyTorch:** PyTorch is a Python library for easy development of deep learning models. It is more popular in research environment, given its quick learning cycle and flexibility in development of models. It is ideally suited for developers already working on Python. For more details, visit https://pytorch.org

4) **MXNET:** MXNET from Apache foundation is yet another very popular deep learning library for quick development and deployment of deep learning models. The advantage of using MXNET is in its APIs for various other languages, making it a perfect solution for integrated development and deployment. For more details, visit https://mxnet.apache.org/

5) **Keras:** Keras is a wrapper for various deep learning libraries. Keras is extremely easy to learn and a new user can get started in minutes. It runs on top of TensorFlow and other deep learning libraries. The syntax is very simple and easy to learn and implement. Keras library is developed in Python, so some knowledge of Python is necessary. More details are available at https://keras.io.

9.6 APPLICATION TO MEDICAL DIAGNOSIS AND TREATMENT

Times are changing fast and a large array of diagnostics are being used for life-threatening and chronic conditions. For many conditions, the indicators may not be so subtle, and doctors may miss out the chance for early diagnosis. In genomics, the data might be too large to make a sense of it without use of complex algorithms. Deep learning provides an opportunity to complement the traditional diagnostic methods by providing early and accurate detection, which may often be missed by the doctors. Deep learning can find its way in most of the life-threatening conditions in hospitals and has been successfully implemented in direct to consumer diagnostics. Some of the areas with high adoptability of deep learning is discussed below.

9.6.1 IMAGING

X-ray, CT scans, MRI, and similar technologies have become a routine part of everyday diagnostics. A radiologist examines the images and inference is used to made diagnosis. Most hospitals struggle to have sufficient radiologists to examine the huge number of images. This leads to delayed diagnosis and treatment. Besides, sometimes the human brain can miss on early diagnosis of cancer or other life-threatening conditions, where early intervention can save lives. Deep learning models can work along the radiologist, acting as a second opinion, and reduce misdiagnosis. Most hospitals also face backlogs, sometimes up to months, especially if the diagnosis by the doctors is not flagged as urgent. Deep learning can examine the images as it is generated and can prioritize cases where it is seen something of concern (Selvikvåg Lundervold and Lundervold, 2019).

Developed countries have resorted to routine mammography for early detection of breast cancer. Such initiatives have been very effective in catching the disease before it has spread. However, it adds huge burden on the radiologist. The likelihood of radiologist to miss on early symptoms is much higher than when the patients come with symptoms. Machines if well trained can outperform radiologist in detecting breast cancer on routine mammography. Besides, it can even risk access the potential of development of breast cancer in future and those patients can go for more frequent mammography (Abdelhafiz et al., 2019).

One in five people in the Western world gets cancer at some point in their life. Early detection is often missed, and time is also lost in going through the GP and oncologist. Often in the busy schedule, people tend to ignore visiting doctors until it is too late. Skin Vision is a company from Amsterdam that has used deep learning and has developed a mobile app which can tell if a skin condition is a cancer, thereby helping people reach out to oncologist earlier than normal. Skin Vision has a sensitivity of 95% in detecting most common types of skin cancer. It also provides opportunity to track skin spots over time if a spot shows indication of being precancerous. Skin Vision is certified medical service and provide low cost home diagnostic solutions (de Carvalho et al., 2019).

Deep learning has the potential for routine screening of tuberculosis where the disease load is very high. It is particularly important in underdeveloped and developing countries, where qualified radiologists are at shortage. Deep learning trained on known tuberculosis X-ray can identify tuberculosis at an early stage. Early stage identification is critical for controlling damage to the lungs. Pasa et al. (2019) used convolution neural network to accurately diagnose tuberculosis; this neural network has a potential of large-scale screening of tuberculosis patients.

9.6.2 GENOMICS

Genomics is a potential area where deep learning can benefit in making intelligent decisions. The data have a very high dimension, making it a perfect problem to be solved using deep learning. However, deep learning models rely on thousands or maybe millions of data points, there are issues in getting such huge amount of data. With the huge genomic datasets come the problem of computing infrastructure. Deep learning is being under study by various groups, and with many research papers and data analysis library have been developed, it must find its applications in hospitals or diagnostic settings. Some of the developments of deep learning in genomics are discussed below.

Sakellaropoulo et al. (2019) used the drug resistance profile from 1000 cell lines to develop a deep learning algorithm to predict chemotherapeutic drug resistance in clinical samples. The study involved multiple mathematical models to develop prediction models and the deep learning models outperformed other models. Since the data was limited and originally developed from a cell line, there is a long way for it to be of clinical importance. However, the study demonstrated that deep learning has the capability to be explored in clinical settings.

Deepchrome (www. deepchrome.org) is a suite of deep learning tools for myriad applications of deep learning networks toward functional genomics. It consists of EpiGenome-DeepDiff, Genome-DeepMotif, Genome-gkmStringKernal, Protein-metaDeep, Protein-MustCNN, and BioText-SemiDeep, each with extensive application of deep learning toward functional prediction from genomics datasets.

DeepVariant (Poplin et al., 2018) is a variant caller for NGS data and it uses convolutional network to accurately identify genomic variation. Accurate SNP calling is often tricky, especially where the overlapping reads are less or the reads are of low quality. DeepVariant uses convolutional network and has ability to learn from one model and implement on another.

9.7 TUTORIAL

Before we start developing deep learning models, we need to set up the environment. This case study uses the Keras Python package, which runs on TensorFlow.

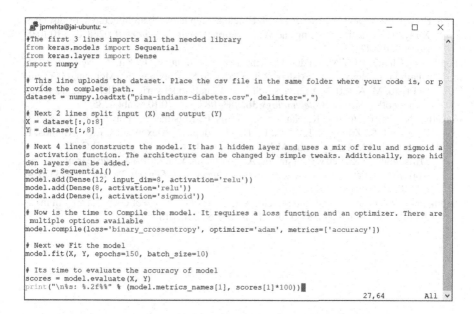

```
 jpmehta@jai-ubuntu: ~                                          —   □   ×
#The first 3 lines imports all the needed library
from keras.models import Sequential
from keras.layers import Dense
import numpy

# This line uploads the dataset. Place the csv file in the same folder where your code is, or p
rovide the complete path.
dataset = numpy.loadtxt("pima-indians-diabetes.csv", delimiter=",")

# Next 2 lines split input (X) and output (Y)
X = dataset[:,0:8]
Y = dataset[:,8]

# Next 4 lines constructs the model. It has 1 hidden layer and uses a mix of relu and sigmoid a
s activation function. The architecture can be changed by simple tweaks. Additionally, more hid
den layers can be added.
model = Sequential()
model.add(Dense(12, input_dim=8, activation='relu'))
model.add(Dense(8, activation='relu'))
model.add(Dense(1, activation='sigmoid'))

# Now is the time to Compile the model. It requires a loss function and an optimizer. There are
 multiple options available
model.compile(loss='binary_crossentropy', optimizer='adam', metrics=['accuracy'])

# Next we Fit the model
model.fit(X, Y, epochs=150, batch_size=10)

# Its time to evaluate the accuracy of model
scores = model.evaluate(X, Y)
print("\n%s: %.2f%%" % (model.metrics_names[1], scores[1]*100))
                                                          27,64      All
```

FIGURE 9.4   Example code for development of deep learning network.

After installing Python 3.6, install PIP and use PIP to install TensorFlow, Keras, and Numpy package, e.g., pip install numpy, tensorflow, and keras. The dataset used is from https://www.kaggle.com/kumargh/pimaindiansdiabetescsv

The first eight columns correspond to pregnancies, glucose, blood pressure, skin thickness, insulin, BMI, diabetes pedigree function, and age and the last column is the outcome, i.e., diabetes versus no-diabetes. The eight parameters are supposed to predict if the person is likely to get diabetes in his lifetime. Once the model is trained, it can be used for making predictions for other patients and early intervention can be made to reduce chances of diabetes development.

Figure 9.4 shows the code which you can run on your computer or use COLAB. Once you execute the code, the model is developed, training performed, and the accuracy is reported. In our test drive, we obtained an accuracy of 76.56%. Try playing with parameters to obtain better prediction accuracy.

REFERENCES

Abdelhafiz, D., Yang, C., and Ammar, R. (2019) Deep convolutional neural networks for mammography: advances, challenges and applications. *BMC Bioinformatics* **20**, 281. doi: 10.1186/s12859-019-2823-4.

Crevier, D (1993), *AI: The Tumultuous Search for Artificial Intelligence*, New York, NY: BasicBooks.

de Carvalho, T.M., Noels, E., Wakkee, M., Udrea, A., and Nijsten, T. (2019) Development of smartphone apps for skin cancer risk assessment: Progress and promise. *JMIR Dermatology* **2** (1), e13376. doi: 10.2196/13376.

Pasa, F., Golkov, V., and Pfeiffer, F. (2019) Efficient deep network architectures for fast chest X-ray tuberculosis screening and visualization. *Scientific Reports* **9**, 6268. doi: 10.1038/s41598-019-42557-4

Poplin, R., Chang, P.C., Alexander, D., Schwartz, S., Colthurst, T., Ku, A., Newburger, D., Dijamco, J., Nguyen, N., Afshar, P. T., Gross, S. S., Dorfman, L., McLean, C. Y., and DePristo, M. A. (2018) A universal SNP and small-indel variant caller using deep neural networks. *Nature Biotechnology* **36**, 983–987. doi: 10.1038/nbt.4235.

Sakellaropoulos, T., Vougas, K., Narang, S., Koinis, F., Kotsinas, A., Polyzos, A., Moss, T.J., Piha-Paul, S., Zhou, H., Kardala, E., Damianidou, E., Alexopoulos, L.G., Aifantis, I., Townsend, P.A., Panayiotidis, M.I., Sfikakis, P., Bartek, J., Fitzgerald, R,C, Thanos, D., Mills Shaw, K.R., Petty, R., Tsirigos, A., Gorgoulis, V.G. (2019) A deep learning framework for predicting response to therapy in cancer. *Cell Reports* **29** (11), 3367–3373.e4. doi: 10.1016/j.celrep.2019.11.017.

Selvikvåg Lundervold, A. and Lundervold, A. (2019) An overview of deep learning in medical imaging focusing on MRI. doi: 10.1016/j.zemedi.2018.11.002.

Part III

Ethics

10 Ethical Issues and Challenges with Artificial Intelligence in Healthcare

Nicolas Brault and Benoît Duchemann

CONTENTS

10.1 MEDICAL ETHICS

10.1.1 A HISTORY OF MEDICAL ETHICS: FROM THE HIPPOCRATIC OATH TO THE NUREMBERG CODE AND BEYOND

10.1.1.1 Definitions

Before we deal with the history of medical ethics, it is important to define some important notions concerning this discipline, as it constitutes the major theme of this chapter. Our reader, who is not necessarily familiar with this field of research, must indeed have some kind of basic knowledge about what we are going to talk about.

First of all, the word "ethics" (ἠθικός or *ethikos* in Greek, *mores* in Latin), which can be used as a synonym of "morality," refers to both a descriptive and a normative aspect:

- The descriptive sense refers to the way people live in a specific group or a specific society, more precisely to a certain code of conduct, or to a certain set of values according to which an individual or a group lives, which specifies, more or less explicitly, the things or conducts that are permitted, valued, or forbidden.
- The normative sense is not about the way people live but rather about the way they should live. The idea is not to describe, for example, what is right or wrong in a given society, but to justify, for example, why a behavior must be considered as right or wrong, or good or bad. In other words, "ethics" in this sense is about the value of values. Some philosophers call it "normative ethics," to be more explicit about its subject.

The concept of "medical ethics" refers more to the field of "applied ethics," and constitutes a framework for the relations between medical doctors and their patients, but also concerning biomedical research. This notion is to be distinguished from the "medical deontology," which is the study of medical doctors' duties toward their patients. In most of the countries around the world, there are, for example, some kind of ethical codes which can concern journalists, lawyers, architects, and of course physicians and health professionals in general. Limits between "medical ethics" and "medical deontology" are quite vague, but we can consider that "medical ethics" refers to the philosophical reflection about what can or should be done in medicine, and the "medical deontology" refers to the legal aspects of the practice of medicine, that is to say what physicians are allowed or forbidden to do in their daily practice, and the disciplinary measures they can face if they are breaking the rules.

The last word to be defined is the word "bioethics": the term was coined by the American biochemist Van Rensselaer Potter (1911–2001) in his book *Bioethics: Bridge to the Future* (1971). According to Potter, bioethics applies to all the living world and Potter wanted to create a new philosophy that would integrate biology, ecology, medicine, and human values. Then, in the United States, bioethics became synonymous with the ethics of biomedical research. That's why Potter, in 1988, chose to use the term "global bioethics" to show more explicitly that his conception of bio-ethics encompasses both the humanity, present and future, and the environment.

The scope of this chapter is clearly about the normative sense of ethics, in the applied context of medicine, which includes both the physician-patient relationship, biomedical research and the healthcare system. We won't talk about animal ethics or environmental ethics: if we use the word "bioethics," it will be to designate the ethics of biomedical research.

10.1.1.2 The Hippocratic Oath and Its Values

Medical ethics has a long history, which dates back to Hippocrates (460–370 BC) and his famous Hippocratic Oath (which has probably not been written by Hippocrates himself). The new physicians, who were members of the Hippocratic School, were supposed to swear to uphold specific ethical standards. As the text of the Hippocratic Oath can be easily found on the Internet,[1] it is not necessary to reproduce it here *in extenso*. The most important aspect for us is that we can distinguish four ethical ideas or principles at stake in this oath:

1) First of all, medical doctors must respect a certain probity or integrity. This includes collegiality, i.e., respect for the other physicians and their family, especially the teachers. Physicians have to help them, morally and finan-cially, in case they need it. Physicians should also respect the profession of physician in itself, and keep away from corruption.
2) The second idea refers to the importance of not doing harm to the patient: "I will abstain from all intentional wrong-doing and harm." This principle is often written in the Latin phrase *Primum non nocere*, which means "First, do not harm." In others words, it refers to the modern principle of non-maleficence. According to the Hippocratic Oath, this principle of not doing harm to the patient prohibits euthanasia, abortion, and even surgery, which must be left to specialists ("craftsmen").
3) The third idea is the corollary of the second: the physician must not do harm to his patient, but he must also do him good. This refers nowadays to the principle of beneficence. Of course, the Hippocratic Oath does not state explicitly this obligation, even if he says that the physician must "help the sick."
4) Finally, the Oath insists on the importance of medical secrecy and confi-dentiality: "And whatsoever I shall see or hear in the course of my profes-sion, as well as outside my profession in my intercourse with men, if it be what should not be published abroad, I will never divulge, holding such things to be holy secrets." This appears as a cardinal virtue, which is still very important today, insofar as it is an essential component of a trustwor-thy relationship between the physician and the patient.

The values Hippocratic physicians promote are clearly centered on the physician-patient relationship, which is quite logical, given the fact that there was no biomedical research or healthcare system at that time. This is also due to the fact that Hippocrates is considered as the founder of clinical medicine (from the Ancient Greek κλίνειν *klinein* meaning to slope, lean or recline): the *klinikos* is thus the physician who visits his patients in their beds. This means that Hippocratic medicine is clearly centered on the patient, his individuality and his relationship with the environment. To put in other words, for Hippocrates, there was no such thing as diseases but only sick individuals. That's probably why his ethics is patient-centered.

10.1.1.3 From the Nuremberg Code to the Oviedo Convention

However, the birth of experimental medicine during the 19th century, due to Claude Bernard, changed the way medicine was conceived. Then, during the 20th century, several experiments were made upon people, most of the time without even their consent and sometimes without even informing them. We can make a short list of the most striking unethical experiments that took place all over the world during this period. First of all, in 1902, a German medical doctor, Albert Moll, dressed a list of more than 600 experiments where medical doctors inoculate pathogenic agents to patients without informing them. Then, in 1929, the French Army vaccinated population in Senegal without their ascent. In 1930, in Lubeck's hospital (Germany), 76 children died because they were vaccinated against tuberculosis. In 1932 began the longest experiment in history: the "Tuskegee Study," whose goal was to study the development of syphilis. This study included 600 poor Afro-American farmers: 399 with syphilis, 201 who did not have the disease. They were left uninformed (researchers told them they were being treated for "bad blood") and the authorities did not ask for their consent. Of course, they were not treated of their diseases, even after penicillin became the drug of choice for syphilis in 1947. The experiment was stopped in 1972 (40 years later), when the *New York Times* revealed the affair. In 1932, Units 731 and 100 were created by the Japan Army in China to make experiments on prisoners. The paroxysm of horror was reached by the Nazis, who made a series of medical experiments on a large number of prisoners, including children. It includes experiments on twins, freezing, malaria, jaundice, mustard gas, sea water, sterilization, poison, incendiary bomb, or high altitude.

Subsequently to the discovery of the horrors and war crimes committed by the Nazis during World War II were held the Nuremberg Trials from 1946 to 1949. One of these trials was dedicated to the physicians who made these experiments and was called the "Doctor's trial." This gave birth to the Nuremberg Code (1947), which states 10 ethical principles in medical research. The most important is the first one which states that "the voluntary consent of the human subject is absolutely essential." The code insists then on the risk-benefit balance of the experiment, and the fact that the experiment must be done for "the good of society" (second principle)

To be clear, the Nuremberg Code has never had any legal value in any country, nor it has been taken as official ethics guidelines by any association. The first international declaration, adopted by the World Medical Association, is the "Declaration of Helsinki" in 1964, which states "ethical principles for medical research involving human subjects, including research on identifiable human material and data," are largely inspired from the Nuremberg Code. Its basic principles are the respect for the individual and his autonomy (Article 8), their right to self-determination, and the right to make informed decisions (Articles 20, 21, and 22) regarding participation in research, both initially and during the course of the research: this is the notion of informed consent. Another important point is that "the subject's welfare must always take precedence over the interests of science and society" (Article 5), and that "ethical considerations must always take precedence over laws and regulations" (Article 9). It also recognizes the importance of not doing research on vulnerable individuals or groups. Its operational principles are that research should be based on a thorough knowledge of the scientific background (Article 11), on a careful assessment of risks and benefits (Articles 16, 17), but also have a reasonable likelihood of benefit to the population studied (Article 19), and be conducted by suitably trained investigators (Article 15), using approved protocols. Research must also be subject to independent ethical review oversight by a properly convened committee (Article 13). Of course, as the Declaration of Helsinki is a product of the World Medical Association, it has no real legal value, but it is considered as a set of ethical principles that every physician around the world should respect.

In fact, the only international legally binding instrument is the Oviedo Convention, or "The Convention for the Protection of Human Rights and Dignity of the Human Being with Regard to the Application of Biology and Medicine." It was created by the Council of Europe and entered into force on December 1, 1999. It has been ratified by 29 countries, although the Council of Europe has 47 members. Countries like the United States, the United Kingdom, the Russian Federation, the Popular Republic of China, the Republic of India, or Germany did not ratify it: this means that the vast majority of the world population did not ratify it. However, this convention is interesting for us, as it is not only about biomedical research, but also about biomedicine in general. It addresses issues such as "Consent," "Private life and right to information," "Human genome," "Scientific research," "Organ transplantation," or even "Public debate."

The Preamble to the Oviedo Convention thus states that "developments in biomedicine must benefit future generations and all of humanity." Its general principles are the primacy of the human being, an equitable access to healthcare, and professional standards. The issue of consent is of course pivotal to the Convention because of the relationship it has with individual autonomy. Medical intervention carried out without consent is a general prohibition within Article 5. Furthermore, consent must be free and fully informed. The Oviedo Convention also focus on the human genome: for example, genetic testing as a tool for discrimination is prohibited under Article 11. Article 12 allows genetic testing only for health or for scientific research linked to health purposes, and is reserved for health-related purposes only. In the same way, modification of the human genome, for reasons other than health-related, is generally prohibited under Article 13. Besides, a specific text about the human genome exists, which was issued by UNESCO in 1997: the "Universal Declaration on the Human Genome and Human Rights," where the human genome is considered as the "heritage of humanity" and forbids reproductive cloning.

To ensure that these ethical principles are being respected all over the word, several ethical committees were created at the end of the twentieth century: there are, for example, National Medical Councils in many countries, and experiments are supposed to be validated *ex ante* by an ethical committee. As already stated, some national and international ethical committees exist. The first committee on bioethical issues was created in France in 1983: it is called the "Comité consultatif national d'éthique" (*National Consultative Ethics Committee*) and was created in 1983. The Council of Europe has a *Committee on Bioethics DH-BIO*, created in 2012 (in replacement of the Steering Committee on Bioethics, created in 1992). And the United Nations has the *International Bioethics Committee* (IBC), which was created in 1993 and is composed of 36 independent experts.

10.1.2 THE PHILOSOPHICAL FOUNDATIONS OF MEDICAL ETHICS: DEONTOLOGY AND TELEOLOGY

10.1.2.1 Ethical Dilemmas in Medical Ethics

After this brief overview on the legal and historical aspects of medical ethics, it is time to enter into its philosophical foundations. Most of the time, medical ethics is taught to students as a way to solve ethical dilemmas that they could face during their career as medical doctors: in this sense, medical ethics could furnish a kind of procedure to solve these dilemmas. Moreover, the recent progress in Artificial Intelligence may lead health professionals and some philosophers (for example, Nick Bostrom) to think that medical ethics (and ethics in general) could be implemented in some kind of Artificial Intelligence, and even a "superintelligence" according to Bostrom (Bostrom 2009). Of course, this implementation means that we could or should let Artificial Intelligence solve these ethical dilemmas, as Artificial Intelligence would be more objective or more powerful than the human brain to solve this kind of complex problems.

This is not the main point of this chapter: we focus here more on the multiple AI artifacts that are now used by physicians, patients, consumers, or the private and public sectors to analyze and improve medical practice, whether in a clinical or a public health context. Moreover, we consider that if some ethical principles are probably implementable, for example, utilitarianism and its calculus of pleasure and pain, it is however difficult, and maybe impossible, that an AI artifact could solve the ethical dilemmas in the medical context. We indeed consider medical ethics not as procedure that could automatically lead physicians to the solution to ethical dilemmas, but rather as a resource (just as AI artifacts) that physicians could use to think about all the moral implications of their decision (or non-decision) and explore the value of the values involved in various clinical or public-health-related issues.

However, it can be useful to state some of the ethical dilemmas physicians could face during their career: should a physician perform an abortion even if it were against his own beliefs? Should a physician tell to one half of a couple that the other half of the same couple is HIV positive, and thus break confidentiality? Should a physician prolong futile care for dying patient, to please, for example, members of his family? Conversely, should a physician stop life-sustaining therapies because of family demands? Should physician-assisted suicide be legalized? Should a physician refuse to take care of a patient because he has no health insurance and can't afford a treatment? Should it be legal to buy and sell organs for transplant?

As we can see, the list of dilemmas is almost infinite and can concern several issues such as confidentiality, professional integrity, medically assisted procreation, euthanasia, health insurance, but there are also some dilemmas concerning experimentations, reproductive technologies, or personalized medicine. The Covid-19 pandemic has also shed light, in a context of uncertainty, on critical choices physicians had to make as there was a shortage of vital equipment and supplies, for example, ventilators. In several countries, physicians had to make life-and-death decisions, according to criteria such as age or comorbidity, which were established in an emergency context.

Of course, most of the ethical dilemmas are in some way resolved by law or guidelines of states, institutions, or committees: for example, in France, the law on medical confidentiality strictly prohibits a physician from revealing HIV seropositivity to half of the couples who are not seropositive. And if the physician does it, he can be judged and put in jail for that. However, the laws and guidelines can vary a lot according to countries and times, and ethical dilemmas can be resolved in many ways according to the dominant culture of a country: abortion can thus be strictly prohibited in religious countries, for example. Another example is the possibility to sell and buy organs for transplant: in certain countries it is legal, in others it is forbidden. But sometimes laws and guidelines are just silent about what to do in certain circumstances, and the physician must be able to resolve a dilemma in order to act. That's why it is important to know and understand the two main positions in medical ethics: deontology and teleology.

10.1.2.2 Deontological Ethics

As we can see, the specificity of problems in medical ethics and bioethics in general is that it is not a choice between the good and the bad, or a problem concerning the weakness of the will (e.g., X did A rather than B, even though X was convinced that B was the better thing to do), but rather a choice between bad and bad: most of the time, you have to choose the lesser evil. Another way to state the problem in medical ethics is in terms of "values conflict": for example, euthanasia can be legal in a country, and a patient can ask you for euthanasia, and you can even be rather a pro-euthanasia person, but it can contradict the fundamental value of medical practice: "First, do not harm." This conflict between different personal, professional, and societal values is also a kind of ethical dilemma.

To simplify, we can say that there are two major ethical positions in medical ethics: deontology and teleology (also called consequentialism).

Deontological ethics is usually associated with the work of Immanuel Kant (1724–1804): according to his theory (Kant 1998), an action is considered as morally good if its intention is good, whatever the consequences of this action. In other words, the action is morally good if it conforms to a law or a principle, if it is made with respect to what he calls the "moral law." This is in relation to the fact that for Kant, the only virtue that can be unqualifiedly good is the "good will." No other virtue has this status because every other virtue can be used to achieve immoral ends (for example, the virtue of loyalty is not good if one is loyal to an evil person).

For him, there is a single obligation, which he calls the "Categorical Imperative," which is derived from the concept of duty. Categorical imperatives are principles that are intrinsically valid and good in themselves: this means that they must be obeyed, whatever the circumstances. Kant gives two different and successive formulations to his categorical imperative:

1) The first formulation of the categorical imperative is that of *universalizability*: "Act only according to that maxim by which you can at the same time will that it should become a universal law" (Kant, 1998, p. 31).
2) The second formulation of the categorical imperative is related to the fact that for Kant, only humans, considered as rational agents, are capable of morality and are to be considered as ends in themselves: "So act that you use humanity, whether in your own person or in the person of any other, always at the same time as an end, never merely as a means" (Kant, 1998, p. 38).

The two formulations are in fact two faces of the same coin. To understand his point, one has to remember that Kant makes a clear distinction between persons and things: persons (by which Kant means human beings) are ends in themselves and as such have a dignity; whereas things are means toward an end, and consequently have a price. This is summed up in Table 10.1.

Therefore, every human being has to defend his dignity and the dignity of any other human beings when he acts: for example, dwarf-tossing is more or less legal in some countries (for example, in Australia), if the person is of course consenting, but in some countries, it is considered as contrary to human dignity and thus prohibited. The rationale for this interdiction is that even if the person of short stature is consenting to this practice, and is thus autonomous, however, by consenting to being tossed, he infringes not only his own dignity but also the dignity of all the other human beings (according to the first formulation of the categorical imperative). In a medical context, it can be applied to euthanasia or medically assisted suicide: in a Kantian perspective, suicide is strictly prohibited because it cannot be universalized: "*First,* as regards the concept of necessary duty to oneself, someone who has suicide in mind will ask himself whether his action can be consistent with the idea of humanity *as an end in itself.* If he destroys himself in order to escape from a trying condition he makes use of a person *merely as a means* to maintain a tolerable condition up to the end of life. A human being, however, is not a thing and hence not something that can be used *merely* as a means, but must in all his actions always be regarded as

TABLE 10.1

Persons and Things

Persons	Things
Ends	Means
Dignity	Price

an end in itself. I cannot, therefore, dispose of a human being in my own person by maiming, damaging or killing him" (Kant, 1998, p. 38).

It is not better if it is medically assisted because, in this situation, it is the physician (or a member of the medical staff) who commits a murder, and murder is also prohibited, even if there are some exceptions. In the same way, one cannot sell his organs (for example, a kidney) because he is a person and as such he cannot use his body as a means to an end, which has a price, and not a dignity.

Finally, Kant distinguishes between three kinds of actions in relation to moral duty (or moral law):

1) *An action that is contrary to duty:* This action is necessarily immoral or bad because it is contradictory to categorical imperative and thus infringes the human dignity. Killing, or lying, or committing suicide are clearly actions contrary to duty.

2) *An action that is in conformity to duty:* This action is morally neutral. For example, a physician who keeps secret the information revealed by his patient because he doesn't want to lose his job acts in conformity to duty but not from duty. He's acting this way because of an interest or by fear and this is more an hypothetical imperative than a categorical one.

3) *An action from duty:* This is the only action that must be considered as good according to Kant. An action from duty is, for example, keeping the medical secret because it is the physician's duty, whatever the consequences. This is the only way to be in conformity with the moral law, and then with reason. It is about doing one's duty for duty sake.

As we can see, the main weakness of Kantian moral is its rigidity: It is quite difficult to apply it to the multiple situations met by health professionals in critical medical contexts, especially in multicultural societies. The other main weakness lies in its formalism: by focusing on principles and rules, Kantian ethics is doomed to be empty and powerless in real life, as principles always underdetermine actions. This critic was already tackled by Kant in a controversy with Benjamin Constant (the problem of lying to the murderer at the door), in his book *On a Supposed Right to Lie Because of Philanthropic Concerns* (1797). Conversely, the main advantage of Kantian moral is that it is quite easy to translate it into laws or norms, whose main function is to authorize or forbid conducts and actions. A second advantage is its appeal to autonomy and the idea, taken from Jean-Jacques Rousseau, that one is free when he obeys a law he prescribed for oneself. Autonomy is indeed a cardinal virtue in the field of medical ethics.

10.1.2.3 Teleological ethics (or consequentialism)

In opposition with the deontological view, the teleological position in medical ethics pays a special attention not to the intention (the good will) of the action, but to its results or its consequences: if the action has produced some good, or more good than harm, or even minimized harm, then this action must be considered as morally good. The most famous consequentialist theory is without a doubt utilitarianism, which was founded by Jeremy Bentham (1748–1832) and developed in his book *An Introduction to the Principles of Morals and Legislation* (Bentham 1789), first published in 1789. The main concept of utilitarianism is logically "utility" and Bentham's work opens with a statement of the principle of utility:

> Nature has placed mankind under the governance of two sovereign masters, pain and pleasure. It is for them alone to point out what we ought to do, as well as to determine what we shall do.
>
> **(Bentham 1789, Introduction, Chapter 1, p. 1)**

This sentence is interesting because Bentham adopts a heteronomous perspective: by "heteronomy," we mean that the ends are assigned by someone or something else than the individual himself—it could be Nature, as in Bentham's case, but it can also be God. Religions are typically heteronomous ethics, because God is supposed to have told humans what he ought and ought not to do (for example, the Ten Commandments). In an autonomous perspective, like in Kant's moral philosophy, any rational agent gives to himself the ends he wants to pursue: for Kant, as we saw, the end is duty, that is respect of the moral law and of the categorical imperative. For Bentham, it is "Nature" who gives us our ends: avoid pain and seek for pleasure, as pain and pleasure are our "sovereign masters who tell us what we ought to do."

By "principle of utility," Bentham means:

> that principle which approves or disapproves of every action whatsoever. According to the tendency it appears to have to augment or diminish the happiness of the party whose interest is in question: or, what is the same thing in other words to promote or to oppose that happiness.
>
> **(Bentham 1789, Introduction, Chapter 1, p. ii)**

And by "utility," Bentham means:

> that property in any object, whereby it tends to produce benefit, advantage, pleasure, good, or happiness (all this in the present case comes to the same thing) or (what comes again to the same thing) to prevent the happening of mischief, pain, evil, or unhappiness to the party whose interest is considered.
>
> **(Bentham 1789, Chapter 1, p. 2)**

As we can see, for Bentham, the concept of utility is synonymous with the concepts of "benefit, advantage, pleasure, good, or happiness" and the goal of every human being and of every society is to augment the happiness or the pleasure, and to diminish the unhappiness or pain. Bentham even creates some kind of "hedonistic calculus" or "felicific calculus" to calculate the amount of pleasure or pain that a specific action is likely to cause. He distinguishes between seven factors, which Bentham calls "circumstances," such as "intensity, duration, certainty or uncertainty" (see Bentham 1789, Chapter 4, p. 27).

Bentham thus proposes a kind of algorithm to calculate the amount of pleasure or pain caused by an action. This constitutes a major outbreak in moral philosophy because, for the first time, it is or it looks possible to quantify what is considered as purely a qualitative phenomenon, i.e., pleasure or pain. And this calculus includes not only the individual who acts but also all other persons who could be affected by this action.

In medical ethics, this idea of a calculus is particularly used in medical experimentation: one of the major criteria to authorize an experimentation on human beings is indeed the risk-benefit balance, which must be positive. The same kind of quantification is used in quality of life scales (QOLS), or also in quality-adjusted life years (QALY), which is a generic measure of disease burden, including both the quality and the quantity of life lived, used in economic evaluation to assess the value of medical interventions. Finally, several ethical dilemmas can be resolved with a teleological or consequentialist approach: selling one's organ can be, for example, morally justified because it saves someone's life, without causing too much harm to the person who gives his organ.

The main strength of teleological approach is that it is practical: its appeal to quantification makes it easy to implement it in public health policies, but also in data-driven approach. The second advantage is the idea that we can define or calculate objectively the good but also the bad: this leads to better take into account the pain and the suffering of the patient, but also his quality of life.

The main weakness of the teleological approach, and especially the utilitarian approach, is that it is not so easy and sometimes not possible to calculate what is a pleasure or what is happiness, and *a fortiori* a certain amount of pleasure or happiness: in multicultural societies, it is difficult to take for granted that every human being has the same conception of what are pleasure and pain. More precisely, there is always a risk of sacrifice: the maximum of happiness for the maximum of people is not the maximum of happiness for the totality of people. In a utilitarian perspective, it is not morally wrong to sacrifice one child to save ten children. Ultimately, utilitarianism can be summed up by the sentence: "The end justifies the means." Besides representing some kind of moral laziness, this moral principle can lead to serious misconducts in a medical context, and even to atrocities, as this was the case with the Nazis doctors, who were probably convinced that their horrible experiments on prisoners would greatly improve science.

10.1.3 FROM "PRINCIPLISM" TO VIRTUE ETHICS:

10.1.3.1 The "Principlism" of Beauchamp and Childress

In 1979, a book was published that is still highly influential in the field of medical ethics: *Principles of Biomedical Ethics* (Beauchamp and Childress 2013), written by philosophers Tom Beauchamp and James Childress. This is an important book because its main idea is to provide a tool for health professionals and patients, both to identify moral problems and to make decisions about what to do. This practical approach for ethical decision-making is thus new, not because it would propose new ethical principles, or a new ethical theory, but because it proposes a set of four principles that are supposed to furnish "an analytical framework of general norms derived from the common morality that form a suitable starting point for biomedical ethics" and thus "general guidelines for the formulation of more specific rules" (Beauchamp and Childress, p. 13). These four principles are as follows:

(1) *Respect for autonomy* (a norm of respecting and supporting autonomous decisions),

(2) *Nonmaleficence* (a norm of avoiding the causation of harm),

(3) *Beneficence* (a group of norms pertaining to relieving, lessening, or preventing harm and providing benefits and balancing benefits against risks and costs), and

(4) *Justice* (a group of norms for fairly distributing benefits, risks, and costs). (Beauchamp and Childress, p. 13)

Nonmaleficence and beneficence are old principles, dating back to Hippocrates, as we saw before. They are also clearly teleological principles, as they are oriented toward the goal or the consequences of the action, i.e., patient's good. Conversely, autonomy and justice, which are more modern principles, are deontological principles: autonomy refers again to the patient and his capacity to an informed consent, whereas justice refers more to the socioeconomic aspect of medicine and healthcare.

By "common morality," Beauchamp and Childress mean "the set of universal norms shared by all persons committed to morality" (Beauchamp and Childress, p. 3), such as the prohibition of murder and of causing pain to others, the obligation of telling the truth, etc. In this sense, this common morality is "applicable to all persons in all places, and we rightly judge all human conduct by its standards." Hence, as the four principles are derived from this "common morality," they are supposed to be also universal. Therefore, the main advantage of principlism is that these four principles can be accepted as a basis for discussion, be it religion, or the moral principles, or the culture in general of all the participants to this discussion. This is crucial in modern multicultural societies. By stating the four principles, it allows the participants to the discussion (patient, patient's family, physician, medical staff, etc.) to be more explicit about the values they cherish the most and make their decision according to their most valuable value.

The main weakness of this theory can be that it is too narrow: maybe four principles are not enough and maybe some people can consider that they do not share neither of these four principles nor the principles of that "common morality" that every human being is supposed to share. For example, in a heteronomous perspective (whether the one fixing the rules is God or Nature, or anything else), these four principles may appear as totally irrelevant. The second weakness is that the conflict between principles may stay unresolved, because there are no unified moral theory from which they are all derived[2]: in other words, not only is there a conflict between teleology and deontology, but there is also a conflict inside teleology and inside deontology between the two principles of each side. For example, the principle of justice can be in contradiction with the principle of beneficence: during the Covid-19 pandemic, physicians had to made difficult choices between their patients, as the resources (for example, ventilators) were rare, according to the criteria that were not necessary fair (age, gender, social insurance, low or high socioeconomic status, etc.). In the same way, the distinction between non-maleficence and beneficence is not always clear: in the case of a terminally ill patient, doing good (beneficence) could lead to help the patient to die, which contradicts the principle of non-maleficence. Conversely, the physician could practice some kind of therapeutic obstinacy or aggressive treatment and thus not respect the principle of maleficence, in order to save a patient in conformity with the principle of beneficence. The formal aspect of principlism cannot furnish a solution to this kind of problems.

10.1.3.2 Virtue Ethics

It is impossible to present in a few pages all ethical theories that have been proposed more or less recently. We can cite *right theories*, which is a variant of contractualism, and focus on the concepts of contract, mutual agreement, and consent; *narrative ethics*, term coined by Adam Newton in his eponymous book (Newton 1997), an approach to ethical problems and practice that involves listening to and interpreting people's stories rather than applying principles or rules to particular situations; and *care ethics*, defended especially by Carol Gilligan from a feminist perspective in her book (Gilligan 1993), which holds that moral action centers on interpersonal relationships: the aim of care ethics is thus in particular to maintain relationships by contextualizing and promoting the well-being of caregivers and care-receivers in a network of social relations.

However, it seems important to mention virtue ethics for two main reasons: first, this is without doubt the oldest ethical theory, dating back to Aristotle and his *Nicomachean Ethics* (Aristotle 2009); second, since the article of E. Anscombe in 1958 (Anscombe 1958), virtue ethics has made a significant comeback in the philosophical discussions about medical ethics and bioethics (and ethics in general), precisely because of the absence, in deontological as well as teleological ethics, of the traditional themes of ethics in history: virtues and vices, moral character, moral wisdom, the problem of happiness, and the fundamental question: what is a good life? In medical ethics, virtue ethics insists not on the principles or the consequences of the action, but on the agent: the goal of ethics is not to know "what virtue is" but "to become good" (Aristotle 2009, p.24).

Virtue is for Aristotle a disposition, or a habit, or a "state of character," and acting virtuously is avoiding excess and deficiency, which are vices:

> Virtue, then, is a state of character concerned with choice, lying in a mean, i.e. the mean relative to us, this being determined by reason, and by that reason by which the man of practical wisdom would determine it
>
> **(Aristotle 2009, p. 31)**

For example, in a dangerous situation, a man must be courageous, which means neither rash, nor coward. But how does one know if he is courageous (i.e., virtuous) or rash or coward (i.e., vicious)?

The criterion here is a real person: the "man of practical wisdom" (the *phronimos*) embodies the virtue of practical wisdom (*phronesis*), which is derived from experience. But there is another criterion to recognize a virtuous action: pleasure. For Aristotle, when we act virtuously, we can feel the emotion of pleasure, and this emotion functions as a sign that we are doing something good. But pleasure is not an end, as it is for utilitarianism: it is rather a means towards a greater end, which is happiness, defined as an "activity in accordance with virtue" (Aristotle 2009, p.194).

The last important point about Aristotelian ethics in the context of medical ethics is the importance given to the specificity of a situation: if virtue is a state of character, this state of character must be in practice to be real, and this practice always refers to specific situations or cases:

For instance, both fear and confidence and appetite and anger and pity and in general pleasure and pain may be felt both too much and too little, and in both cases not well; but to feel them at the right times, with reference to the right objects, towards the right people, with the right motive, and in the right way, is what is both intermediate and best, and this is characteristic of virtue.

(Aristotle 2009, p. 30)

For physicians and healthcare professionals, the main advantage of virtue ethics is that it insists on their moral character (and physicians, for example, are supposed to have values and act virtuously, as their main goal is to cure patients and take care of them), their practical wisdom (acquired through experience), and also on the specificity of each patient and of each situation: the physician knows what to do, taking into account both general principles and the particular circumstances of a case.

The main weakness of virtue ethics is that it depends too much on the moral character of the agent and is too prone to individual definitions. It is thus extremely difficult to systematize or generalize and cannot furnish clear or explicit guidelines or healthcare professionals.

10.1.3.3 Synthetic Tables of Ethical Theories (Table 10.2)

TABLE 10.2
The Three Main Ethical Theories

Name	Deontology	Teleology	Virtue
Origin of moral principles	Autonomy	Heteronomy	Heteronomy
Motive of the action	Duty	Pleasure	Virtue
End of the action	Justice	Good	Happiness
Criterion of morality	Principles	Consequences	Mean between excess and deficiency
Weaknesses	*Rigidity:* difficulty to apply it to real situations, especially in the medical context *Formalism:* lacks empirical content	Sacrificial effects Difficulty to define what is good and bad	Depends too much on the moral character of the agent: too individual. Difficulty of systematization: cannot furnish explicit guidelines for action
Strengths	Easy to translate into laws and codes Appeal to freedom and consent	Objectivity of the good through quantification Easy to put in practice	Insists on the moral character and the practical wisdom of healthcare professionals. Attention paid to the specificity of each case
Main representative author	Kant	Bentham	Aristotle

10.2 ETHICS OF ARTIFICIAL INTELLIGENCE

10.2.1 ETHICS OF TECHNOLOGY AND ETHICS OF AI

Technology has been perceived as a vehicle for economic, human, as well as social progress since 18th century. By showing the solar system through his telescope and by demonstrating a heliocentric theory of the universe, Galileo Galilei has highlighted our human senses fallibility and has freed us from it. Somehow the industrial revolution machinism freed us from ungrateful physical tasks and enhanced our individual and collective capabilities to perform tasks requiring more and more energy, force, and dexterity.

Nevertheless, this progressive dimension has been recurrently questioned. Lewis Mumford (Smith 1994)[3] has argued that technological innovations might threaten social and spiritual progress; similar conceptions, highlighting technicist issues, have also been put forth by other thinkers such as Langdon Winner, Jacques Ellul, or Ivan Illich.[4]

As Johnson and Powers (2005) dismiss the idea that technical innovation might be axiologically neutral, Langdon Winner's quote in Smith (1994) completes their statements:

> Technological systems, with their inherent political qualities, are not value neutral (…), societies, if they are to be equitable and effective, must understand precisely what sorts of implications new technologies may carry with them before they are introduced.
>
> **(Smith 1994)**

Hence, if a new technological system is not neutral, the value system it carries must be dependent on the societal environment in which it is to be implemented. The ethical responsibility for the development and implementation of such a system should refer to the political will for social justice. In order to remain ethically valuable, technological innovations should thus comply with regulations supporting the society's value system. In so doing, those regulations are society-driven and external to the technology itself, and should be the means to submit technology to some higher moral principles. Condorcet already mentioned this need for an "improved legislation" almost two centuries ago:

> In short, does not the well-being, the prosperity, resulting from the progress that will be made by the useful arts, in consequence of their being founded upon a sound theory, resulting, also, from an improved legislation, built upon the truths of the political sciences, naturally dispose men to humanity, to benevolence, and to justice?
>
> **(Condorcet 1791)**

Technical progress should then be coconstructed *de facto* by the Aristotelian necessary causes,[5] which lead the technical production as well as an outer ethical order that should be enforced by governments.

As any technology, AI should be subject to outer rationalized ethical policies. Moreover, as a disruptive technology which will potentially—and already does—change drastically working and leisure environments, there is a fundamental need for a normative framework guaranteeing the ethical production and usage of AI.

10.2.2 FROM THE MYTHS OF ARTIFICIAL INTELLIGENCE TO NEO-LUDDISM: A PLEA FOR REGULATION OF AI

Further to our senses limitations as shown by Galileo Galilei, Herbert Simon (Simon 1955) has brought to light and modelized our limited rationality, "the psychological limits of the organism."[6] His theory was later echoed and developed by scientists of decision such as Tversky (1969), Kahneman and Tversky (1979), and Evans (1990), highlighting how human cognition is imperfect and subject to irrationality and biases.

The initial AI project[7]—in which H. Simon participated—was to deliver a clear understanding of our cognition and to create *in silico* a "common sense" at least equal to ours, and possibly better or at least more regular. AI then seems to be an innovative object aiming at extending our capabilities by freeing us from our cognitive limitations. It is the latest promise for technical progress, a systemic agent of our present and future modernity. This project is part of the present AI storytelling, the constructed myth of an enhancing technology meant for human good.

In the early 19th century, Luddites destroyed textile machines which were accused of replacing human labor and know-how; this idea has been regularly echoed by Marxist thinkers and in particular by Anders (2018a; 2018b), hence speaking of the alienation of human workers. Quite differently, Arendt (2018) considers that technology alienates our relationship with the world, and Kitcher (2001) considers that a more contemporary Luddite "lament" to science and technology is to see them as dehumanizing. On the other hand, instead of considering humans as being submitted to an anonymous system led by a technical rationality, Jonas' approach (Jonas 1985) considers a consequentialist "ethic of the future" where human responsibility is necessary to balance the potential consequences of our technique-driven actions.

While our societies are faced with these historical warnings against possible technical misdeeds of particular technical innovations, amplified by a form of technophobia that irrigates certain sectors, some new dangers and risks are emerging with the rise of AI technology. Some voices today[8] fear that AI will help replace humans in most industries not yet concerned by sole machinism. They fear that no human activity—even the cognitive ones—will actually be free from being performed by alternative machinic or AI processes. Some voices, conveyed by Bostrom (2014), warn against AI and the emergence of a new order that would sound the death knell for human sovereignty or at least for human autonomy. Some others still highlight the fear of job destruction[9]; it is then no longer only a matter of a "Luddite" fear of human labor replacement by the means of mechanization, but more broadly of the transformation of the very concept and the very value of labor. Finally, some are concerned with the transparency of AI solutions, the respect of privacy and confidentiality of information, and the manipulation of people.

Both ethical and legislative frameworks still remain deficient while facing such historical and emerging fears for machinism and AI. As a matter of fact, legislations from most countries have trouble keeping pace with the fast changes brought on by AI and the development of new applications. It is what Floridi (1999) calls a "policy vacuum," which is also noticed by Johnson and Powers (2005), Müller (2016), and Morley et al. (2020). In such circumstances, all actors are therefore calling for the foundation of a specific ethics that will enable AI to face these challenges. The industrial and institutional actors are trying to fill the gap but without any real coordination. Furthermore, besides the marketing promise of responsible innovations, the actual ethical purpose does not always appear clearly established.

Some private companies[10] and professional organizations[11] have so far managed to develop ethical principles in order to frame the AI innovations. Some governments together with professional organizations have also succeeded in legislating on certain AI-related innovations or so-called intelligent systems[12]; however, this remains limited to specific industries and oriented only toward an efficient while ethical use of technology. On top of this, many workshops and roundtables have been held in various countries, collecting the general public's perception of AI-related issues and relaying it in a bottom-up mode[13] to governments. Morley et al. (2020) identified nearly 70 AI ethics programs from major AI players,[14] institutional programs at a national or an international level, and the "AI for Good" program launched by the United Nations in collaboration with the ITU.[15]

However, this search for an AI ethics goes along with its myth. AI is considered mostly as an ethical object as it is presently designed. But it is assigned some capabilities that go far beyond its actual achievements and some voices want to rule AI as a possible futuristic—and much fantasized—autonomous subject.

10.2.3 AI FOR SOCIAL GOOD: A NEW PRINCIPLISM?

10.2.3.1 What Ethics for AI ?

Is not a mistaken interest the most frequent cause of actions contrary to the general welfare?

(Condorcet 1791)

Hence, establishing an AI ethic and further implementing an AI applied ethic should consist in "hearing" the interest so that the action of an AI artifact remains in conformity with the general welfare.

It would involve answering questions: how do we define welfare we want to aim at; and consequently, how can we model an AI that complies with such a welfare or such a social good?

Answering such questions requires first to choose an ethical theory. A consequentialist version—as in Jonas (1985)—should involve a moral responsibility toward the future consequences of technology-driven actions. A contractualist would include some sort of a social contract built upon democratic deliberation in order to establish what general good is. A utilitarian one would necessitate a consensual value system in order to evaluate and balance the positive and negative impacts of technology. A virtue ethics would be based on character virtues of the individual and collective actors involved in the AI development and implementation. Finally, a principlist version is built upon clear ethical principles and their efficient usage.[16] The latter functions itself as a technical scheme, with a cybernetic feedback loop regulating the potential differences between practical misdeeds and the ethical axiomatic.

Broadly, knowledge engaged in the definition of general good principles is on the order of moral axiomatic. It can be considered in a transcendental way as resulting from a higher value system, for example, religious, or immanent, for example, conditional to a given sociocultural context. Whatever ethical theory is involved,[17] it is originated consensually from a public. We may note at this point the difference between the idealistic contractualism[18] based on Rousseau's social contract and the Hobbesian contractarianism[19] based on a self-interested deal. But there remains an ambiguity in the word "public" that needs to be clarified: besides the obvious group of all members from a society, there may be several publics as much as there may be several interest groups such as the industry, governmental institutions, activists, scientists, consumers etc. Thus, general good is based on a system of value within a given society and a given public. We may note a possible tension here as different publics within a common society may have different sets of values, this tension could be reinforced when considering different publics from different societies.

10.2.3.2 Principles and Factors

Further to Google's and IEEE's initiatives already mentioned, let us mention as well the Asilomar AI Principles[20] following the Conference for Beneficial AI, or else the Partnership on AI eight "tenets"[21] delivering a general creed for ethical AI developments.

Aiming at a synthesis of 47 AI ethical principles identified in four major international reports, Floridi et al. (2018) grouped them into five major categories: *beneficence*, *non-maleficience*, *justice*, *autonomy*, and *explicability*. The first four principles are precisely those edicted by Beauchamp and Childress (2013) in their foundational work for a biomedical ethics, with Floridi et al. adding the explicability as a principle specific to AI.

In doing so, Floridi et al. (2018) as well as Taddeo and Floridi (2018) propose a structural basis to standardize ethical behaviors in the chain of production and usage of AI. Then they categorize the action prescriptions into four groups: *to assess, to develop, to incentivize*, and *to support*; upstream evaluation of the capacity to manage risk, evaluation of the capacity to repair, evaluation of tasks that should never be delegated to the AI, evaluation of existing legislation and their capacity to deal with ethics; development of mechanisms that are still deficient or missing, whether technical (explicability), industrial (dynamic evaluation of misdeeds, unsuspected bias, etc.), institutional (reparation, financial responsibility), or academic (metric of trust in AI); emulate research; and finally support the "development of self-regulatory codes of conduct for data and AI-related professions, with specific ethical duties" or support training. It is therefore an important work of foundation of an ethical framework in order to support the development of an AI for good.

Cowls et al. (2019) resume the research initiated by Floridi et al. (2018), no longer on the theme of AI4People but similarly on that of AI4SG ("for Social Good").

Based on the study of 27 research projects dealing with examples of AI4SG, Cowls et al. (2019) propose a series of seven essential and presumed robust factors "that should characterise the design of AI4SG projects":(1) falsifiability and incremental deployment; (2) safeguards against the manipulation of predictors; (3) receiver-contextualized intervention; (4) receiver-contextualized explanation and transparent purposes; (5) privacy protection and data subject consent; (6) situational fairness; and (7) human-friendly semanticisation. The analysis of these factors is provided with "recommended best practices," the first of which, very Popperian in its formulation, is addressed to designers (efficient cause) to set up methods for testing their development (formal cause) in order to ensure users' trust (trustworthiness) in their object. To varying degrees, all other instructions are addressed to designers; even when it comes to considering the object appropriation by the user (receiver), it is a question of devising ergonomic strategies so that the solution, its expected beneficence, and its supposed non-maleficence are optimized according to the specifications.

10.2.3.3 Implementation

Following Floridi et al. (2018), Taddeo and Floridi (2018), and Cowls et al. (2019), we have established five general categories of ethical principles and four categories of action prescriptions and determined seven deontological factors aiming at a responsible AI design. Their proximity to biomedical principles will obviously serve our purpose of establishing an ethics of AI in a healthcare context.

In order to become applicable, they further require a detailed view of what concepts those ethical categories—beneficence, non-maleficence, or even justice—actually refer to. In a given context, they should refer to a social contract or agreement made between publics, institutional, and industrial actors. The 2018 *Montréal Declaration for a Responsible Development of Artificial Intelligence*[22] is an example of such an agreement proposal. It was born through the cooperation of "citizens, experts, public officials, industry stakeholders, civil organizations and professional associations" in order to guide AI toward a responsible industry. Such a concertation includes ten principles: well-being, respect for autonomy, protection of privacy and intimacy, solidarity, democratic participation, equity, diversity inclusion, caution, responsibility, and sustainable development. The well-being principle, which belongs to the category beneficence, is itself developed with five do's and don'ts guidelines such as "AIs must help individuals improve their living conditions, their health, and their working conditions,"[23] thus being focused on how AI can affect our societies in a utilitarian way. Hence, there is a need for a bridge between Floridi et al.'s principlistic deontology for an efficient ethical AI production and the Montréal contractualistic declaration for a responsible AI. Furthermore, the deontology factors framing technically an ethical AI production should refer specifically to the social agreement which is a result of a democratic concertation in a given industry and a given context, i.e., British healthcare system, human resources in Germany, IOT in France, etc.

This democratic control as specified in the "Democratic Participation" principle requires in particular that "the decisions made by AIs affecting a person's life, quality of life, or reputation should always be justifiable in a language that is understood by the people who use them or who are subjected to the consequences of their use."

This brings us to explicability as a principle category. It emphasizes a necessary commitment of AI designers to knowledge accessibility, hence calling for a bridge between ethics and epistemology. It requires also that the meaning of symbols conveyed by a given language from an artifactual emitter should be understood by the message receiver. It is then crucial that there exists a language common to AI developers as well as to AI artifacts and AI users, should the latter particularly be physicians. This is not only about ergonomics but also about creating the conditions of a meaningful access to the artifactual output so that the calculated result is justifiable.

10.2.3.4 Tensions

We have just seen how the AI deontology should be submitted to the democratically edicted ethical framework. Here is a point of friction between the economic and technical constraints related to the development processes and the ethical requirements initiated by the publics. It is as well a point of tension between sets of values that are possibly different or even divergent. The issue here is to resolve at least locally the tension emerging when putting agreed-upon principles into practice.

Whittlestone et al. (n.d.) has further identified four main tensions in the process of ethical principles implementation:

- Accuracy versus fair and equal treatment
- Personalization versus solidarity and citizenship
- Quality and efficiency of services versus privacy and informational autonomy
- Convenience versus self-actualization and dignity

In particular, can we solve these dilemmas involving conflicting values? For each of these dilemmas, is there a way to maximize both values or else is it possible to draw a clear ethical line maximizing the overall benefits while minimizing the costs? This would mean defining a metrics allowing us to quantify the ethical compliance with different sets of values.

For example, research on some CNN[24] artifacts dedicated to melanoma detection using digital dermoscopy images show overall some very accurate sensitivities and specificities.[25] However, the learning process is based on labeled image datasets from existing recorded cases. Wolff (2009) reports that the lifetime risk of dying from a melanoma is about 10 times higher for light skin individuals compared to dark skin ones. As a consequence, there are far less labeled images of dark skin melanomas available for the neural networks learning process and the diagnosis accuracy of such CNNs cannot be equivalent for all skin colors. In this case, overall accuracy is comparable to most dermatologists, but there is a lack of fairness in the accuracy expectations for a dark skin patient. Is this acceptable? What kind of trade-off would optimize the accuracy benefits without compromising the fairness principle?

10.2.3.5 Limitations

Based on Cowls et al. (2019), organizing the results of numerous studies published on arXiv and Scopus, among others, and of more than 70 "Ethical Codes of Practice" identified by Morley et al. (2020) in institutions and industry, we can observe that these applied research methodologies are only targeting the designer and the ethical modalities for developing an algorithm with the technical ambition of fitting the ethical principles. It may be objected that arXiv is dedicated to developers and scientists, but this is not the case with Scopus. Subsequent research on the Internet and in technology ethics journals has not given any more results in this direction. Hence, the current AI applied ethical factors present a first limitation in their scope: they are located only at the technical development level. On the one hand, it seems like an effective management strategy of the functional realization of explicitly pre-established principles; on the other hand, it denies both the user and the systemic environment the possibility to have an autonomy in their interaction with the AI artifact. The user is not considered an autonomous agent who can legitimately appropriate the AI object in an unplanned way. He/she is not considered a moral agent addressed by the ethical framework. The applied ethical system is intended for the "designer" as the only possible observer, as if the ethical approach is focused only at his/her position of action. And, in fact, all the recommendations are addressed exclusively to designers. Besides its projected technical efficiency, this applied technical ethics is unable to consider the implicit behaviors that might emerge apart from the intentional function the artifact has been programmed to fulfil.

Further to this limitation in the scope of AI, another limitation is directly related to the ethical theory choice. So far, the ethical frameworks were based on democratic social contracts, or else on principlistic deontology or contractarianism. Based on Beauchamp and Childress foundational work, this methodology aimed at establishing a technical framework ensuring compliance with ethical principles. We might then recall that Beauchamp and Childress' *The Principles of Biomedical Ethics* is presently in its 8th edition and has been extended in particular since its 4th edition in 1994. A new chapter was then arguing for the addition of five virtues—*trustworthiness, compassion, discernment, conscientousness*, and *integrity*,[26] thus advocating for the extension of principlistic ethics to virtue ethics. In doing so for AI ethics, it would be no longer only a question of constituting an ethical model for the AI development, but also of dealing with the responsibility that results from the action of every agent in the chain of production and use of AI, and therefore of refusing the modern substitution of *acting* by *doing*.[27] By adding those virtues, it is then a matter of acting responsibly and not only of doing ethics or even managing an ethical system.

The construction of an ethical system for AI should therefore be dual, principlistic as the only evaluable modality with demonstrable effectiveness, and reflective in the way responsible ethical behavior must be conducted, which is perhaps what Floridi et al. (2018, p. 692) referred to when mentioning the objective of "Enhancing Human Agency, Without Removing Human Responsibility."

10.3 PRINCIPLISM, VIRTUE ETHICS, AND AI IN MEDICINE

10.3.1 A New Principlism for AI in Medicine

Whether it concerns medicine or AI, it seems quite obvious that these two fields and industries raise many ethical problems, and thus generate a long list of declarations, conventions, codes, principles, guidelines, etc. For the different stakeholders working in the field of AI in healthcare, this great amount of texts probably makes their task more complex than it should be, though most of them may feel the necessity for an ethical regulation. That's why in this last part a framework for an ethical discussion is proposed, using as a basis what has been previously done in medical ethics and AI ethics. This framework is intended primarily for developers or engineers working in the field of AI related to healthcare, but also to users, i.e., both physicians (or healthcare professionals in general) and patients. More generally, it also encompasses, as medicine depends largely on a healthcare system in modern societies, the relationships between AI and healthcare in society. Our main goal is clearly not to supply the reader with some kind of recipe or method to solve ethical problems, a method or recipe that could be itself implemented in an Artificial Intelligence, but rather to make more explicit what is at stake in this nascent field of AI in healthcare and to point what should be considered as the major ethical principles which could or should be mobilized in any ethical discussion inside this field.

As a matter of fact, the most suitable tool or device is principlism, first proposed by Beauchamp and Childress (2013) and then completed by Floridi et al. (2018). Its main advantage is to put words on sometimes vague ideas and to allow people (computer and data scientists, engineers, physicians, patients, etc.) to state, discuss, and choose between different and sometimes contradictory values. As we saw, the four initial principles of principlism are beneficence, non-maleficence, autonomy, and justice. To these four principles, Floridi et al. (2018) added the principle of explicability, which is specific to AI and refers to both "the epistemological sense of *intelligibility* (as an answer to the question 'how does it work?') and in the ethical sense of *accountability* (as an answer to the question: 'who is responsible for the way it works?')" (Floridi and Cowls 2019). These five principles appear necessary to deal with the ethical issues raised by AI, but insufficient to tackle the specific issues raised by AI in healthcare.

More precisely, we may criticize the fact that the principle of explicability is too demanding or too stringent, not from an ethical point of view, but from an epistemic point of view. In other words, the "epistemological sense of intelligibility" is a good ethical principle but is very difficult or even impossible to realize in practice: most of the time, it is indeed not possible for the AI artifact's designer(s) and developer(s) to explain how it works in practice. As it is explained in the chapter on the epistemological issues of AI in healthcare, there is a gap between statistical correlations on which AI reasonings are based and a true causal relationship. And it appears that this gap is almost unsurmountable from an epistemic point of view. Therefore, it seems better and more efficient to adopt a semiological interpretability rather than a causal explicability: we thus propose to replace the principle of explicability by the principle of explainability. Explainable AI (XAI) has generated quite a huge literature in the last few years,[28] and many definitions of XAI can be found. For example, Barredo Arrieta et al. (2020) defined explainability as follows: "Given an audience, an **explainable** Artificial Intelligence is one that produces details or reasons to make its functioning clear or easy to understand.[29]" Wikipedia defines XAI as "methods and techniques in the application of artificial intelligence technology (AI) such that the results of the solution can be understood by humans."[30] We won't discuss that definition: the main idea is that XAI is opposed to the concept of "black box" where even the designers cannot explain the outcomes of AI reasoning, and thus is opposed to the principle of explicability. We thus consider that the principle of explainability is less stringent from an epistemic point of view than the principle of explicability, but as demanding as it is from an ethical point of view.

Furthermore, we consider that a sixth principle must be added, in order to restore an equilibrium: the principle of predictibility. By "predictibility," we do not refer to the "predictability" of AI, defined by the European High Level Expert Group guidelines, as the fact that for a system, "the outcome of the planning process must be consistent with the input," and which is considered "as a key mechanism to ensure that AI systems have not been compromised by external actors" (Fjeld et al. 2020). On the contrary, by "predictibility" we mean the capacity of AI to predict a result or an outcome, for example, in the medical context, of a disease, of a treatment, etc. This criterion of predictibility is originally a technical one: for example, in Machine Learning, prediction refers to the output of an algorithm after it has been trained on a historical dataset and applied to new data when forecasting the likelihood of a particular outcome. It the predicted outcome happens, it is a proof that the software is working properly. From an epistemological point of view, it refers to the criteria of verification or confirmation: if a scientific theory predicts correctly some events, then this theory must be considered as correct. From an ethical point of view, it is a way to morally judge AI not on the basis of its algorithm, or the way it works (and judge who is responsible for that) but to judge it on its results or on its consequences, without having to open the black box, i.e., account for the way it works. This appears particularly important in a medical context: in this context, medical predictions and medical decisions, whether they are or not produced or aided by AI, are a matter of life and death.

It has been noticed before that among the four principles of principlism defined by Beauchamp and Childress, two of them were deontological, namely, autonomy and justice, and two of them were teleological, namely, nonmaleficence and beneficence. This categorization can also be applied to the principles of explainability and of predictibility: explainability can be considered as a deontological principle and predictiblity as a teleological principle. Explainability indeed refers to the idea of responsibility: Barredo Arrieta et al. (2020) put, for example, this principle in relation to those of fairness and accountability. In other words, explainability appears as a matter of principle and not of consequences. Conversely, the principle of predictibility focuses on the results or the consequences of AI, and thus pertains to teleological ethics: the problem is not to know how it works or why it works that way, but to be sure that it produces good, or more good than harm.

10.3.2 THE NEW PRINCIPLISM IN A CLINICAL AND PUBLIC HEALTH CONTEXT

To test the operationality of these six ethical principles, it is important to apply them first to the clinical or medical context, where the three actors are the physician, the patient, and an Artificial Intelligence; and then to the context of public health in a broad sense, where the private companies and the state are involved through

AI technologies (for example, the Big Tech), health insurance (private or public), and through several instances of regulation such as associations (of physicians or of patients) or diverse health agencies (for example, in the United States, the Food and Drug Administration and the Center for Disease Control and Prevention). The issues regarding the physician-patient relationship are individual, whereas the issues regarding public health are collective and societal. It appears that the six principles stipulated here constitute a simple and efficient solution to tackle the ethical issues at both the individual and the collective level.

For example, if we focus on the physician-patient relationship, the principle of autonomy commands that all the information (or almost all) given by the patient to his physician stay confidential, due to medical secrecy. This rule of confidentiality applies equally to the data provided by users of, for example, mobile health applications, even if there are clearly more actors involved here and if the ownership of the data is a tricky issue. The principle of autonomy can be linked to the principle of explainability: the idea here is that the functioning of an AI artifact can be understood, and can be understood differently according to the "audience," i.e., a patient or a physician. A last issue related to the principle of autonomy is the notion of informed consent: to be informed, the person consenting to something must know and understand what he consents to; the principle of explainability can serve as a way to inform the person on how an AI artifact is functioning and thus permit the consent to be valid. A similar reasoning can be made about the deontological principle of justice: the function of the principle of explainability is to ensure that every user is treated fairly and is not subject to several bias produced by an AI artifact. From a public health and populational perspective, the conciliation of the principles of justice and explainability is supposed to guarantee that the allocation of resources is fair, or, in other words, that the resources go to those who need it more. Ultimately, beyond the ethical issue, there is a social and political issue: in case there is a breach in the confidentiality, or bias that would lead to medical errors, or inequalities in the treatment of patients or in the allocation of resources, someone (an individual or a company) has to pay for it, that is has to be responsible for it. Blaming the algorithm cannot be a way to escape one's responsibility.

From a teleological perspective, the principles of beneficence and non-maleficence constitute an essential feature of the physician-patient relationship. Though it is merely science fiction, we can think about the first law of the Three Laws of Robotics created by Isaac Asimov which states that "A robot may not injure a human being or, through inaction, allow a human being to come to harm"(Asimov 1950). This could be applied to any AI artifact, especially in a medical context: though it is not sure if it can be implemented, these two principles must be considered if AI is to be considered as responsible. The principle of predictibility intervenes at this point to evaluate ex post if an AI artifact has done good, or has not done harm, or has done more good than harm. This can be applied to both a medical (drugs, surgery, etc.) or a public health action (vaccination, public health insurance) intervention, and both to a preventive or a curative action. Every action must indeed be evaluated or assessed on both its principles and its consequences on the global health of an individual patient or of a population.

10.3.3 THE NEW PRINCIPLISM AND VIRTUE ETHICS: FOR A RESPONSIBLE AI IN HEALTHCARE

If the six principles stipulated here are necessary to address ethical issues regarding the use of AI in healthcare, they are however not sufficient. As seen before in Section 10.1.3.1, many conflicts between principles exist, for example, between teleological and deontological principles (such as beneficence and justice), or even between deontological principles or teleological principles themselves (for example, beneficence and non-maleficence). The two principles proposed here, explainability and predictibility, can of course be in conflict in certain medical situations: it is probable that, for example, the ability to predict an outcome can be achieved at the expense of the explainability of the outcome. According to us, this is why deontological and teleological ethics must be supplemented or balanced with virtue ethics.

As we saw in Section 10.1.3.2, virtue ethics, by referring to the "practical wisdom" of the actors involved in response to a specific action (or set of actions) in a specific situation, seems particularly adapted to clinical or public health situations or interventions. The main argument here is that insofar as a physician or a patient or other stakeholder has to choose between different ethical principles in a situation when there is no good solution, the only way to justify an ethical choice between principles in a specific situation is to appeal to the practical wisdom of the participants to this situation (physician, patient, etc.), i.e., to virtue ethics. In other words, principlism (the 6 principles) permit to name the values and to discuss about the value of these values for the participants, but the tensions that may arise between conflicting values, which determines the action to be done, can be ultimately resolved based on such practical wisdom. Thus, if the principle of beneficence or non-maleficence is chosen after a discussion, the patient must trust the virtue of the physician. Conversely, if the principle of autonomy is chosen, it is the physician who must trust the practical wisdom of the patient. The same argument applies to a public health context where the government would have to choose between, for example, beneficence and justice: in this case however, virtue ethics must be balanced by some kind of democratic procedure. The last point is that in relation to AI, it could also be a choice of the physician or of the patient (or of the government and the citizens) to choose between predictibility and explainability: the main point here is that AI artifacts should not decide by themselves and should propose different options, leaving the choice to its human operators.

Virtue ethics is probably the least implementable ethics, precisely because it refers to something that is specifically human: life experience, a kind of wisdom, an attention given to specific situations, and, finally, a sense of mankind. In a medical context as well, there are specific virtues which "derive primarily from experience with health care relationships": Beauchamp and Childress (2013) mention "five focal virtues: compassion, discernment, trustworthiness, integrity, and conscientiousness, all of which support and promote caring and caregiving." These virtues are surely a fundamental part of the practice of any healthcare professionals. That's why virtue ethics can constitute an invaluable help to put the six principles into practice, in order to create a responsible AI in healthcare. Of course, this won't solve automatically all

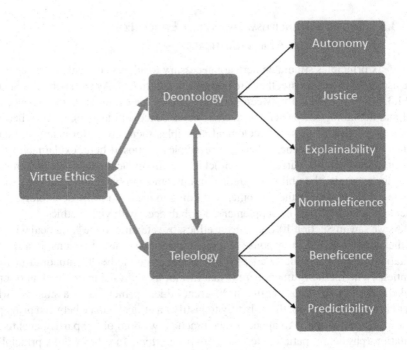

FIGURE 10.1 A proposal for an ethical AI in medicine.

the ethical dilemmas that exist in daily medical practice. But as it is about ethics, it is always about how things ought to be rather than how things are.

Figure 10.1 shows the proposal for an ethical AI in medicine.

NOTES

1. For example, https://en.wikipedia.org/wiki/Hippocratic_Oath.
2. For such a critic, see Clouser and Gert (1990).
3. See p. 28.
4. For further representative readings regarding the critical stance of Technic, see Ellul 1964; Illich 1973; Adorno and Horkheimer 1994; Marcuse 1991; Winner 2020; and Habermas 1987.
5. Formal, material, efficient and final causes which tell us the how, with what, who, and why of the physical emergence of an artifact. For more details, see Aristotle (2008).
6. Simon (1955, p. 101): "Because of the psychological limits of the organism (...), actual human rationality-striving can at best be extremely crude and simplified approximation to the kind of global rationality that is implied, for example, by game theoretical models."
7. As stated at the Dartmouth AI Conference, August 31, 1955, by J. McCarthy et al.
8. See, for instance, Arnaud Montebourg's candidacy to the French socialist party nomination for the 2017 Presidential election.
9. See Anders (2018a).
10. See Google's AI ethics principles: https://ai.google/principles/.
11. See IEEE's "Global Initiative on Ethics of Autonomous and Intelligent Systems": https://standards.ieee.org/develop/indconn/ec/autonomous_systems.html.

12. See regulatory framework for "Sofware as Medical Devices," initiated by the IMDRF (International Medical Device Regulators Forum), approved in 2018 by the American FDA and the UE.
13. See in particular the *Déclaration de Montréal IA Responsable*, retrieved on 24/ 09/2019 at: https://www.declarationmontreal-iaresponsable.com/rapport-de-la-declaration.
14. Such as the GAFAM: Google, Apple, Facebook, Amazon, Microsoft.
15. *International Telecommunication Union.*
16. A deontological ethics is thus principlistic.
17. Except for religious morality.
18. Ashford and Mulgan (2018): "According to contractualism, morality consists in what would result if we were to make binding agreements from a point of view that respects our equal moral importance as rational autonomous agents."
19. Ashford and Mulgan (2018): "Under contractarianism, I seek to maximise my own interests in a bargain with others."
20. See https://futureoflife.org/ai-principles/.
21. See www.partnershiponai.org/tenets/.
22. Retrieved on 24/09/2019 from https://www.montrealdeclaration-responsibleai.com/the-declaration.s
23. Ibid. p. 8
24. Convolutional Neural Networks.
25. See Haenssle et al. (2018); Esteva et al. (2017).
26. See Garchar and Kaag (2013).
27. See Arendt (2018).
28. For an overview of the literature on XAI, see Barredo Arrieta et al. (2020).
29. Italics in the original text.
30. https://en.wikipedia.org/wiki/Explainable_artificial_intelligence#cite_note-guardian-1 (retrieved on 09/01/2020).

REFERENCES

Adorno, Theodor W, and Max Horkheimer. 1994. *Dialectic of Enlightenment*. New York: Continuum.
Anders, Günther. 2018a. *Die Antiquiertheit des Mensche. Band 2: Über die Zerstörung des Lebens im Zeitalter der dritten industriellen Revolution*. 4., durchgesehene Auflage. München: C.H.Beck.
Anders, Günther. 2018b. *Die Antiquiertheit des Menschen. Band 1: Über die Seele im Zeitalter der zweiten industriellen Revolution*. 4., durchgesehene Auflage. München: C.H.Beck.
Anscombe, G E M. 1958. "Modern Moral Philosophy." *Philosophy* 33 (124): 19.
Arendt, Hannah. 2018. *The Human Condition*. 2nd edition. Chicago and London: The University of Chicago Press.
Aristotle. 2008. *Physics*. Translated by Robin Waterfield and David Bostock. Oxford World's Classics. Oxford and New York: Oxford University Press.
Aristotle. 2009. *The Nicomachean Ethics*. Translated by W. D. Ross and Lesley Brown. Oxford and New York: Oxford University Press.
Ashford, Elizabeth, and Tim Mulgan. 2018. "Contractualism." In *The Stanford Encyclopedia of Philosophy*, edited by Edward N. Zalta, Summer 2018. Metaphysics Research Lab, Stanford University. https://plato.stanford.edu/archives/sum2018/entries/contractualism/.
Asimov, Isaac. 1950. *I, Robot*. Garden City, NY: Doubleday.
Barredo Arrieta, Alejandro, Natalia Díaz-Rodríguez, Javier Del Ser, Adrien Bennetot, Siham Tabik, Alberto Barbado, Salvador Garcia, et al. 2020. "Explainable Artificial Intelligence (XAI): Concepts, Taxonomies, Opportunities and Challenges toward Responsible AI." *Information Fusion* 58 (June): 82–115. doi: 10.1016/j.inffus.2019.12.012.

Beauchamp, Tom L., and James F. Childress. 2013. *Principles of Biomedical Ethics*. 7th ed. New York: Oxford University Press.

Bentham, Jeremy. 1789. *An Introduction to the Principles of Morals and Legislation*. 1st ed. London: T. Payne.

Bostrom, Nick. 2009. "Ethical Issues in Advanced Artificial Intelligence." In *Science Fiction and Philosophy: From Time Travel to Superintelligence*, edited by Susan Schneider, 277–84. Hoboken, NJ: Wiley-Blackwell.

Bostrom, Nick. 2014. *Superintelligence: Paths, Dangers, Strategies*. 1st edition. Oxford: Oxford University Press.

Clouser, K. D., and B. Gert. 1990. "A Critique of Principlism." *Journal of Medicine and Philosophy* 15 (2): 219–36. doi: 10.1093/jmp/15.2.219.

Condorcet, Marie-Jean-Antoine-Nicolas Caritat, Marquis de. 1791. *Outlines of an Historical View of the Progress of the Human Mind*. The Online Library Of Liberty. http://oll-reso urces.s3.amazonaws.com/titles/1669/Condorcet_0878_EBk_v6.0.pdf.

Cowls, Josh, Thomas King, Mariarosaria Taddeo, and Luciano Floridi. 2019. "Designing AI for Social Good: Seven Essential Factors." *SSRN Electronic Journal*. doi: 10.2139/ ssrn.3388669.

Ellul, Jacques. 1964. *The Technological Society*. Translated by John Wilkinson. Knopf. A Vintage Book. New York, NY: Vintage books.

Esteva, Andre, Brett Kuprel, Roberto A. Novoa, Justin Ko, Susan M. Swetter, Helen M. Blau, and Sebastian Thrun. 2017. "Dermatologist-Level Classification of Skin Cancer with Deep Neural Networks." *Nature* 542 (7639): 115–18. doi: 10.1038/nature21056.

Evans, Jonathan St B. T. 1990. *Bias in Human Reasoning: Causes and Consequences*. Essays in Cognitive Psychology. Hove and London, LEA.

Fjeld, Jessica, Nele Achten, Hannah Hilligoss, Adam Nagy, and Madhulika Srikumar. 2020. "Principled Artificial Intelligence: Mapping Consensus in Ethical and Rights-based Approaches to Principles for AI." *Berkman Klein Center for Internet & Society*. http:// nrs.harvard.edu/urn-3:HUL.InstRepos:42160420

Floridi, Luciano. 1999. "Information Ethics: On the Philosophical Foundation of Computer Ethics." *Ethics and Information Technology* 1 (1): 33–52. doi: 10.1023/A:1010018611096.

Floridi, Luciano, and Josh Cowls.2019. "A Unified Framework of Five Principles for AI in Society." *Harvard Data Science Review*, 1(1). https://doi.org/10.1162/99608f92.8c d550d1

Floridi, Luciano, Josh Cowls, Monica Beltrametti, Raja Chatila, Patrice Chazerand, Virginia Dignum, Christoph Luetge, et al. 2018. "AI4People—An Ethical Framework for a Good AI Society: Opportunities, Risks, Principles, and Recommendations." *Minds and Machines* 28 (4): 689–707. doi: 10.1007/s11023-018-9482-5.

Floridi, Luciano, Josh Cowls, Thomas King, Mariarosaria Taddeo. 2020. "How to Design AI for Social Good: Seven Essential Factors." *Science and Engineering Ethics* 26 (3): 1771–1796. doi: 10.1007/s11948-020-00213-5. Epub 2020 Apr 3. PMID: 32246245; PMCID: PMC7286860.

Garchar, and Kaag. 2013. "Classical American Philosophy and Modern Medical Ethics: The Case of Richard Cabot." *Transactions of the Charles S. Peirce Society* 49 (4): 553. doi: 10.2979/trancharpeirsoc.49.4.553.

Gilligan, Carol. 1993. *In a Different Voice: Psychological Theory and Women's Development*. Cambridge, MA: Harvard University Press.

Habermas, Jürgen. 1987. *Knowledge and Human Interests*. Cambridge: Polity Press.

Haenssle, H A, C Fink, R Schneiderbauer, F Toberer, T Buhl, A Blum, A Kalloo, et al. 2018. "Man against Machine: Diagnostic Performance of a Deep Learning Convolutional Neural Network for Dermoscopic Melanoma Recognition in Comparison to 58 Dermatologists." *Annals of Oncology* 29 (8): 1836–42. doi: 10.1093/annonc/mdy166.

Illich, Ivan. 1973. *Tools for Conviviality*. London and New York: Marion Boyars.

Johnson, Deborah G., and Thomas M. Powers. 2005. "Ethics and Technology: A Program for Future Research." In *Encyclopedia of Science, Technology, and Ethics*, edited by Carl Mitcham. Detroit, MI: Macmillan Reference USA.

Jonas, Hans. 1985. *The Imperative of Responsibility: In Search of an Ethics for the Technological Age*. Chicago: University of Chicago Press.

Kahneman, Daniel, and Amos Tversky. 1979. "Prospect Theory: An Analysis of Decision under Risk." *Econometrica* 47 (2): 263. doi: 10.2307/1914185.

Kant, Immanuel. 1998. *Groundwork of the Metaphysics of Morals*. Translated by Mary J. Gregor. Cambridge Texts in the History of Philosophy. Cambridge, UK and New York: Cambridge University Press.

Kitcher, Philip. 2001. *Science, Truth, and Democracy*. Oxford Studies in Philosophy of Science. Oxford and New York: Oxford University Press.

Marcuse, Herbert. 1991. *One-Dimensional Man*. Boston: Beacon Press.

Morley, Jessica, Luciano Floridi, Libby Kinsey, and Anat Elhalal. 2020. "From What to How: An Initial Review of Publicly Available AI Ethics Tools, Methods and Research to Translate Principles into Practices." *Science and Engineering Ethics* 26 (4): 2141–68. doi: 10.1007/s11948-019-00165-5.

Müller, Vincent C., ed. 2016. *Fundamental Issues of Artificial Intelligence*. Synthese Library, Studies in Epistemology, Logic, Methodology, and Philosophy of Science, vol. 376. Cham: Springer.

Newton, Adam Zachary. 1997. *Narrative Ethics*. 1. Harvard Univ. Press paperback ed. Cambridge, MA: Harvard Univ. Press.

Simon, Herbert A. 1955. "A Behavioral Model of Rational Choice." *The Quarterly Journal of Economics* 69 (1): 99. doi: 10.2307/1884852.

Smith, Merritt Roe. 1994. "Technological Determinism in American Culture." In *Does Technology Drive History? The Dilemma of Technological Determinism*, edited by Merritt Roe Smith and Leo Marx, 1–35. Cambridge, MA: MIT Press.

Taddeo, Mariarosaria, and Luciano Floridi. 2018. "How AI Can Be a Force for Good." *Science* 361 (6404): 751–52. doi: 10.1126/science.aat5991.

Tversky, Amos. 1969. "Intransitivity of Preferences." *Psychological Review* 76 (1): 31–48. doi: 10.1037/h0026750.

Whittlestone, Jess, Rune Nyrup, Anna Alexandrova, Kanta Dihal, and Stephen Cave. n.d. "Ethical and Societal Implications of Algorithms, Data, and Artificial Intelligence: A Roadmap for Research," 59.

Winner, Langdon. 2020. *The Whale and the Reactor: A Search for Limits in an Age of High Technology*. 2nd ed. Chicago: University of Chicago Press.

Wolff, Tracy. 2009. "Screening for Skin Cancer: An Update of the Evidence for the U.S. Preventive Services Task Force." *Annals of Internal Medicine* 150 (3): 194. doi: 10.7326/0003-4819-150-3-200902030-00009.

11 Epistemological Issues and Challenges with Artificial Intelligence in Healthcare

Nicolas Brault, Benoît Duchemann,
and Mohit Saxena

CONTENTS

11.1 KEY ISSUES IN PHILOSOPHY OF ARTIFICIAL INTELLIGENCE (AI)

11.1.1 A SHORT HISTORY OF AI: FROM 17TH CENTURY'S CALCULATORS TO THE DARTMOUTH ARTIFICIAL INTELLIGENCE CONFERENCE (2005)

11.1.1.1 From Pascal to Turing: A Prehistory of AI

Some set the computer science birth (without the actual naming) in the early 19th century and Charles Babbage's Analytical Engine,[1] the first mechanical programmable calculator using punch cards. We could go further in the past with Pascal's Pascaline[2] or Leibniz's Arithmetic Machine[3] as technical artifacts aimed at computing calculations. Those inventions were already simulating basic computations normally performed by human minds.

Much later, the turning point of computer science is more likely to be attributed to Alan Turing. With his 1936 abstract "a-machine,"[4] he is considered as the "mythological" father of computer science. He is the initiator of computer science as a theoretical and scientific discipline. With his abstract machine, he could prove the uncomputability of the *Entscheidungsproblem* ("decision problem")[5] and further the fundamental limitations in the power of performing mechanical computations. It was the first time a symbolic language combined with a complex logic system was conceived specifically for an automatic machine in order to represent and symbolize problems and the whole computation procedure leading to their solutions.

As for Artificial Intelligence, his contribution was more of a predictive and philosophical one.

In his 1950 publication, *Computing Machinery and Intelligence* (Turing 1950), he detailed his famous Imitation Game, or Turing Test dedicated to challenge future computers in their ability to ape human beings in their speech proficiency. Hence, he offered a first—although reductionist—definition of intelligence and implicitly a first definition of Artificial Intelligence.

In his test, a first human is considered as the blind evaluator. Facing him are a computer and another human. The computer succeeds if the evaluator cannot distinguish its communication with the other human's. John Searle later challenged the Turing Test validity with his Chinese Room model (Searle 1980). According to him there is no necessary correlation between mechanically answering the questions of the evaluator and understanding the questions and the answer delivered, even if right, hence putting the emphasis on the meaning rather than on the procedure.

11.1.1.2 From Turing to Dartmouth: A First Definition of AI

The period of time from Turing to Dartmouth is marked by the emergence of the first electronic[6] computers, such as the EDSAC created in 1949 by Maurice Wilkes' team at the University of Cambridge Mathematical Laboratory (the first computer with an internally stored program) or the EDVAC (*E*lectronic *D*iscrete *V*ariable *A*utomatic *C*omputer) at the Ballistics Research Laboratory with the collaboration of the University of Pennsylvania and based upon Von Neumann's theoretical project. ENIAC (Electronic Numerical Integrator And Computer) is considered the very first fully electronic computer, which was developed in 1945 at the Moore School of Electrical Engineering from UPenn, but it had to be recabled in order for every other program to be executed.

The aim of a computer is to process calculations that are normally processed by human minds. The very concept of computer is thus developed as a human mind imitation.

To that extent, this period is marked by the tension between two theories of the mind, between connexionists and cognitivists, and between a neurological and a symbolic conception of the mind.

Connexionists were willing to modelize it as a "black box" gifted with feedback or retraction mechanisms. The main success of this research is the mathematical modelization[7] of basic constituents of the brain: formal neurons (Figure 11.1).

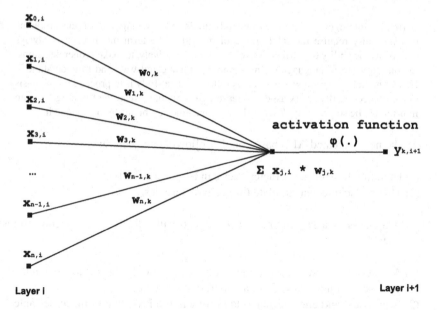

FIGURE 11.1   Mathematical modelization of a formal neural network.

McCulloch and Pitts proposed to simulate the brain behavior through a model using billions of basic neurons. Further to their research, the neuropsychologist Donald Hebb invented in 1949 the Hebb rule that enabled the neurons to learn:

> When an axon of cell A is near enough to excite B and repeatedly or persistently takes part in firing it, some growth process or metabolic change takes place in one or both cells such that A's efficiency, as one of the cells firing B, is increased.
>
> **(Hebb 1949)**

Using the Hebb rule, Franck Rosenblatt invented in 1957 the Perceptron: the first neural network with one layer and capable of learning.

On the other hand, cognitivists considered that thought can be described at an abstract level as a manipulation of symbols, whatever the materiality of the manipulation medium (brain or electronic machine). This approach supposes *a priori* a relationship between thought and language that can be formalized as a system of symbols.

One cognitivist (or symbolic) scheme consists in having machines manipulate language through symbols.

In 1956, four scientists, John McCarthy (Dartmouth College), Marvin Lee Minsky (Harvard University), Nathaniel Rochester (from IBM Corporation), and Claude Shannon (Bell Labs and theorist of Information Theory), invited some of their colleagues to a summer seminar at the Dartmouth College (New Hampshire, USA) to work on a new computation modality that is named for the first time : Artificial Intelligence. This is considered as the birth date of the AI field.

The seminar conclusions contain a formal definition for AI, thus including as a prerequisite a general definition for intelligence:

> "Artificial intelligence comprises methods, tools, and systems for solving problems that normally require the intelligence of humans. The term intelligence is always defined as the ability to learn effectively, to react adaptively, to make proper decisions, to communicate in language or images in a sophisticated way, and to understand."[8] Hence the field program was defined as follows: "The study is to proceed on the basis of the conjecture that every aspect of learning or any other feature of intelligence can in principle be so precisely described that a machine can be made to simulate it."

Thus, the newly created AI is based on the following conjecture:

(1) Human intelligence characteristics can be accurately described.
(2) That a machine can simulate these characteristics.

The AI appears at a key moment when two parallel fields are emerging almost simultaneously:

(1) A theoretical and scientific field dedicated to study the nature of intelligence and human mind from a materialistic perspective.
(2) A practical and engineering field aiming at the invention of machines able to process information and to calculate.

At that moment, Newell and Simon are fully convinced that real AI is within reach: "There are now in the world machines that think, that learn and that create" (Simon and Newell 1958).

11.1.1.3 Neural Networks versus Expert Systems

The short history of AI has been highlighted by the tension between connexionist and cognitivist theories. Is has thus been marked by the tension between those willing to simulate the brain behavior through its atomistic neural components and those willing to emulate the symbolic knowledge and reasoning.

On the one hand, the connexionist theory has known major impediments in the 1970s through the logical XOR crisis and a lack of practical achievements.

On the other hand, symbolic reasoning systems gave birth to expert systems. Restricting those programs to limited domains and with a small level of reasoning ambiguities managed to set limits to the combinatory explosion of rule production systems. An expert system encapsulates knowledge structured as rules and facts and can reason on that knowledge base by using some inference mechanisms as follows: if fact F is asserted, then action A. Its aim was then to emulate the human expert cognition within a limited domain.

For instance, DENDRAL (*Dendritic Algorithm*)[9] contained all the expert chemist knowledge and used it to solve problems of chemical components identification based on physical measurements. MYCIN[10] was dedicated to blood infectious diseases diagnosis (later to meningitis) and their associated medical prescription. For the first time, the inference engine is clearly separated from the knowledge and the expert system is able to explain its reasoning. In 1978, a clinical trial was conducted where MYCIN was challenged by nine physicians in the diagnosis of 80 patients suffering from meningitis. The results then evaluated by eight meningitis specialists were in favor of the algorithm. Many more examples of expert system achievements are available: PROSPECTOR in 1976 in Stanford, TAXMAN in 1977, or DELTA (Diesel Electric Locomotive Troubleshooting Aid) by General Electric in the beginning of the 1980s for assisting locomotive failure diagnosis.

Those systems were efficient for specific tasks where no algorithmic procedure was known in a specific narrow and technical knowledge domain.

11.1.1.4 Emergence and Development: Neural Networks and Machine Learning (ML)

In 1982, John Hopfield's research got neural networks research back on track. As a solution to neural network limitations, Hopfield proposed a fully connected (but non-reflexive) multilayer neural network. To make his point, he made an analogy with energy states of atoms in statistical physics and made it clear that physics was a field for a direct application of neural networks.

For every layer, neuron nods still work the same way as for the Perceptron, but some hidden layers are added and connected one to another.

The fundamental research that followed this moment, the emergence of personal computers, and the Internet bringing more and more computer power and foremost more and more data related to human behaviors created the conditions of development of modern AI, based on neural networks, and modern computers for the mathematical and technical part and so-called Big Data as the necessary fuel to Machine Learning, to the machine imitating human cognitive behaviors. As of today, we can classify AI learning in three main categories:

- *Unsupervised learning:* Can use examples without labels, or can generate its own examples. Needs the rules (of the game), in order to be able to play and evaluate an example, i.e. AlphaGo Zero learnt by playing against itself.
- *Supervised learning:* The system learns a labeled dataset (pairs input + expected output), it builds up the matrix of neural weights that will optimize a function f relating the input to its ideal output.
- *Reinforcement learning:* Optimization of cumulative reward.

11.1.2 THE MODERN CONCEPTS OF ARTIFICIAL INTELLIGENCE AND BIG DATA

The main AI industrial applications are nowadays based on supervised learning. The aim is to predict an expected output y for an input x or rather to compute an approximated output y_e, which should be a good approximation of the ideal y with a maximum acceptable error ε, and a minimum acceptable probability p_e: $p(y_e - y < \varepsilon) < p_e$. In order to achieve this end, during the learning stage, the program must calculate the matrix of neural weights at all neural nods.

To do so, a training dataset is input. This is a set of pairs of inputs and their expected outputs. In the case of a melanoma detection program, the dataset is a set of pairs (x_i, y_i), where x_i is an image of a cutaneous lesion and y_i is its known related diagnosis.

Neural weights are initiated stochastically. Initial outputs with initial weights are computed. So it is the initial error ε_0 to the expected output for every input. Using most often the retro-propagation of gradient, with output layer being layer number n, weights of layer $n - 1$ are tuned to reduce the initial error (cost function); according to layer $n - 1$, weights of layer $n - 2$ are tuned as well; and so on. When the full weight matrix has been recalculated, a new output is once again calculated with a new cost function ε_1, and so on, step by step, until the statistical error on the whole dataset is within range.

The main issue of those computations is obviously the dimensionality.

The dimensionality problem is correlated with the input data: a 2D image is worth approximately 10^6 pixels, an audio file 10^6 bits per mn, as for a text, a mole of matter is worth 10^{24} bits.

If the input data is to be represented using vectors,[11] it will first be represented atomistically in the input space. For instance, an image will be represented in a n-dimension space where n is the number of atoms of data present in the input. A black and white image of 10^6 pixels will be initially represented in a 10^6-dimension space where its coordinates will be the black color ratio for a given pixel.

Obviously, the dimensionality needs to be reduced in order to perform computations efficiently. There is a necessity to find regularities that will enable the system to represent parsimoniously the data, by compressing it in a reasonably big dimensional latent space without losing relevant data.

Hence, the learning stage is about the simultaneous mechanized construction

- of the parsimonious statistical representation of a given dataset in the latent space and
- of the neural weights matrix that enables to represent any given input not already present in the dataset.

This dual representation processing gives rise to a model, as defined by Minsky[12]. The probable prediction the AI program is aiming at concerning the input x is actually the output of a computation based on its representation or its model x^* in the latent space. This model can also be seen as a multidimensional measurement of its original input. For a given model, a chosen prediction[13] program should compute the probable end result.

11.1.3 AI: FROM DATA TO KNOWLEDGE

11.1.3.1 Truth and Proof

The epistemological issue related to software computations concerns the insurance that the end computed result is as expected; hence, it is true or a good enough reflection of the truth that shall be ascertained by proof.

A first way to consider the proof concept is the *tekhnê*'s "right rule"[14] that shall be used to produce a technical artifact. Software Verification and validation as defined by Mackall, Nelson, and Schumman 2002) is "the process of ensuring that software being developed or changed will satisfy functional and other requirements (verification) and each step in the process of building the software yields the right products (validation). In other words:

- Verification—Build the Product Right
- Validation—Build the Right Product"

A second version of the proof concept may be considered as in Tarski (1969, p. 70) as "a procedure of ascertaining the truth of sentences which is employed primarily in deductive science." In this case, the proofs show how the end result can be deducted logically from axiomatic premises.

Tymoczko claims:

> If we view proofs as abstract patterns, it seems obvious that the mere existence of a proof of a theorem guarantees the truth of the theorem (modulo axioms, etc.). There aren't any "gaps" in the (real) proof; it is rigorous, indeed the standard of "rigor." In the case of formal proofs, the idea of rigor can be explained in terms of logical validity.
> **(Tymoczko 1980)**

Would the difference in proof value be then only a matter of "rigor" ?

We find the difference to be more conceptual. While V&V proposes procedures managing the software development organization and testing the code for bugs or failures until their absence is reached, the deductive process aims at proving positively that the end result is logically true. Thus, there is an epistemic tension about the way of ascertaining truth between a technical approach based on pragmatic verification and validation and a scientific approach based on formal logic. The former's semantics is validity and evidence, while the latter's is truth and proof. The former is based on synthetic statements grounded on real phenomena, while the latter is based on analytic statements grounded on axioms and meanings. The former is aiming at decision and action, while the latter is aiming at certainty.

This is not a new tension in computer science as the past decades have shown numerous pessimistic arguments regarding the lack of proof of computer programs and the significant number of potential accidents related to unproven software. (Wiener 1985) mentions the original argument for proving limitations in a program development[15]; Dijkstra (1972) mentions the logical bias of program testing[16] not able to prove the absence of a faulty code; Thom (1971) mentions the human "impossibility of verifying all its steps."[17]

The tension rose dramatically in the late 1970s with the computer-assisted resolution of the 4-color problem.[18] It made even more pronounced the formal proof issue. This event is about the resolution of a mathematical problem with the help of mechanized computations. The question that arises is whether the proof should comply with mathematical proving norms or whether other scientific or technological norms could be used as a proving scheme. Tymoczko (1980) claims that "what has been checked is not rigorous" and that "what is rigorous hasn't been checked" and furthermore cannot be humanly checked. Thus, the computer-assisted proof does not comply with the standards of an acceptable mathematical demonstration proof. The noted lack of rigor draws a line between the possibility error, although small, and certainty.

We may consider as well the main proofs characteristics as in Tymoczko (1979) and in particular that they should be "convincing," "formalizable," and "surveyable," in particular that "a proof is a construction that can be looked over, reviewed, verified, by a rational agent." To that respect, the four-color demonstration proof is not formalizable and particularly not humanly surveyable.

By presenting this way the four-color problem resolution, our aim was not to criticize its demonstration[19] but to show that the way to manage proof in computer science was and is not self-evident.

In the end, we may regard this issue as related to our view of the computer science nature. Is computer science purely applied mathematics, does it relate to natural sciences with an empirical content, or is it merely an engineering discipline aiming at reliability and quality ? And should it be proven accordingly?

11.1.3.2 Machine Learning: Logic, Reliability, and Knowledge

This tension is slightly more complex where Machine Learning is concerned. Hoare (1996) noted that:

> the most dramatic advances in the timely delivery of dependable software are directly attributed to a wider recognition of the fact that the process of program development

can be predicted, planned, managed and controlled in the same way as in any other branch of engineering.

However, development of an ML software involves at least two objects. The first object is about the learning program which is the result of specific software engineering grounded on management rules and norms. The second object is the trained software. For neural networks with supervised learning, it is inherently a process grounded on a dataset which is itself a reduction of a limited series of experiments. It is also a process that is not directly programmed by human engineers but the result of step-by step complex computations.

The first programmed object (object P) is subject to engineering development standards such as verification and validation IEEE[20] Standard 1012[TM21] and testing IEEE Standard 829[TM].[22] As a programmed software, the epistemic tension here is released by the application of engineering development management schemes. The program is planned, managed, controlled, and evaluated and then given evidence for the validity of its function, architecture, and interface.

As for the second object (object T), it is the result of an experimental training of object P using a chosen dataset as an empirical grounding. Object T must be evaluated in order to prove that the acquired but unformalized knowledge leads to proper results, that its outputs are as the existing human knowledge would predict them. If we consider object T as an engineering artifact, it should be V&Ved following previously mentioned standards. If we consider it to be the result of a natural science experiment, it should be proven as per the epistemic standards of the considered object, i.e., an AI software dedicated to detecting a melanoma in a dermoscopy image should be validated according to the clinical trials standards. Finally, if we consider it to be an artifact dedicated to formally modelizing knowledge by using applied mathematics, it should be proven using logic.

For example, similar experiments considering the AI software as a technical device or as a medical device will propose different ways of proving its reliability and truthfulness.[23]

On the other hand, if we were to have a logical approach to the Machine Learning processes, the question should arise as to what kind of logic could be used to validate formally the program resulting from the training stage, i.e., that the program produces true results. Truth is an assertion that needs a proof. And proofs can be given in different manners: first of all, by showing the reality of the assertion in all its occurrences, or through a formal causal argument using Aristotelian syllogistic, modal logic, or any other valid formal inference theory.

ML training using supervised learning is based on a dataset, i.e., on a set of individual experimental results in order to infer a general ability to compute any result from any input not present yet in the dataset. It is thus about inferring general propositions from particular ones, thus induction. Let us remind Mill's (1882, p. 208) definition for induction: "Induction may be defined the operation of discovering and proving general propositions."

By "proving," Mill meant inferring in accordance to his *System of Logic*. Hence, qualifying Machine Learning processes as inductive because they go from particular propositions to general processes goes without saying but qualifying the actual logic being used as induction seems a bit excessive without the formal proof that should go along with it.

However, there exists several theorems proving formally some of the behaviors of Machine Learning programs.

Those theorems supply a logical framework to the computations taking place during the training stage. However, they prove formally neither the validity of the dataset representation in the chosen space nor the validity of the predictions output from the unlearnt data, although there are proofs that under certain conditions an infinite size knowledge domain is learnable,[24] that the learning process can converge toward a final model, and that its predictions can be "probably approximately correct" (Shalev-Shwartz and Ben-David 2014). They do not prove, for example, that a domain is learnable within a reasonable machine-time cost, that the point of convergence is optimal, or that the learnt knowledge is bias-free.

Finally, the ambiguous Machine Learning epistemic position is well summarized by Stéphane Mallat (2019) in his lesson: "Machine Learning gives stunning results but we do not know why".[25] This situation is analogous to the steam engines of late 18th and early 19th centuries when steam power was efficiently used, although before the birth of the thermodynamics theory.

11.1.3.3   From Proof to Trustworthiness

Proof can be considered as a relevant decidability criterion for the truth proposition. Then what is it meant for? To communicate the guaranteed validity of the assertion, have a scientific community trust the result, be able to build more research, results, and theory upon those results. Proof means guaranteed truth or verified validity, which means trustworthiness.

But the question remains as to what community shall be targeted by the proof? Whose trust shall be looked for? The target is related to the way the proof itself has been built. Depending on the proof construction, the AI community or the community of practice related to the final usage of the AI artifact[26] may be aimed by the published research articles. Regardless of its construction, the proof may be forwarded using non-scientific or non-professional media in order to establish AI trustworthiness within the general public.

Furthermore, trustworthiness seems to be built as well upon performance taken in all its meanings: past performance as validating a general behavior, but also acting as stage performance where the results are exhibited in an implicit challenge with human performance given as the reference value. To that extent, it is now based on subjective arguments, socially and artificially constructed.

11.1.3.4   Explicability and Dependability

Proof, V&V, or statistic performance may not be enough. An AI artifact does not have a technical function by itself and for itself, it is not enough that its efficiency be validated in a white room. Such an artifact is meant to be in relationship with the world, interrelated with its working environment and its users. Decisions taken according to AI findings might engage human lives, i.e., in a deliberative physician-patient relationship, the detection of a breast cancer should be explained to the patient, this might be the case in high-reliability organizations such as nuclear and chemical industry, or in decisions with significant ethics content such as recidivism risk assessment in trials. Hence, an AI artifact should be able to communicate the results of its reasonings in a comprehensible manner including a "why" or at least a "how" to the computed outcome instead of being a "black box" delivering a *Pythian* prediction.

AI "reasonings" are a form of an artificial *mimésis* of cognitive activities normally performed by humans and already ruled by explicit and implicit knowledge, norms, cultures, etc. Hence, there is a tension between a new artificially conceptualized activity and its counterpart in the real world. Either the results communication is supported only by its assumed trustworthiness or else this communication comes with an explicit explanation. The former creates a situation of human dependence toward the machine authority. The latter supposes the possibility of a causal explanation and the possible commensurability of both artificial and human models. To that extent, if the AI "explicability" is considered as an ethical concept, its possibility is an epistemic issue based on causal inferences.

Let us recall that those AI "reasonings" are based on the computation of statistical correlations between empirical samples present in the dataset which are applied onto any new sample for a prediction. However, correlations between two events A and B do not disclose any directionality or directional temporality between A and B. Thus, causality cannot be inferred solely from correlations: "one cannot substantiate causal claims[27] from associations alone".[28] However, Fisher (1935) had assumed the possibility to draw valid statistical inferences from particular observations of their causes. Following Suppes (1970), Rothman (1976), Spirtes, Glymour, and Scheines (2000), or Pearl (1995; 1998; 2000; 2009), Halpern (2005a; 2005b), Pearl (2009), and later Pearl and Mackenzie (2018) have attempted to give a mathematical grounding to causal inferences in statistics based on the structural causal model (SCM), differentiating the "necessary cause"[29] from the "actual cause."[30]

In parallel, attempts from Hempel and Oppenheim (1948), Salmon (2006), Halpern (2005b), Pearl and Mackenzie (2018), and Pearl (2018) have also been made to supply causal explanations in statistic models.

In Hempel and Oppenheim (1948), the explanatory power is the possibility to deduce logically an *explanandum*[31] from an *explanans*,[32] the constitutive sentences of which must be true. Further to Hempel's *deductive-nomological* model (Hempel 1965) or Salmon's (Salmon 2006) *statistical relevance* model, Halpern and Pearl (2001b) developed their explanation scheme based again on the SCM. Although it is not fully clear from tensions, their model enables the display of clear graphical networks with directional relations disclosing the statistically "proven" causal path(s) between a cause X and its consequence Y.

However, the question remains as to what AI proposition needs to be explained and how. For example, let us consider an AI software capable of detecting melanomas in dermoscopy images of cutaneous lesions. Ideally, the user—dermatologist or physician—should be explained an individual categorization[33] using a "standard" medical interpretative theory.[34] However, the AI has built its own computed model using only selected images with their labels as learning material and such a "standard" theory has not been programmed as such. Thus, the AI software is unable to deliver an explanation comparable to the one a dermatologist would deliver to his/her patient. Further to this point, let us remind that the very notion of causal explanation as defined by Halpern and Pearl (2001b) cannot account for the correlation between the image of lesion and diagnosis as the symptom is not the disease cause just as the ABCDE theory is semiotic and not causal. All the detection AI software can account for is the way correlations are computed between representations of the learning dataset and a new image to be interpreted. The explainable interpretation does not account for the real phenomenon itself using existing theories but on a distant model, hence needing the construction of a distant semiology theory.

In our view, this necessity for a renewed semiology is acceptable. As any medical imaging device does not present the reality but a model to be queried using distant interpretation schemes, the computed AI digital representation is a model to be queried and requires the structuration of new semiotic rules in order to humanly infer the outcome thus to explain it. Here the explanation is a matter of semiology rather than a matter of epistemic causality and if the explained diagnosis refers to a real disease, its explanation and the semiotic rules shall refer to its computed virtual representation. The explanation syntax shall be directly related to the computations, while the meaning involved remains to be theorized.

11.1.3.5 Biases and Errors

We have just seen that performance and efficiency were the keys to trustworthiness. But this very performance may be biased.

As in Weisberg (2010), by bias we mean "the extent to which a particular measure of a causal effect has been systematically distorted." Thus, the concept of bias assumes a systematic error in a process evaluating a statistical cause. In Fisher's view (Fisher 1935; 1965), a "faulty" experiment is either due to an error in the statistics interpretation or an error in the experiment design or execution. The latter statistical error is directly related to what Fisher calls "Bias of Systematic Arrangements" (Fisher 1935), thus located in what he calls the *design of experiment.*

The AI training being based on mechanized statistical correlations, we may wonder what differentiates AI statistical biases from epidemiology's or social sciences'. AI as a general methodology can be considered as a class of *design of experiment.* A specific AI experiment would then be subject to errors in the process of statistical evaluation or in its own design process, or else in its execution—development and implementation. The statistical errors may reside in the initial data[35] or their label assignment, in the assumptions made to represent the data, or in the inability to identify confounding variables.

In our AI case, errors might first be located in the AI technique itself and then in the development methodology, the algorithm design, in wrong technical choices of software bricks or parameters during the development process. Those errors and biases can be related to human fallibility in a technical activity which is still at the research or at best at the innovation stage, still aiming at better solutions and better performance, hence not fully codified even when considering IEEE Standard 1012[TM]. If they remain implicit and undetected, they might cause inaccurate data representation. Biases may also be located in the training itself. They may be related to wrong assumptions on hyperparameters value settings during the training stage. The training dataset itself may be biased. Its labeling structure may bear untested correlation hypothesis. It may involve information bias with inaccurate or even culturally biased labels. It may also be statistically too small, or integrating too small a number of certain minorities, of female versus male labels, of certain diseases. The bias may as well be located in the testing scheme, e.g., in the testing dataset, supplying wrong V&V results.[36] Those dataset biases are all too well-known in statistics as selection bias.

AI involving somehow some mechanized statistics technics, AI-related biases are consequently similar to biases in statistics but may be made implicit within veiled development choices and parameters, within hidden data representation and classification.

11.1.4 AI and Big Data: From the Myth to a New Paradigm?

We have seen how the original AI project had been built around the hypothesis that human thoughts or mental states were complex but mere calculations[37] and that computer models could eventually simulate such complex calculations and even explain them, thanks to memory and computation power continuous improvements.

Nowadays we live in an era saturated with data. Data are being produced firsthand by our individual Internet and mobile activities. Facebook reported warehousing 300 petabytes of data in 2014.[38] Data are also generated by social, professional, and scientific activities: commercial sales, electricity consumption, stock markets, medical data, scientific experiments, sociological data, etc. Together with the belief that knowledge is encapsulated within the data, the *Zeitgeist* or spirit of our time is that any knowledge is accessible through Big Data by the means of Machine Learning and furthermore that human intelligence can be outreached by AI agency.

Some say this myth is about to become a new paradigm. The question arises as to what paradigm and in what scientific field. It is probable that as a technology it will alter profoundly many sectors of activity that shall adopt it and even change the worldview. However, to that extent, it remains difficult to use the Kuhnian concept of paradigm. A profound environment alteration is not necessarily the crisis that should precede the scientific revolution. Furthermore, the knowledge representations involved in AI software shall be different one from another as they have been developed and trained with different processes, parameters, and datasets. In a given domain and for a given theory, what AI representations and scientific concepts should supersede the others and should an AI representation supersede the human theory given the AI representation do not deliver an explainable theory.

More generally, as a methodology, it could be some sort of a modern version of the 18th century empiricism, with the use of mechanized inductive processes simulating human reason. If we consider Galileo to have encrypted Nature regularities in a mathematical language, the AI project would be to further enable the artificial encoding of any human, social, or natural phenomenon. If so, the new AI paradigm would be about a new scientific methodology aiming at the mechanized encryption of general phenomena.

To this claim, we might object the absence of a formal proof, although it is the very proof that makes a proposition or a theory either surely true or surely false. AI is technically verified and validated, but that does not mean that its technical processes are proven formally using deductive or inductive logic. In that case, we may address this objection by using Peirce's pragmatic conception of an object as subsumed under its effects in the world: "Consider what effects … we conceive the object of our conception to have. Then, our conception of these effects is the whole of our conception of the object" (Peirce 1978).

In this case, the effects being the whole of the artifact conception, a verification and validation based on the equivalence between what an AI artifact is and what its effects are in the world should be relevant considering Peirce's commitment to the truth or even to Dewey's instrumental commitment to "warranted assertibility."[39] The possible emergence of an AI paradigm as a scientific methodology would then result in the resurgence of scientific instrumentalism.

Given that AI has a claim for truth—or warranted assertibility—we might consider now the claim of AI as a neurobiological paradigm if AI happened to simulate entirely human thoughts. As Putnam (2001) puts it, "truth is not just a notion of folk psychology; it is the central notion of logic." But human intelligence is about psychology, i.e., not only logic but also heuristics and rationally limited cognitive processes.[40] Putnam adds that "intentionality is only a feature of folk psychology" and that according to Brentano's thesis, "intentionality won't be reduced and won't go away," where "intentionality is a primitive phenomenon that relates thought and thing, minds and the external world" (Putnam 2001). Thus, there is an essential contradiction here in aiming at simulating human reasoning while having a claim for truth.

Those non-exhaustive objections might be considered as what Hughes (1993, pp. 79–80) calls "reverse salient," i.e., impediments or components of a system which endangers the technical endeavor. However, in the history of a technical system, "reverse salients" can and must be resolved in order to develop, stabilize, and gain "momentum." Present AI is at the crossroads with many well-documented successes properly communicated in order to convince potential customers about its trustworthiness, with a technology that is still producing inventions and enhancements while already commercialized. But it still needs to solve its "reverse salients" in order to become a paradigm as such or at least a successful technological system that will change the "worldview."[41]

11.2   KEY ISSUES IN PHILOSOPHY OF MEDICINE: MEDICINE, HEALTH, AND DISEASE

11.2.1   The Hippocratic Conception of Medicine, Health, and Disease

11.2.1.1   Hippocrates and the Birth of Clinical Medicine

The first scientific revolution in medicine is due to Hippocrates of Kos (460–370 BC). Hippocrates is famous for being the founder of rational medicine, or more emphatically as the "Father of Medicine." At a time when medicine was strictly intertwined with religion and magic, he was the first to regard disease as a natural, rather than a supernatural, phenomenon. He thus encouraged the physicians to look for the physical causes of the disease and to use both clinical observation and inductive/deductive reasoning. By doing this, Hippocrates applied to medicine the method of the philosophers of his time, namely, Democritus (460–370 BC) and the sophist Gorgias (483–375 BC), whom he knew personally; but also, of course, Socrates (470–399 BC). This method consists in the replacement of a mythical explanation of phenomena by a logical or natural explanation; in the transition from "mythos" (the stories of gods, goddesses, and heroes, such as in Homer's *Iliad* and *Odyssey*) to "logos" (the development of rational philosophy and logic, such as pre-Socratic philosophers or, later, Plato and Aristotle's works).

More specifically, Hippocrates is considered as the father of clinical medicine: the word "clinical" refers to the patient in his bed (from Ancient Greek *klinikós*: "pertaining to a bed," from *klínein*: "to lean, incline"), and clinical medicine is defined as medicine at the bedside. By founding clinical medicine, Hippocrates insists on the necessity for physicians to use their five senses when examining their patient, as stated at *Surgery* 1.1: "It's the business of the physician to know … [things] which are to be seen, touched, and heard; which are to be perceived in the sight, and the touch, and the hearing, and the nose, and the tongue, and the understanding" (Thumiger 2018). Hippocrates distinguishes three steps in the examination of the ill:

(1) First, the "sensorial appraisal of the patient's physical state (body temperature, wetness and dryness; sweating or tremors; sensitivity of individual parts) and of the quality of his or her discharges (urine, faeces, and other bodily fluids) to be observed, touched, smelled, and even tasted by the physician" (Thumiger 2018).

(2) Second, a clinical interrogation or interview with both the patient and his family and friends. A passage at *Epidemics* 1.23 states the "things to be observed" according to Hippocrates: "the following were the circumstances attending the disease, from which I framed my judgements, learning from the common nature of all and the particular nature of the individual, from the disease, the patient, the regimen prescribed and the prescriber – for based on these things may become more favourable or less so; … from the custom, mode of life, practices and ages of each patient; from talk, manners, silence, thoughts, sleep or absence of sleep, the nature and times of dreams, plucking, scratching, tears" (Thumiger 2018). As we can see, the interview is about both what the patient is saying (the content of the interview) and the way he is saying it (the form of the interview), the latter being a rich source of information about the physical and mental state of the patient. This also includes what the patient is not saying, and could be said by his family or friends, or guessed by the physician.

(3) Third, taking the patient's history: this refers to of course the patient's previous illnesses but also to his "regimen," to his habits, his occupations, his familial situation, or in Hippocrates' words, "the custom, mode of life, practices and ages of each patient."

11.2.1.2 Hippocrates and the Theory of Four Humors

Hippocrates' conception of health and disease is based on the theory of four humors (blood, phlegm, yellow bile, black bile), which constitute the basis of the physiology of man, or, in other words, its nature. Health and disease are directly related to these humors: health is defined as an equilibrium or a balance of humors within the body (which Hippocrates calls "eucrasia"), whereas disease is due to a disequilibrium or a disbalance in the humoral composition of the body (which Hippocrates calls "dyscrasia"), which means that a humor is either in excess or in default, as Hippocrates states it at *Nature of Man* 4:

> "The human body has within itself blood and phlegm and yellow and black bile, and these are the nature of the body, and because of them it suffers and is healthy. So it is particularly healthy when these things maintain a balance of their power and their quantity in relation to one another, and when they are thoroughly mixed together. It suffers when one of them becomes either too small or too great, or is separated in the body and is not mixed with all the others."
>
> **(Hankinson 2018)**

These four humors are put in relation with the theory of the four elements (earth, water, air, fire), which was proposed by Empedocles (494–434 BC). The novelty of Hippocrates is to establish a correspondence between the four elements in nature with the four humors or fluids in the human body. Hippocrates goes even further by relating these elements and humors with the four ages of life, the four seasons, and also the four couple of qualities. This allows Hippocrates to distinguish between internal factors of disease (humors, for example) and external factors (season, for example). We can draw a table to see the correspondence between these different items (Table 11.1).

So, for example, if the physician has a patient who is a child, and if we are in the spring season (which is hot and wet), there is a high risk of the humor "blood" to be in excess: the physician can thus prescribe preventively a dietary habit such as the prohibition of eating red meat, or he can prescribe bloodletting as a preventive or curative treatment. This table of correspondence allows the physician to adapt the regimen of the patient to his individual characteristics but also to his environment. The occurrence of specific disease can also be prognosed, according to criteria such as season and thus avoided by prevention: the fact that the first printed medical book,

TABLE 11.1

Hippocrates and the Theory of Four Humors

Element	Humor	Couple of Qualities	Season	Age of Life
Air	Blood	Hot and moist	Spring	Infancy
Fire	Yellow bile	Hot and dry	Summer	Youth
Earth	Black bile	Cold and dry	Autumn	Maturity
Water	Phlegm	Cold and moist	Winter	Old age

by Gutenberg in 1457, is the *Laxiercalender,* a calendar of the bloodletting and purgation. That's also why regimen is the central concept of Hippocratic medicine, considering that regimen includes not only dietary habit but also habits of life, physical exercise, and even the art of sleeping and dreaming.

11.2.1.3 Hippocrates' Conception of Health and Disease

The last important point about Hippocratic medicine is that, ultimately, the real physician is Nature. We just showed that for Hippocrates, health and disease are directly related to the four humors and to the good balance of these humors within the body: the patient and the physician must thus find a way to maintain that balance, either through preventive or curative measures. But there is a serious limit to that, and especially to the power of the physician. Hippocrates is supposed to have said that "Nature is the true physician of diseases," which has been translated in Latin under the expression "*Vis medicatrix naturae.*" The exact citation is: "The body's nature is the physician in disease. Nature finds the way for herself, not from thought. ... Well trained, readily and without instruction, nature does what is needed" (*Epidemics* VI, section 5, chapter I[42]). This means that the role of the physician is not to go against nature but to help the patient and his body to restore his equilibrium, for example, by regimen or by bloodletting. This also shows that for Hippocratic physicians, each patient has to be considered both as an individual or particular patient and also as a whole organism in relation with his environment, with, for example, *Airs, Waters and Places* (Hippocrates and Jones 2010), to cite one of the books of the Hippocratic Corpus dedicated to that kind of environmental issues. This is also why the physician-patient relationship is so important in the Hippocratic tradition. The first aphorism of his famous book named *Aphorisms* is a good summary of the difficult art of medicine: "Life is short, and Art long; the crisis fleeting; experience perilous, and decision difficult. The physician must not only be prepared to do what is right himself, but also to make the patient, the attendants, and externals cooperate" (Hippocrates and Jones 2005).

11.2.2 THE MODERN CONCEPTION OF MEDICINE, HEALTH, AND DISEASE: FROM ANATOMO-CLINICAL TO EXPERIMENTAL MEDICINE

11.2.2.1 Bichat and the Foundations of Anatomo-Clinical Medicine

The second scientific revolution in medicine takes place more than 2000 years after the clinical revolution initiated by Hippocrates, at the end of the 18th century. This revolution is the product of many evolutions that cannot be described in this chapter. Two of them can nonetheless be emphasized: the first one is the development of anatomy in the 16th century, thanks to Andreas Vesalius (1514–1564) and his famous book *De Humani Corporis Fabrica* (*On the Fabric of the Human Body*), published in 1543. At a time when the anatomy of Galen is still the medical orthodoxy, even if Galen only dissected animals and not humans, Vesalius establishes anatomy as a scientific discipline by insisting on direct observation as the only reliable source of anatomical knowledge, and no longer the authority of Galen or Hippocrates. The second evolution is more due to political and social reasons and takes place after the

French Revolution of 1789: according to Michel Foucault (2003), between the end of the 18th century and the beginning of the 19th century, hospitals in France ceased be a place for charity toward the poor, the homeless, or the orphans, to become a genuine medicalized place. The advantage of this evolution is that physicians can observe a vast number of patients but also dissect them when they die. These two evolutions largely explain the advent of anatomo-clinical medicine.

Anatomo-clinical medicine is defined as the systematic correlation between the clinical data and the autopsy data, or, in other words, between the medicine at the bedside and anatomo-pathology. The founder of modern anatomical pathology is Giovanni Battista Morgagni (1682–1771), who has been for 56 years Professor of Anatomy at the University of Padua (as Vesalius before him), one of the most prestigious faculties of medicine in the world at this time. His main thesis is that most diseases are not vaguely dispersed throughout the body, but originate locally, in specific organs and tissues. However, it is the French anatomist Xavier Bichat (1771–1802) who is considered as the true founder of the anatomo-clinical method: as Morgagni, Bichat dissected hundreds of corpses and was able to find the lesions which were the causes of the disease. More precisely, Bichat, who founded histology and histopathology, was convinced that diseases were due to some specific lesions in the various tissues of the human body. The works of Bichat modified the vision that physicians had of the body: the human body became more transparent to them, as they were able to identify the lesion inside the body through clinical examination, at least for some diseases.

The last important point about Bichat is that he was a vitalist. Vitalism is traditionally opposed to mechanism: the mechanistic doctrine was defended, for example, by René Descartes (1596–1650) who considered that all living beings, except humans, are just machines. This theory of beast-machine states that only human beings have a soul, but also that all biological phenomena (even if the word "biology" appears only during the 18th century and become common during the 19th century) are reducible to physical laws or physico-chemicals laws. On the contrary, vitalism considers that living phenomena are subject to specific laws or that vital properties could not be explained through physics or chemistry. The difference is that some kind of "vital principle" (or "vital force" or "élan vital" in French) exists and distinguishes living beings from all other beings. We can distinguish three main thesis in vitalism:

(1) Vital phenomena are not reducible to physicochemical phenomena.
(2) Vital phenomena can only be observed and cannot be experimented: any experimentation on vital phenomena just distort them.
(3) Vital phenomena must be conceived in their totality: each organism is an organized totality, with hierarchized functions.

That's why Bichat, in his *Physiological Researches upon Life and Death* (Bichat 1809), defines life as "the totality of those set of functions which resist death": each living being has from his birth a certain quantity of vital energy, which decreases throughout life and through the struggle with everything that is dead.

11.2.2.2 C. Bernard and the Foundations of Experimental Medicine

One of the greatest revolutions in the history of medicine is clearly operated by Claude Bernard (1813–1878), in his book *An Introduction to the Study of Experimental Medicine*, published originally in 1865 (Bernard 1927). This revolution can be divided into three aspects: first, a revolution in the method; second, a revolution in physiology, through the discoveries Bernard made; and finally, a revolution in the conception of health and disease.

Bernard's main goal is to establish the use of scientific method, i.e., experimental method inherited from Isaac Newton and Descartes, in medicine through the knowledge of physiology. The purpose of physiology is no longer to understand how the human body is organized through organs or tissues, but to understand how the human body functions or works, and the various organs and tissues work together, or, in other words, to understand their determinism. For Bernard indeed, and contrary to Bichat's thesis, vital phenomena are as much determined as non-vital phenomena. He considers that this determinism is an "experimental axiom" that could give physiology and medicine the status of a scientific discipline:

> We must acknowledge as an experimental axiom that in living beings as well as in inorganic bodies the necessary conditions of every phenomenon are absolutely determined. That is to say, in other terms, that when once the conditions of a phenomenon are known and fulfilled, the phenomenon must always and necessarily be reproduced at the will of the experimenter. Negation of this proposition would be nothing less than negation of science itself.
>
> **(Bernard 1927)**

Moreover, for Bernard, the vitalistic concept of a "vital force" is not an explanation of the phenomenon of life: "what we call vital force is a first cause analogous to all other first causes, in this sense, that it is utterly unknown" (Bernard 1927). However, Bernard agrees with Bichat on the specificity of vital phenomena. He considers that physical and chemical sciences provide the foundation for physiology, although physiology is not reducible to them. But the specificity of the object (vital phenomena) does not correspond to a specificity of the scientific method:

> So, if the sciences of life must differ from all others in explanation and in special laws, they are not set apart by scientific method. Biology must borrow the experimental method of physico-chemical sciences, but keep its special phenomena and its own laws.
>
> **(Bernard 1927)**

This unity of scientific method is in strict correlation with the way Bernard considers what a good scientific method is: it is only through experiments and through the hypothetico-deductive method, that science can make progress. Bernard thus distinguishes different steps of any experimentation: first, the experimenter makes empirical observations, then he proposes hypotheses to explain these observations (a cause-effect relationship), then he tests his hypotheses through an experiment, and it is only the experiment that can tell if the initial hypotheses are confirmed and infirmed. When a hypothesis is confirmed, then we have a theory. But the theory is always subject to future revisions: "Theories are only hypotheses, verified by more or less numerous facts. Those verified by the most facts are the best, but even then they are never final, never to be absolutely believed" (Bernard 1927).

This method justifies for Bernard the passage from dissection to vivisection in order to study physiological determinism: dissection only gives information about dead structures, but not about how an organ properly performs its function. It is through the practice of vivisection that Bernard discovered, for example, the glycogenic function of the liver. This led him to create the concept of "internal secretion" and then to the concept of "milieu intérieur" or "internal environment":

> The living body, though it has need of the surrounding environment, is nevertheless relatively independent of it. This independence which the organism has of its external environment, derives from the fact that in the living being, the tissues are in fact withdrawn from direct external influences and are protected by a veritable internal environment which is constituted, in particular, by the fluids circulating in the body.
>
> **(Bernard 1974)**

It is important to note at this point that Bernard's experimental medicine did not have a real impact on medicine as it was daily practiced in the second half of the 19th century. If physiology is today legitimately considered as a science, the scientific status of medicine is still debated.[43] The main progress was the fact that the laboratory was at that time introduced at the hospital. Physicians thus got used to going back and forth from the bedside to the laboratory. The laboratory played also a major role in the development of microbiology and bacteriology with the works of Louis Pasteur (1822–1895), who discovered the principle of vaccination (against rabies), microbial fermentation, and pasteurization; or Robert Koch (1843–1910) who identified the specific causative agents of anthrax (*Bacillus anthracis*), tuberculosis (*Mycobacterium tuberculosis*), and cholera (*Vibrio cholerae*) and theorized what is known as the "Koch's four postulates":

(1) The organism must always be present, in every case of the disease.
(2) The organism must be isolated from a host containing the disease and grown in pure culture.
(3) Samples of the organism taken from pure culture must cause the same disease when inoculated into a healthy, susceptible animal in the laboratory.
(4) The organism must be isolated from the inoculated animal and must be identified as the same original organism first isolated from the originally diseased host.

This exemplifies the statement of Bernard, for whom a good physician is first a good scientist and a good experimenter. However, contrary to Bernard's work, bacteriology had a huge impact on clinical medicine and "Pasteur, a chemist without medical training, inaugurated a new era in medicine" (Canguilhem 2000).

11.2.2.3   The Modern Conception of Health and Disease

Talking about a modern conception of health and disease should not mislead the reader: by "modern," we refer to the conceptions that evolved from the end of the 18th century to the beginning of the 20th century. It started with the anatomo-clinical medicine that identifies disease with the lesion of an organ, lesion that prevents the organ to perform fully or normally its function. It continued with the conception of the physiology of the human body defended by Bernard. According to him, the only difference between physiology and pathology is a quantitative one. Disease is not a result of disequilibrium or a disbalance in the humoral composition of the body as in the Hippocratic tradition (though the idea of internal secretion and internal environment are quite similar to the fluidic conception of health and disease defended by Hippocrates), or the result of a lesion, as in anatomo-clinical medicine, but the result of the deregulation of a normal function, or a dysfunction of an organ. In other words, the normal and the pathological are identical if we except quantitative variations: there is only a difference of degree between health and disease, and not a difference of nature. These two conceptions of disease (lesion of an organ and quantitative variation of a physiological variable) have in common that the individual patient is erased behind his disease. In other words, the patient is reduced to his organs and its functions, or to his physiological variables such as blood pressure, heart rate, blood sugar levels, etc. This conception was clearly reinforced during all the 20th century with the invention of a huge quantity of monitoring devices (starting with the electrocardiogram) and of paraclinical exams which reduced the patient to a set of numerical values and intervals of normality. Health and disease have thus become a quantitative notion, and not anymore, as in the Hippocratic conception, a qualitative one. As Canguilhem says:

> Contemporary medicine is founded, with an efficacy we cannot but appreciate, on the progressive dissociation of disease and the sick person, seeking to characterize the sick person by the disease, rather than identify a disease on the basis of the bundle of symptoms spontaneously presented by the patient.
>
> **(Canguilhem 2012)**

Finally, the bacteriology of Pasteur and Koch "led to a profound epistemological revolution in medicine" (Canguilhem 2000), and on the way health and disease are conceived. Canguilhem says that, after bacteriology, "the object of medicine was no longer so much disease as health" (Canguilhem 2000). The reference to this passage from a "medicine of disease" to a "medicine of health," described by Canguilhem and Foucault, is crucial to understand contemporary conception of medicine, health, and disease.

11.2.3   The Contemporary Conception of Medicine, Health, and Disease

There were so much of discoveries and progress in all areas of medicine and science in general during the 20th century that it is almost impossible to list them. However, we can distinguish two major—and contradictory—trends in the evolution of medicine throughout the 20th century: the molecularization of medicine and the advent of modern epidemiology, understood here as a mix of new statistical methods and study design applied to medicine and a new conception or a new approach of epidemiology often characterized as "risk factor epidemiology" (Giroux 2011).

11.2.3.1 The Molecularization of Medicine in the 20th Century

First, the molecularization of medicine is a by-product of the molecularization of biology and of life in general, in relation to the progress of genetics made during the 20th century, often epitomized by the discovery of DNA Double Helix by J. Watson, F. Crick, and R. Franklin in 1953. This molecularization culminated in the human genome sequencing achieved in 2003 through the Human Genome Project. As N. Rose explains:

> This new genetics was bound up with a mutation in the very image that we have of life. The body that 20th-century medicine inherited from the 19th century was visualized via a clinical gaze, as it appeared in the hospital, on the dissection table and was inscribed in the anatomical atlas. The body was a vital living system, or a system of systems. … In the 1930s, biology came to visualize life phenomena at the submicroscopic region—between 10^{-6} and 10^{-7} cm …. Life, that is to say, was molecularized.
>
> **(Rose 2001)[44]**

This molecularization can be considered as the logical continuation of the reduction of disease to lesions or quantitative variations of physiological variables. Now, the disease is located at a molecular level: it could concern the cell or, at a lower level of reality, the gene. For example, Linus Pauling published a paper in *Science* titled: "Sickle cell anemia, a molecular disease" (Pauling et al. 1949), where he shows that "hemoglobin from patients with sickle cell anemia (Hemoglobin S or HbS) differs from hemoglobin of normal patients" (Strasser and Fantini 2020), due to a "difference in the physicochemical properties of the protein, namely the different numbers of electric charges of the macromolecule" (Strasser and Fantini 2020). In 1959, J. Lejeune, M. Gautier, and R. Turpin published the first study which identifies a genetic disease: trisomy 21 (each cell in the body has three separate copies of chromosome 21 instead of the usual two copies) showed that a numerical chromosome abnormality could be responsible for the disease. This study constitutes a landmark in the beginnings of medical genetics. In other words, the progress made by molecular biology during the 20th century gave birth to a new medicine: biomedicine. This concept of "biomedicine" is not just a kind of merging of biology and medicine but embraces a whole worldview. S. Valles shows, in his article "Philosophy of Biomedicine," three key features of biomedicine:

(1) "First, specific to biomedicine: the domain of disease and its causes is restricted to solely biological, chemical, and physical phenomena;

(2) Second, shared with many natural sciences: an emphasis on laboratory research and technology and, as translated to health research, a discounting of research questions that cannot be studied by randomized clinical trials (or their analogs, e.g., 'natural experiments'); and

(3) Third, an embrace of 'reductionism,' a philosophical and methodological stance ... that holds that phenomena are best explained by the properties of their parts" (Valles 2020).

Biomedicine thus appears as the reductionist medicine: patient is once again reduced to the physical, chemical, and biological constituents—there is no place for his individuality and his relation to environment. Moreover, the experimental methodology, inherited from Bernard, is completed by the introduction of new statistical methodologies just after World War II, which profoundly modified the conception of the etiology of diseases but also the way drugs are evaluated.

11.2.3.2 The Quantification of Medicine[45] and the Birth of Evidence-Based Medicine (EBM)

Just after World War II, a new way to understand the causes of disease appears: in 1950, one of the most famous articles in the history of epidemiology was published: it was written by R. Doll and A.B. Hill (1950) which demonstrated a correlation between smoking and lung cancer and paved a new way to understand the etiology of a disease by using statistical method. It provides a new methodology for observational studies: the "case-control study," which is retrospective. In 1954, Doll and Hill published a new article (Doll and Hill 1954) about the correlation between smoking and carcinoma of the lung. Due to several critics addressed by prominent statisticians such as J. Berkson[46] or R. A. Fisher[47], to the methodology of case-control study and the risk of bias it introduces, Doll and Hill decided to adopt "some entirely new approach ... characterized by looking forward into the future" (Doll and Hill 1954), or, in other words, a prospective study, also known later as a cohort study. A few years before, A.B. Hill has conducted, with his colleagues of the Medical Research Council, what is considered as the first randomized clinical trial in history (Hill 1990), which evaluated the potential of streptomycin to treat tuberculosis. The double-blind randomized clinical trial (random allocation of subjects to the two groups, treatment versus placebo, neither the researchers nor the subjects know who receives the treatment and who receives the placebo) soon became the gold standard in medical experiments (Jones and Podolsky 2015). The introduction of these new methodologies, both to assess the etiology of disease and to evaluate the safety and benefit of new drugs (Marks 2000), modified both the conception of the etiology of several diseases and the way medicine was practiced. This gave rise to a new epidemiology, called "risk factor epidemiology" (Giroux 2011).

The problem is that it generated an enormous amount of medical literature, from observational to experimental studies: for example, if in 1950 there were around 86,000 articles indexed in PubMed, in 2018, there are more than 1.3 million[48]: how does the clinician is supposed to find his way through all these results? Besides this problem of quantity, there is a problem of quality: how is the clinician supposed to assess the scientificity of an observational or an experimental study? How is he supposed to choose between the results of a cohort study and the results of randomized clinical trial? How is he supposed to be sure that such behavior, or such substance (tobacco for example, or alcohol), cause a disease, but only in a probabilistic manner?

It was to answer these questions that EBM appeared at the beginning of the 1980s. The term "Evidence-Based Medicine" was coined by Gordon Guyatt in 1992, and it was first considered as a new "approach to teaching the practice of medicine" (Guyatt 1992). However, it soon became a new to practice medicine and its definition changed:

> Evidence based medicine is the conscientious, explicit, and judicious use of current best evidence in making decisions about the care of individual patients. The practice of evidence based medicine means integrating individual clinical expertise with the best available external clinical evidence from systematic research.
>
> **(Sackett et al. 1996)**

This EBM is historically a product of two main evolutions in medicine, in relation to the development of observational and experimental studies after World War II: the first one is the development of what is called "clinical epidemiology," defined by Sackett as "the application, by a physician who provides direct patient care, of epidemiologic and biometric methods to the study of diagnostic and therapeutic process in order to effect an improvement in health" (Sackett 1969), and which A. Feinstein prefers to call "clinimetrics," whose domain is "concerned with quantitative methods in the collection and analysis of comparative clinical data, and particularly with improved 'measurement' of the distinctively clinical and personal phenomena of patient care" (Feinstein 1983). In other words, clinical epidemiology or clinimetrics is an attempt to quantify clinical medicine and to make it more scientific.[49]

The second main evolution is the notion of "critical appraisal" of the medical and clinical literature, praised by E.A. Murphy (Murphy 1976) and D. Sackett essentially to avoid bias. Sackett considers that critical appraisal constitutes the origin of EBM: "By the early 1990s we began to extend the Critical Appraisal concepts to include clinical decision making for and with individual patients. This was labelled Evidence-Based Medicine by our former graduate student, Gordon Guyatt" (Haynes and Goodman 2015). This double evolution led to the hierarchization of the levels of evidence, starting from the opinion expert to the observational studies (case-control study, cohort study), and to the experimental studies (non-randomized and randomized clinical trials) to finish by the category of critical appraisal which includes systematic reviews and meta-analysis. This pyramid of evidence is thus a way to assess the quality of evidence, and a tool for the physician to make better decisions and provide the best treatment to his patient. However, EBM appears as a pure product of biomedicine and tends to adopt a reductionist approach to the patient. Once again, the patient is forgotten.

11.2.3.3   From the Medicine of Disease to the Medicine of Health

G. Canguilhem is probably the most prominent critics of both the reduction of medicine to a science and the reduction of health and disease to a quantitative or objective definition. These two theses are strictly intertwined, and are due to the definition of health and disease (or normal and pathological) given by Canguilhem. He opposes to

Bernard's thesis "that in biology the normal and the pathological are, but for minor quantitative differences, identical" (Canguilhem 2000). For Canguilhem, "there is no objective pathology. Structures or behaviors can be objectively described but they cannot be called 'pathological' on the strength of some purely objective criterion" (Canguilhem 1989). Health is indeed not identical to normality:

> Health is more than normality; in simple terms, it is normativity. Behind all apparent normality one must look to see if it is capable of tolerating infractions of the norm, of overcoming contradictions, of dealing with conflicts. Any normality open to possible future correction is authentic normativity, or health.
>
> **(Canguilhem 2000)**

In other words, "life is this polarized activity of debate with the environment, which feels normal or not depending on whether it feels that it is in a normative position or not"(Canguilhem 1989). Thus, health cannot be defined statistically or mechanistically, but is rather the ability to adapt to one's environment. In this sense, every patient is unique and must be treated as such, and the main goal of medicine and therapeutics is to establish or restore the normal, by which he means "the subjective satisfaction that a norm is established." Health is therefore something eminently subjective, and the patient knows better than the physician if he is healthy or not. And the difference between the normal and the pathological is one of nature and not of degree. The difference between these two states is clear-cut for the patient, because it is a "new way of life for the organism" (Canguilhem 1989): for example, diabetes is not just a biochemical problem of high blood sugar level, or a set of symptoms such as frequent urination or increased thirst: in reality diabetes modifies completely the way of living of the patient and has a global impact on his daily life. In other words, there are no diseases, only sick individuals.

Therefore, medicine is not an objective science, but "a technique or art at the crossroads of several sciences" (Canguilhem 1989). For him, clinical medicine, or medicine at the bedside, comes first, long before any pathological science:

> In pathology the first word historically speaking and the last word logically speaking comes back to clinical practice. Clinical practice is not and will never be a science even when it uses means whose effectiveness is increasingly guaranteed scientifically. Clinical practice is not separated from therapeutics, and therapeutics is a technique for establishing or restoring the normal whose end, that is, the subjective satisfaction that a norm is established, escapes the jurisdiction of objective knowledge. One does not scientifically dictate norms to life. ... The physician has sided with life. Science serves him in fulfilling the duties arising from that choice. The doctor is called by the patient. It is the echo of this pathetic call which qualifies as pathological all the sciences which medical technology uses to aid life. Thus, it is that there is a pathological anatomy, a pathological physiology, a pathological histology, a pathological embryology. But their pathological quality is an import of technical and thereby subjective origin.
>
> **(Canguilhem 1989)**

In other words, it is because health and disease are subjective that pathological sciences exist: pathological refers etymologically to the suffering (the pathos) of someone, and the very existence of medicine is to relive this suffering, to care much more than to cure.

One of the main points of Canguilhem's conception of health and disease is the importance given to the environment. For him, the environment—and not the body—comes first and that it is the relation with the environment that determines the normal or the pathological:

> Thus, in order to discern what is normal or pathological for the body itself, one must look beyond the body. With a disability like astigmatism or myopia, one would be normal in an agricultural or a pastoral society but abnormal for sailing or flying. Hence we cannot clearly understand how the same man with the same organs feels normal or abnormal at different times in environments suited to man unless we understand how organic vitality flourishes in man in the form of technical plasticity and the desire to dominate the environment.
>
> **(Canguilhem 1989)**

The distinctive feature of man is that his environment is not only and not essentially biological but social: this means that social norms (technological, economic, juridical, political, or moral norms) are more important than vital norms. Yet, one of the most prominent traits of modern societies is the medicalization of society, criticized by both Canguilhem and M. Foucault, that every aspect of life is now susceptible to receive a medical treatment. Foucault says, for example, that "the medicine of the last decades, already acting beyond its traditional boundaries defined by the patient and by the diseases, begins to no longer have any domain outside it."[50] Canguilhem describes how this process of medicalization modifies both the medical act itself and medicine in general. Medicine is no more the response to a pathetic appeal from a patient, but is now a response to a demand.

> This gave new impetus to a medical discipline that had enjoyed prominence in England and France since the end of the eighteenth century—public health or hygiene. ... The political pressures stemming from public health concerns gradually resulted in changes in medicine's objectives and practices. The accent was shifted from health to prevention to protection. The semantic shift points to a change in the medical act itself. Where medicine had once responded to an appeal, it was now obedient to a demand. Health is the capacity to resist disease; yet those who enjoy good health are nevertheless conscious of the possibility of illness. Protection is the negation of disease, an insistence on never having to think about it. In response to political pressures, medicine has had to take on the appearance of a biological technology. Here, for a third time, the individual patient, who seeks the attention of clinician, has been set aside.
>
> **(Canguilhem 2000)**

In other words, the traditional medicine of diseases has become nowadays a medicine of health. This means that now medicine is relying essentially on prevention and prediction. This is partly due to what is called "epidemiological transition" (Omran 1971), whose most prominent manifestation is the replacement of infectious diseases by chronic diseases. Contemporary medicine is founded on a new individualization of the patient: the patient is now identified according to his risk factors (blood pressure, body mass index, genes of predisposition to some diseases, etc.). The object of contemporary medicine is no longer the sick individual or the diseases, but the risk of disease: every individual is now a potential sick individual. Consequently, all the behaviors of all the individuals are now the target of public health policies and advertisements: every citizen is supposed to do sport or physical activity, to eat fruit and vegetables, to avoid smoking or any risky behaviors, etc. The problem is that these policies of health promotion[51] or of empowerment tend to make the individual responsible of his state of health or of disease, without considering his familial, social, economic, or ecological background. In other words, it can lead to a form of guilt for getting sick. Lastly, the main objective of this medicine of health is to produce a normalization of the behaviors by exerting a pression on the individuals in order for him to adapt to the existing social norms and to be physically and psychically performant in a competitive world. The concept of biopower and biopolitics, theorized by M. Foucault, and defined as the practice of modern nation states and their regulation of their subjects through "an explosion of numerous and diverse techniques for achieving the subjugations of bodies and the control of populations" (Foucault 1978), has never been so relevant, when the Covid-19 pandemic imposes unprecedent measures of restriction on civil liberties for the sake of public health.

11.3 CONCLUSION: PERSONALIZED MEDICINE OR THE INTRODUCTION OF AI AND BIG DATA IN MEDICINE

The sequencing of human genome achieved in 2003, whose main goal was to identify and map all the genes of the human genome from both a physical and a functional standpoint, opened a new era in biology and medicine called the "post-genomics era." It gave birth to "omics" sciences: genomics, transcriptomics, metabolomics, interactomics, epigenomics, proteomics, pharmacogenomics, etc. The main progress of "omics" sciences is that, instead of analyzing a single gene, protein, or metabolite, it analyzes the entirety of a genome, a proteome, or a metabolome. According to the US National Academy of Sciences, there are two main reasons to conduct omics research:

> One common reason is to obtain a comprehensive understanding of the biological system under study. For instance, one might perform a proteomics study on normal human kidney tissues to better understand protein activity, functional pathways, and protein interactions in the kidney. Another common goal of omics studies is to associate the omics-based molecular measurements with a clinical outcome of interest, such as prostate cancer survival time, risk of breast cancer recurrence, or response to therapy.
>
> **(Committee on the Review of Omics-Based Tests for Predicting Patient Outcomes in Clinical Trials et al. 2012)**

In other words, the general idea is the individualization of the diagnosis, prognosis, and therapeutics according to the genetic profile of a patient. Many authors consider that these omics sciences opened a new era in medicine and constitute a scientific revolution. Some authors called this new medicine "personalized medicine"[52]

(Langreth and Waldholz 1999); its aim was to "target drug for each unique genetic profile." Ten years later, for the anniversary of the article, the tone was less optimistic: "we know that it was a new era that started, and we have already seen the first important results, even though the promise of 'targeting drugs for each unique genetic profile' is far from being fulfilled yet" (Jørgensen 2009). However, the main characteristics of personalized medicine is that it first continues the molecularization of medicine which started in the 20th century, and then it inaugurates the computerization of medicine (Lemoine 2017) through the use of Artificial Intelligence and Big Data. In 2008, L. Hood proposed to call this new medicine "P4 medicine," defined as "a result of two convergences: systems medicine and the digital revolution" (Hood 2013). But to what correspond these four P's?

1. *The first P stand for "predictive":* "Within the next 10 years, we should be able to sequence entire genomes in less than an hour's time at the cost of a few hundred dollars. ... In 10 years, we may have a little hand-held device that will prick your finger, make 2,500 blood measurements, and will longitudinally follow the organ-specific proteins for 50 different organs. This will allow us to detect many diseases at the earliest detectable phase, weeks, months, and maybe years before symptoms appear" (Hood 2013).
2. *The second P corresponds to "personalized":* "In the future, diseases will be stratified according to the genetic make-up of the individual, and, in turn, treatments will be individually optimized" (Hood 2013).
3. *The third P is for "preventive":* "Instead of medicine focusing on disease as it does today, the focus in the future will be on wellness" (Hood 2013).
4. *The last P stands for "participatory":* "Patient-driven networks are going to be the driving force of this revolution in medicine" (Hood 2013).

In other words, the main idea behind P-medicine is that all medical decisions, practices, interventions, or products would be tailored to the individual patient. For some authors, P-medicine will radically transform the healthcare sector and society: with the emergence of mHealth through the multiplication of wearable devices (smart watches, for example, which integrate more and more sensors), which makes possible "mathematically sophisticated 'big data' analyses of billions of data points generated for each individual in the population" (Flores et al. 2013) and thus a continuous self-monitoring of each individual which could be cross-checked with his genetic data, the possibilities are great. In this sense, it could surely "make disease care radically more cost effective by personalizing care to each person's unique biology and by treating the causes rather than the symptoms of disease" or "provide the basis for concrete action by consumers to improve their health as they observe the impact of lifestyle decisions"(Flores et al. 2013).

But the risks are as much great as the possibilities: for the moment, nothing guarantees that the analysis and reasonings of Artificial Intelligence are not prone to random and systematic errors. Nothing guarantees neither that these new technologies, in a sector entirely controlled by the Big Tech companies, could not be used in another way, not only to make profit, but to exert some kind of huge biopower on the population and increase social and health inequalities between the individuals. In other words, what we need, from an epistemological point of view, is a real critical appraisal of Big Data and Artificial Intelligence in healthcare (Brault and Saxena 2020) to assess the validity of the Big Data and the way Artificial Intelligence thinks or reasons. What is needed is not only to open the black box of Artificial Intelligence, but to make it explicable, explicability referring here to both "the epistemological sense of *intelligibility* (as an answer to the question 'how does it work?') and in the ethical sense of *accountability* (as an answer to the question: 'who is responsible for the way it works?')" (Floridi and Cowls 2019). At least, as we explained in the previous chapter, we can make AI "explainable," by which we mean the semiological interpretability of Artificial Intelligence technologies. This explainability appears to us as the only way to make AI understandable by the public, and to make possible for the public and the citizens to exert a democratic control on it. As health is defined by the World Health Organization as "a state of complete physical, mental and social well-being and not merely the absence of disease or infirmity," physicians and patients, and not just algorithms, should be the main actors of this well-being, in all its dimensions.

NOTES

1. Menabrea Luigi Federico (1843).
2. Pascal (1645).
3. Leibniz (1710).
4. Namely a Turing Machine.
5. In mathematics and computer science, the *Entscheidungsproblem* ("decision problem") is a challenge posed by David Hilbert in 1928. The problem requests an algorithm to be able to decide whether a given statement is provable from the axioms using the rules of logic.
6. That is, not electromechnical.
7. By Warren McCulloch and Walter Pitts. See McCulloch and Pitts (1943).
8. For the full text, see: www-formal.stanford.edu/jmc/history/dartmouth/dartmouth .html.
9. Developed by Edward Feigenbaum, Bruce Buchanan, Joshua Lederberg, and Carl Djerassi.
10. Developed (starting) in 1972 by Edward H. Shortliffe, mentored by Bruce Buchanan.
11. Which is rather common but the representation can be made using tensors as well.
12. Marvin Minsky, *Matter, Mind and Models*, 1963: *"To an observer B, an object A* is a model of an object A to the extent that B can use A* to answer questions that interest him about A"*, in (Minsky 1968).
13. Depending on the request, for instance: categorization, probability computation, etc.
14. The Aristotelian *orthos logos*.
15. "A proof represents a logical process which has come to a definitive conclusion in a finite number of stages. However, a logical machine following definite rules need never come to a conclusion."
16. But program testing can be a very effective way to show the presence of bugs, but is hopelessly inadequate for showing their absence.
17. René Thom (1971) as quoted in (Tymoczko 1981): "Let us suppose that we have been able to construct for a formal theory S an electronic machine M capable of carrying out at a terrifying speed all the elementary steps in S. We wish to verify the correctness of one formula F of the theory. After a process totaling 1030 elementary operations,

completed in a few seconds, the machine M gives us a positive reply. Now what mathematician would accept without hesitation the validity of such a 'proof,' given the impossibility of verifying all its steps?"

18. See (Appel and Haken 1977).
19. It is not considered a problem anymore but a theorem.
20. Institute of Electrical and Electronics Engineers, see also ISO standards.
21. Standard for System, Software, and Hardware Verification and Validation, last version in 2016.
22. Standard for Software and System Test Documentation, last version in 2008.
23. As examples we might consider Li et al. (2016) and Haenssle et al. (2018).
24. See Shalev-Shwartz and Ben-David (2014).
25. Translation by the author.
26. That is, dermatologists in the case of a melanoma detection software, oncologists in the case of breast cancer detection, etc.
27. Such as explicability.
28. See Pearl (2009, p. 99).
29. X is a necessary cause of Y if Y would not have occurred provided X had not occurred.
30. X is an actual cause of Y if X is at the origin of a logical sequence of events ending in the occurrence of Y.
31. Empirical phenomenon.
32. Mainly general laws derived from general regularities.
33. To make it simple: melanoma or non-melanoma.
34. For example, the ABCDE semiology model.
35. Sampling bias.
36. Often, the whole dataset is split: two-third of the dataset is used for training, while the last third is used for testing. In that case, bias in the training dataset is probably present in the testing dataset as well.
37. See Hobbes, Putnam.
38. See https://engineering.fb.com/core-data/scaling-the-facebook-data-warehouse-to-300-pb/ (retrieved August 28, 2020).
39. See Dewey (1941).
40. See Simon (1955).
41. See Kuhn (1970).
42. Hippocrates and Smith 1994.
43. See, for example, Canguilhem (1989).
44. On the molecularization of biology and medicine, see also Chadarevian (2003).
45. For a history of quantification in medicine, see Matthews 1995) and Jorland, Opinel, and Weisz (2005).
46. See, for example, Berkson (2014 [1947]; 1955; 1958; 1963). For a short history of Berkson's bias, see Brault (2020).
47. See, for example, Fisher (1959). On the controversy around the association of smoking with cancer of the lung, see, for example, Parascandola (2004); White (1991); and Vandenbroucke (2009). For a general history of epidemiology, see Morabia 2004); Leplège, Bizouarn, and Coste 2011); and Brault (2017).
48. Alexandru Dan Corlan. Medline trend: automated yearly statistics of PubMed results for any query, 2004. Web resource at http://dan.corlan.net/medline-trend.html (accessed November 29, 2020).
49. For an overview of link between public health epidemiology and clinical epidemiology, see Giroux (2012) and Brault (2017).
50. "Crise de la médecine ou anti-médecine ?", in Foucault (2000).

51. See, for example, "The Ottawa Charter for Health Promotion," published in 1986, accessible at: https://www.who.int/teams/health-promotion/enhanced-wellbeing/first-global-conference.
52. For an overview of the philosophy of personalized medicine, see Lemoine (2017); Darrason (2017); Giroux (2017); Chadwick (2017); and Guchet (2017).

REFERENCES

Appel, Kenneth, and Wolfgang Haken. 1977. "The Solution of the Four-Color-Map Problem." *Scientific American* 237 (4): 108–21. doi: 10.1038/scientificamerican1077-108.

Berkson, J. 1955. "The Statistical Study of Association between Smoking and Lung Cancer." *Proceedings of the Staff Meetings. Mayo Clinic* 30 (15): 319–48.

Berkson, Joseph. 1958. "Smoking and Lung Cancer: Some Observations on Two Recent Reports." *Journal of the American Statistical Association* 53 (281): 28. doi: 10.2307/2282563.

Berkson, Joseph. 1963. "Smoking and Lung Cancer." *The American Statistician* 17 (4): 15–22.

Berkson, Joseph. 2014. "Limitations of the Application of Fourfold Table Analysis to Hospital Data.*,†.*" *International Journal of Epidemiology* 43 (2): 511–15. doi: 10.1093/ije/dyu022.

Bernard, Claude. 1927. *An Introduction to the Study of Experimental Medicine.* Translated by Henry Copley Greene. MacMillan & Co.

Bernard, Claude. 1974. *Lectures on the Phenomena of Life Common to Animals and Plants.* American Lecture Series, Publication No. 900. A Monograph in the Bannerstone Division of American Lecture Series in the History of Medicine and Science. Springfield, Ill: Thomas.

Bichat, Xavier F.M. 1809. *Physiological Researches Upon Life and Death.* Translated by Tobias Watkins. Philadelphia: Smith and Maxwell.

Brault, Nicolas. 2017. "Le Concept de Biais En Épidémiologie." Paris VII.

Brault, Nicolas. 2020. "Le biais de Berkson, ou l'histoire d'un quiproquo épistémologique." *Bulletin d'histoire et d'épistémologie des sciences de la vie* Volume 27 (1): 31–49. doi: 10.3917/bhesv.271.0031.

Brault, N., Saxena, M. "For a critical appraisal of artificial intelligence in healthcare: The problem of bias in mHealth." *J Eval Clin Pract.* 2020 December 23. doi: 10.1111/jep.13528. Epub ahead of print. PMID: 33369050.

Canguilhem, Georges. 1989. *The Normal and the Pathological.* New York: Zone Books.

Canguilhem, Georges. 2000. *A Vital Rationalist: Selected Writings from Georges Canguilhem.* Edited by François Delaporte. 1st pbk. ed. New York: Zone Books.

Canguilhem, Georges. 2012. *Writings on Medicine.* New York: Fordham University Press.

Chadarevian, Soraya de. 1998. *Molecularizing Biology and Medicine: New Practices and Alliances, 1920s to 1970s.* 1st ed. London: Taylor & Francis. doi: 10.4324/9780203304235.

Chadwick, Ruth. 2017. "What's in a Name: Conceptions of Personalized Medicine and Their Ethical Implications." *Lato Sensu: Revue de La Société de Philosophie Des Sciences* 4 (2): 5–11. doi: 10.20416/lsrsps.v4i2.893.

Committee on the Review of Omics-Based Tests for Predicting Patient Outcomes in Clinical Trials, Board on Health Care Services, Board on Health Sciences Policy, and Institute of Medicine. 2012. *Evolution of Translational Omics: Lessons Learned and the Path Forward.* Edited by Christine M. Micheel, Sharly J. Nass, and Gilbert S. Omenn. Washington, D.C.: National Academies Press. doi: 10.17226/13297.

Darrason, Marie. 2017. "Médecine de précision et médecine des systèmes: La médecine personnalisée se trompet-elle de cible ?" *Lato Sensu: Revue de la Société de philosophie des sciences* 4 (2): 66–82. doi: 10.20416/lsrsps.v4i2.983.

Dewey, John. 1941. "Propositions, Warranted Assertibility, and Truth." *The Journal of Philosophy* 38 (7): 169. doi: 10.2307/2017978.

Dijkstra, Edsger W. 1972. "The Humble Programmer." *Communications of the ACM* 15 (10): 859–66. doi: 10.1145/355604.361591.

Doll, R., and A. B. Hill. 1950. "Smoking and Carcinoma of the Lung: Preliminary Report." *British Medical Journal* 2 (4682): 739–48. doi: 10.1136/bmj.2.4682.739.

Doll, R., and A. B. Hill. 1954. "The Mortality of Doctors in Relation to Their Smoking Habits: A Preliminary Report." *British Medical Journal* 1 (4877): 1451–55. doi: 10.1136/bmj.1.4877.1451.

Feinstein, Alvan R. 1983. "An Additional Basic Science for Clinical Medicine: IV. The Development of Clinimetrics." *Annals of Internal Medicine* 99 (6): 843. doi: 10.7326/0003-4819-99-6-843.

Fisher, Ronald A. 1935. *The Design of Experiments*. London: Oliver & Boyd.

Fisher, Ronald A. 1959. *Smoking. The Cancer Controversy: Some Attempts to Assess the Evidence*. Edinburgh, Scotland: Oliver and Boyd.

Fisher, Ronald A. 1965. "The Place of the Design of Experiments in the Logic of Scientific Inference." *Sankhyā: The Indian Journal of Statistics, Series A (1961-2002)* 27 (1): 33–38.

Flores, Mauricio, Gustavo Glusman, Kristin Brogaard, Nathan D Price, and Leroy Hood. 2013. "P4 Medicine: How Systems Medicine Will Transform the Healthcare Sector and Society." *Personalized Medicine* 10 (6): 565–76. doi: 10.2217/pme.13.57.

Floridi, Luciano, and Josh Cowls. 2019. "A Unified Framework of Five Principles for AI in Society." Harvard Data Science Review, June. doi: 10.1162/99608f92.8cd550d1.

Foucault, Michel. 1978. *The History of Sexuality. Volume 1: An Introduction/The Will to Knowledge*. 1st American ed. New York: Pantheon Books.

Foucault, Michel. 2000. *Dits et écrits: 1954 - 1988*. 3: 1976 –1979. Nachdr. Bibliothèque des sciences humaines. Paris: Gallimard.

Foucault, Michel. 2003. *The Birth of the Clinic: An Archaeology of Medical Perception*. London: Routledge. http://site.ebrary.com/id/10639215.

Giroux, Élodie. 2011. "A Contribution to the History of Risk Factor Epidemiology." *Revue d'histoire des sciences* 64 (2): 219–24. doi: 10.3917/rhs.642.0219.

Giroux, Élodie. 2012. "De l'épidémiologie de santé publique à l'épidémiologie clinique. Quelques réflexions sur la relation entre épidémiologie et clinique (1920–1980)." *Bulletin d'histoire et d'épistémologie des sciences de la vie* 19 (1): 21. doi: 10.3917/bhesv.191.0021.

Giroux, Élodie. 2017. "Médecine de précision et Evidence-Based Medicine : quelle articulation ?" *Lato Sensu: Revue de la Société de philosophie des sciences* 4 (2): 49–65. doi: 10.20416/lsrsps.v4i2.683.

Guchet, Xavier. 2017. "Médecine personnalisée versus médecine de la personne : une fausse alternative." *Lato Sensu: Revue de la Société de philosophie des sciences* 4 (2): 36–48. doi: 10.20416/lsrsps.v4i2.813.

Guyatt, Gordon. 1992. "Evidence-Based Medicine: A New Approach to Teaching the Practice of Medicine." *JAMA* 268 (17): 2420. doi: 10.1001/jama.1992.03490170092032.

Haenssle, H. A., C. Fink, R. Schneiderbauer, F. Toberer, T. Buhl, A. Blum, A. Kalloo, et al. 2018. "Man against Machine: Diagnostic Performance of a Deep Learning Convolutional Neural Network for Dermoscopic Melanoma Recognition in Comparison to 58 Dermatologists." *Annals of Oncology* 29 (8): 1836–42. doi: 10.1093/annonc/mdy166.

Halpern, J. Y. 2005a. "Causes and Explanations: A Structural-Model Approach. Part I: Causes." *The British Journal for the Philosophy of Science* 56 (4): 843–87. doi: 10.1093/bjps/axi147.

Halpern, J. Y. 2005b. "Causes and Explanations: A Structural-Model Approach. Part II: Explanations." *The British Journal for the Philosophy of Science* 56 (4): 889–911. doi: 10.1093/bjps/axi148.

Hankinson, Jim. 2018. "Aetiology." In *The Cambridge Companion to Hippocrates*, edited by Peter E. Pormann, 1st ed., 89–118. Cambridge: Cambridge University Press. doi: 10.1017/9781107705784.006.

Haynes, R. Brian, and Steven N. Goodman. 2015. "An Interview with David Sackett, 2014–2015." *Clinical Trials: Journal of the Society for Clinical Trials* 12 (5): 540–51. doi: 10.1177/1740774515597895.

Hebb, D. O. 1949. *The Organization of Behavior: A Neuropsychological Theory*. New York: John Wiley & Sons, Inc.

Hempel, Carl G. 1965. *Aspects of Scientific Explanation and Other Essays in the Philosophy of Science*. New York: MacMillan & Co.

Hempel, Carl G., and Paul Oppenheim. 1948. "Studies in the Logic of Explanation." *Philosophy of Science* 15 (2): 135–75. doi: 10.1086/286983.

Hill, Sir Austin Bradford. 1990. "Memories of the British Streptomycin Trial in Tuberculosis." *Controlled Clinical Trials* 11 (2): 77–79. doi: 10.1016/0197-2456(90)90001-I.

Hippocrates, and William H. S. Jones. 2005. *Hippocrates. Volume IV*. Reprinted. Loeb classical library 150. Cambridge, MA: Harvard Univ. Press.

Hippocrates, and William H. S. Jones. 2010. *Hippocrates. Volume I*. Nachdr. Loeb Classical Library 147. Cambridge, MA: Harvard University Press.

Hippocrates, and Wesley D. Smith. 1994. *Hippocrates. Volume VII*. Loeb Classical Library LCL477. Cambridge, MA: Harvard University.

Hoare, C. A. R. 1996. "How Did Software Get so Reliable without Proof?" In *FME'96: Industrial Benefit and Advances in Formal Methods*, edited by Marie-Claude Gaudel and James Woodcock, 1051: 1–17. Berlin, Heidelberg: Springer Berlin Heidelberg. doi: 10.1007/3-540-60973-3_77.

Hood, Leroy. 2013. "Systems Biology and P4 Medicine: Past, Present, and Future." *Rambam Maimonides Medical Journal* 4 (2): e0012. doi: 10.5041/RMMJ.10112.

Hughes, Thomas Parke. 1993. *Networks of Power: Electrification in Western Society, 1880 - 1930*. Softshell Books ed. Softshell Books History of Technology. Baltimore, MD: John Hopkins Univ. Press.

Jones, David S., and Scott H. Podolsky. 2015. "The History and Fate of the Gold Standard." *The Lancet* 385 (9977): 1502–3. doi: 10.1016/S0140-6736(15)60742-5.

Jørgensen, Jan Trøst. 2009. "New Era of Personalized Medicine: A 10-Year Anniversary." *The Oncologist* 14 (5): 557–8. doi: 10.1634/theoncologist.2009-0047.

Jorland, Gérard, Annick Opinel, and George Weisz, eds. 2005. *Body Counts: Medical Quantification in Historical and Sociological Perspective / La Quantification Medicale, Perspectives Historiques et Sociologiques*. Montréal ; Ithaca: McGill-Queen's University Press.

Kuhn, Thomas S. 1970. *The Structure of Scientific Revolutions*. [2d ed., Enl. International Encyclopedia of Unified Science. Foundations of the Unity of Science, v. 2, No. 2]. Chicago: University of Chicago Press.

Langreth, null, and null Waldholz. 1999. "New Era of Personalized Medicine: Targeting Drugs for Each Unique Genetic Profile." *The Oncologist* 4 (5): 426–7.

Leibniz, Gottfried. 1710. "Brevis description Machinæ Arithmeticæ, cum figura", in *Miscellanea Berolinensia ad incrementum scientiarum*, Berlin (Germany): Berlin-Brandenburgischen Akademie der Wissenschaften, 317–19.

Lemoine, Maël. 2017. "Neither from Words, nor from Visions: Understanding p-Medicine from Innovative Treatments." *Lato Sensu: Revue de La Société de Philosophie Des Sciences* 4 (2): 12–23. doi: 10.20416/lsrsps.v4i2.793.

Leplège, Alain, Philippe Bizouarn, and Joël Coste. 2011. *De Galton à Rothman: les grands textes de l'épidémiologie au XXe siècle*. Paris: Hermann.

Li, Yunzhu, Andre Esteva, Brett Kuprel, Rob Novoa, Justin Ko, and Sebastian Thrun. 2016. "Skin Cancer Detection and Tracking Using Data Synthesis and Deep Learning." *ArXiv:1612.01074 [Cs]*, December. http://arxiv.org/abs/1612.01074.

Mackall, Dale, Stacy Nelson, and Johann Schumman. 2002. "Verification & Validation Of Neural Networks For Aerospace Systems." Dryden Flight Research Center and NASA Ames Research Center.

Mallat, Stéphane. Lesson at the Collège de France, January 23rd 2019.

Marks, Harry M. 2000. *The Progress of Experiment: Science and Therapeutic Reform in the United States, 1900–1990*. Cambridge History of Medicine. Cambridge: Cambridge Univ. Press.

Matthews, J. Rosser. 1995. *Quantification and the Quest for Medical Certainty*. Princeton, NJ: Princeton University Press.

McCulloch, Warren S., and Walter Pitts. 1943. "A Logical Calculus of the Ideas Immanent in Nervous Activity." *The Bulletin of Mathematical Biophysics* 4 (5): 115–33.

Menabrea Luigi Federico, Lovelace Ada. 1843. "Sketch of the Analytical Engine invented by Charles Babbage... with notes by the translator." Translated by Ada Lovelace. In Richard Taylor (ed.), *Scientific Memoirs*, London: Richard and John E. Taylor, 666–731.

Mill, John Stuart. 1882. *A System of Logic*. New York: Harper and Brothers.

Minsky, Marvin Lee. 1968. *Semantic Information Processing*. Cambridge, MA: MIT Press.

Morabia, Alfredo, ed. 2004. *A History of Epidemiologic Methods and Concepts*. Basel and Boston: Birkhauser Verlag.

Murphy, Edmond A. 1976. *The Logic of Medicine*. Baltimore, MD: Johns Hopkins University Press.

Omran, A. R. 1971. "The Epidemiologic Transition. A Theory of the Epidemiology of Population Change." *The Milbank Memorial Fund Quarterly* 49 (4): 509–38.

Parascandola, Mark. 2004. "Skepticism, Statistical Methods, and the Cigarette: A Historical Analysis of a Methodological Debate." *Perspectives in Biology and Medicine* 47 (2): 244–61. doi: 10.1353/pbm.2004.0032.

Pascal, Blaise. 1645. *La Machine d'arithmétique. Lettre dédicatoire à Monseigneur le Chancelier.*

Pauling, L., H. A. Itano, S. J. Singer, and I. C. Wells. 1949. "Sickle Cell Anemia, a Molecular Disease." *Science* 110 (2865): 543–8. doi: 10.1126/science.110.2865.543.

Pearl, Judea. 1995. "Causal Diagrams for Empirical Research." *Biometrika* 82 (4): 669–88. doi: 10.1093/biomet/82.4.669.

Pearl, Judea. 1998. "Graphs, Causality, and Structural Equation Models." *Sociological Methods & Research* 27 (2): 226–84. doi: 10.1177/0049124198027002004.

Pearl, Judea. 2000. *Causality: Models, Reasoning, and Inference*. Cambridge, U.K. ; New York: Cambridge University Press.

Pearl, Judea. 2009. "Causal Inference in Statistics: An Overview." *Statistics Surveys* 3: 96–146. doi: 10.1214/09-SS057.

Pearl, Judea, and Dana Mackenzie. 2018. *The Book of Why: The New Science of Cause and Effect*. New York: Basic Books.

Peirce, Charles S. 1978. *Collected Papers of Charles Sanders Peirce. Volume 5: Pragmatism and Pragmaticism*. 4. print. ed. by Charles Hartshorne ...; Vol. 6. Cambridge, Mass: Belknap Press of Harvard Univ. Press.

Putnam, Hilary. 2001. *Representation and Reality*. Reprinted. Representation and Mind. Cambridge, MA: MIT Press.

Rose, Nikolas. 2001. "The Politics of Life Itself." *Theory, Culture & Society* 18 (6): 1–30. doi: 10.1177/02632760122052020.

Rothman, Kenneth J. 1976. "Causes." *American Journal of Epidemiology* 104 (6): 587–92. doi: 10.1093/oxfordjournals.aje.a112335.

Sackett, David L. 1969. "Clinical Epidemiology." *American Journal of Epidemiology* 89 (2): 125–28.

Sackett, David L., William M. C. Rosenberg, J. A. Muir Gray, R. Brian Haynes, and W. Scott Richardson. 1996. "Evidence Based Medicine: What It Is And What It Isn't: It's About Integrating Individual Clinical Expertise And The Best External Evidence." *BMJ: British Medical Journal* 312 (7023): 71–2.

Salmon Wesley. 1970. "Statistical Explanation", in Robert Colodny (ed.). *The Nature and Function of Scientific* Theories, Pittsburgh: University of Pittsburgh Press, 173–232.

Salmon, Wesley C. 2006. *Four Decades of Scientific Explanation.* 1. Univ. of Pittsburgh Press paperback ed. Pittsburgh, PA: Univ. of Pittsburgh Press.

Searle, John R. 1980. "Minds, Brains, and Programs." *Behavioral and Brain Sciences* 3 (3): 417–24. doi: 10.1017/S0140525X00005756.

Shalev-Shwartz, Shai, and Shai Ben-David. 2014. *Understanding Machine Learning: From Theory to Algorithms.* New York: Cambridge University Press.

Simon, Herbert A. 1955. "A Behavioral Model of Rational Choice." *The Quarterly Journal of Economics* 69 (1): 99. doi: 10.2307/1884852.

Simon, Herbert A., and Allen Newell. 1958. "Heuristic Problem Solving: The Next Advance in Operations Research." *Operations Research* 6 (1): 1–10. doi: 10.1287/opre.6.1.1.

Software and Systems Engineering Standards Committee. 2016. *IEEE Std 1012™-2016,* IEEE Computer Society.

Spirtes, Peter, Clark N. Glymour, and Richard Scheines. 2000. *Causation, Prediction, and Search.* 2nd ed. Adaptive Computation and Machine Learning. Cambridge, MA and London: The MIT Press.

Strasser, Bruno J, and Bernardino Fantini. 2020. "Molecular Diseases and Diseased Molecules: Ontological and Epistemological Dimensions," 27.

"Streptomycin Treatment of Pulmonary Tuberculosis. A Medical Research Council Investigation." 1948. *British Medical Journal* 2 (4582): 769–82.

Suppes, Patrick. 1970. *A Probabilistic Theory of Causality.* Acta Philosophica Fennica, Fasc. 24. Amsterdam: North-Holland Pub. Co.

Tarski, Alfred. 1969. "Truth and Proof". *Scientific American* 220: 63–7.

Thom, René. 1971. "'Modern' Mathematics: An Educational and Philosophic Error?" *American Scientist* 59 (6): 695–99.

Thumiger, Chiara. 2018. "Doctors and Patients." In *The Cambridge Companion to Hippocrates,* edited by Peter E. Pormann, 1st ed., 263–91. Cambridge: Cambridge University Press. doi: 10.1017/9781107705784.013.

Turing, Alan M. 1950. "Computing Machinery and Intelligence." *Mind* 59 (236), 433–60.

Tymoczko, Thomas. 1979. "The Four-Color Problem and Its Philosophical Significance." *The Journal of Philosophy* 76 (2): 57. doi: 10.2307/2025976.

Tymoczko, Thomas. 1980. "Computers, Proofs and Mathematicians: A Philosophical Investigation of the Four-Color Proof." *Mathematics Magazine* 53 (3): 131–38.

Tymoczko, Thomas. 1981. "Computer Use to Computer Proof: A Rational Reconstruction." *The Two-Year College Mathematics Journal* 12 (2): 120. doi: 10.2307/3027374.

Valles, Sean. 2020. "Philosophy of Biomedicine." In *The Stanford Encyclopedia of Philosophy (Summer 2020 Edition),* edited by Edward N. Zalta, Summer 2020. Stanford: Metaphysics Research Lab, Stanford University. https://plato.stanford.edu/archives/sum2020/entries/biomedicine.

Vandenbroucke, J. P. 2009. "Commentary: 'Smoking and Lung Cancer'–the Embryogenesis of Modern Epidemiology." *International Journal of Epidemiology* 38 (5): 1193–96. doi: 10.1093/ije/dyp292.

Weisberg, Herbert I. 2010. *Bias and Causation.* Hoboken, NJ, USA: John Wiley & Sons, Inc.

White, Colin. 1991. "Research on Smoking and Lung Cancer: A Landmark in the History of Chronic Disease Epidemiology." *Lung Cancer* 7 (3): 180. doi: 10.1016/0169-5002(91)90089-O.

Wiener, Norbert. 1985. *Cybernetics or Control and Communication in the Animal and the Machine.* 2d ed., 4. print. Cambridge, MA: MIT Press.

Index

Printed in the United States
by Baker & Taylor Publisher Services